NORTH

*Finding my way while running
the Appalachian Trail*

SCOTT JUREK

BOOKS

1 3 5 7 9 10 8 6 4 2

Random House Books
20 Vauxhall Bridge Road
London SW1V 2SA

Random House Books is part of the Penguin Random House group of companies
whose addresses can be found at global.penguinrandomhouse.com.

Penguin
Random House
UK

First published in the UK by Random House Books in 2018
First published in the USA by Little, Brown in 2018

www.penguin.co.uk

A CIP catalogue record for this book is available from the British Library.

ISBN 9781847948007

Printed and bound by Clays Ltd, St Ives plc

Penguin Random House is committed to a sustainable future for
our business, our readers and our planet. This book is made from
Forest Stewardship Council® certified paper.

For Jenny, my true north

Remote for detachment, narrow for chosen company, winding for leisure, lonely for contemplation, it beckons not merely north and south, but upward to the body, mind and soul of man.

—Harold Allen, early Appalachian Trail planner

Happy Birthday
from
Jim n Helen
2018

CONTENTS

CONTENTS

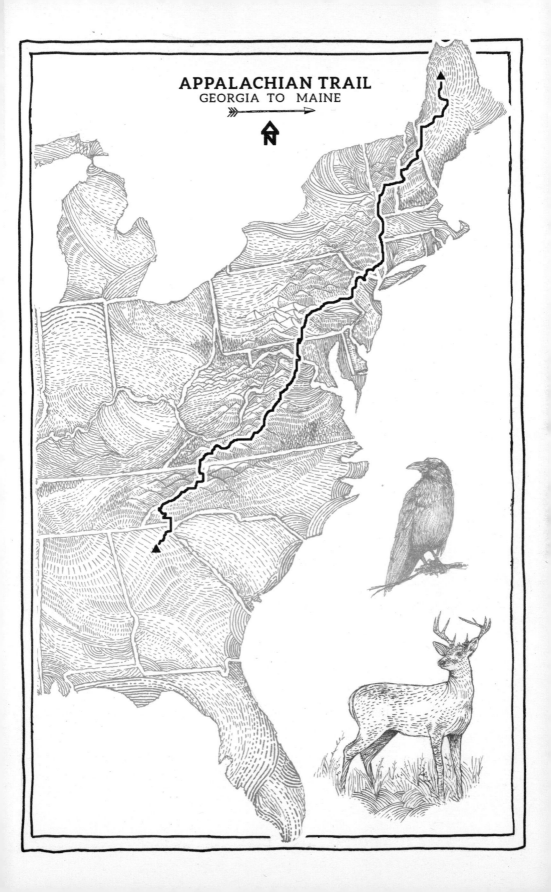

APPALACHIAN TRAIL
GEORGIA TO MAINE

NORTH

PROLOGUE

Day Seven

WHERE IS HE? *He should be here by now.*

He should have emerged from the sea of trees and met me at this road crossing more than an hour ago. It's been pouring all day, a bona fide deluge, and I'm not sure if he's twisted his ankle in the mud or taken a bad fall and is sitting on a rock waiting for me to find him. I call him "Big Thump" for a reason—he's constantly catching his size 11½ feet on some root or rock, sending his six-foot-two frame crashing to the ground with a resounding thud. Somehow, maybe thanks to his twenty-five years of trail-running experience, he always manages to avoid serious injury. But maybe his luck has finally run out.

I last saw him at a parting between two mountains, which out here in the Deep South they call a gap. Being from the West, I had never heard the term before. What Southerners call a gap is what I call a pass and the French call a col; the lowest point of a ridge, or a saddle between two peaks. At Sams Gap, I noticed he had the slightest limp, but I shrugged it off because he started every morning stiff as a board until his muscles loosened up around midday. According to our calculations, he should be able to cover the 13.4 miles of trail to Spivey Gap in just over three hours. But what I've come to realize over the past seven days is that every section is taking a lot longer than we expected and that a steady pace of four miles an hour is surprisingly hard to maintain, even for him.

On the Appalachian Trail he goes by El Venado, Spanish for "the deer." It's the spirit animal bestowed on him in the Copper Canyon by the late Caballo Blanco for the style of his running gait. But almost everyone knows him as Scott Jurek, one of the greatest ultramarathon runners ever, they say. To me, he's always been Jurker, starting way back in 2001 when we met in Seattle. That's what his friends called him, a play on his last name and a jab at his stereotypical Minnesotan niceness. He has accomplished things that no other male runner has even attempted, like winning the Western States 100-Mile Endurance Run seven years in a row. One year he sprained his ankle mid-race; one year he chased a bear up a tree; and one year, less than two weeks after he won, he set a course record at the Badwater 135. He ran laps on a one-mile loop for twenty-four hours straight to set an American record. He won the Hardrock Hundred on a sprained ankle, and he holds three of the fastest times (behind only the great Yiannis Kouros) in the 152-mile Spartathlon race. But now he's taking on a challenge that could permanently damage his body, not to mention our marriage. He said he wants this to be his masterpiece, but secretly, I wonder if he means it.

Jurker, where are you?

CHAPTER 1

GIVE AND TAKE

A Year Earlier

NO MATTER WHAT direction I looked, I could see forever.

And out past the place where forever ended, beyond the hazy horizon where sky and earth commingled, I knew the desert kept going: more rolling mountains, more vast valleys, more everything. West meant the Pacific Ocean and my old stomping ground in the Cascade Mountains outside Seattle; east meant my childhood home, back in the woods of Minnesota and beyond. South was more desert, more sun, more sand, less water.

North, though, felt new again.

Deserts have always been a mystifying and spiritual landscape for me. I didn't set foot in a desert until I was twenty-two, and two decades later, deserts have retained their wonderful otherworldliness. I can see why many a spiritual seeker has chosen to walk through the desert for purification and reflection.

The still and barren Anza-Borrego Desert in Southern California could coax anyone toward enlightenment.

As I marveled at the measure of eternity, I realized it was possible that I wasn't feeling enlightenment so much as mild heat mania. It was ninety-five degrees and only getting hotter. Almost every other living thing had taken refuge either belowground or in whatever meager shade could be found. The only creatures out and about were two bipedal mammals hiding under portable shade, rhythmically striding along the trail. Many Pacific Crest Trail (PCT) thru-hikers take a break during the heat of the day, but we were short on time. We could get away from work and life for only a week, and we wanted to hike as much as possible.

Light and smooth was the name of our game. Quick, but easy. Desert hiking demands that you submit to paradoxes. You must move hastily through the sun and the heat, yet slowly enough to avoid producing too much heat of your own. You need to ration the water you haul on your back but not so much that you are burdened by its weight. Move too fast under the scorching sun and you'll go through your water so quickly that you'll wind up with dehydration and heatstroke. Carry too little water and you'll shrivel up like a raisin, and the desert floor will swallow you whole. Out there, balance isn't just a beautiful idea; it's necessary for survival.

It can also look silly. We were the wacky-looking ultralight-weight hikers—what Jenny calls outdorky—wearing long-sleeved cotton shirts and hiding under umbrellas in the bone-dry heat. We were also carrying what could pass for daypacks, each filled with only twenty pounds of gear, food, and water. We had stripped down to the bare essentials so we could move efficiently, cover more miles, and enjoy them without being dragged down by huge packs. We had even left our camp stove at home. We rehydrated our meals while we hiked.

I'd always dreamed of doing a long trail, of hiking for weeks and months on end with no specific schedule. I'd walk all day, camp where I wanted, live in the moment, feel the flow of unrestricted movement. I felt an urge to live close to the land and forget what society thought was normal. To transcend like Thoreau and Muir, with the Christopher McCandless ideals from *Into the Wild,* chasing a romantic goal to "move around, be nomadic, make each day a new horizon."

I especially loved daydreaming about the ultralight-hiking approach pioneered by Ray Jardine and outlined in his 1996 bible on the subject, *The Pacific Crest Trail Hiker's Handbook.* Now, fifteen years after I first borrowed Jardine's guide from the Seattle Public Library, I was finally here, out on the PCT. It was everything I'd wanted.

But I already wanted more. We hiked the trail in sections, a week at a time, so at this rate it would take us about twenty years to finish the 2,600-mile trail. The more we hiked and hung out with the PCT thru-hikers, the more we both yearned to put our lives on hold for three months and keep walking all the way north.

I turned around and looked south for my umbrella-carrying companion. Sometimes hours and miles passed without us talking. We didn't need to. We were immersed in the rhythm of our strides and in the wildness around us. Like the ancient Taoist philosophy *wu wei*, we were doing without doing. More of that desert paradox. Often, we both did our own things, lost in our own thoughts or our own thoughtlessness, only to return to ourselves and suddenly strike up a conversation as if no time had passed. I loved it either way. I loved walking with her stride for stride, telling stories of our pasts and passing the arduous miles with silly games, like quizzing each other on runners' nicknames and Instagram handles and reciting movie dialogue and song lyrics. And then we would lapse into deep silence again, calmed by the desert.

This was one of those times we were beating our PCT drums alone, separated by a quarter mile of mesquite bushes and sand.

Her maiden name is Jennifer Lee Uehisa, but I call her JLu (pronounced "jay-loo"), like her climbing buddies coined from her initials. She calls me Jurker. People sometimes can't believe we call each other by those casual nicknames that get hollered over canyons and campfires, but I think it's fitting. No sappy, lovey-dovey endearments, no traditional "sweetie" or "dear." We are buddies to each other first and foremost. Sometimes adversaries, but always best friends, even through the deep canyons and high summits of life. We are a team, and we know each other better than anyone else on the planet knows us.

Uehisa is Japanese for "perpetually rising" or "always up." The name fits; she's got a positive attitude no matter the situation, and, like the desert sun, she's always rising. Hiking twenty miles a day with twenty pounds on your back isn't typically how people recover after emergency surgery, but JLu isn't your typical gal. Behind that cute, high-pitched voice is an absolute lion that roars past every challenge.

I'm sure she inherited some of that strength from her family. Her Japanese grandparents lost their home and farm in California and were sent to internment camps during World War II. Her mother emigrated from the barangay of Manila to the United States at age eighteen. Nothing was handed to JLu, and the only thing she knew how to do was go out and earn things the old-fashioned way. That drive is what made our lives compatible. I always chuckle when people assume I turned JLu vegan and made her into an ultrarunner, because she became a vegetarian when she was thirteen and she started running before I ever met her. And she'll let people know it too! I don't blame her. She has scratched and clawed her way through life, and she's done it with grace and wit. She's also got a hard edge, and that hard edge can be razor-sharp. She comes across all sweet and nice, but she can hang with the toughest guys. She says that she isn't competitive, but watch out when it comes to table tennis, crossword puzzles, board games, card games, or, really, any game at all.

And two months ago, she almost died in my arms.

I'd never felt more helpless. In the middle of the night, I'd caught her when she passed out and held her when she vomited on our kitchen floor. She slipped in and out of consciousness as I pleaded with her, "Don't leave me now, don't leave me now." She didn't.

Neither of us knew what was going on, so I drove her to the ER. After hours of testing and waiting, we finally had an answer.

"You're pregnant," the ER doctor said. We sat in stunned silence. "But it's in the wrong place, so we need to terminate it."

Unbeknownst to either of us, she was approximately seven weeks pregnant, but the embryo had been growing in her left fallopian tube. When it got too big, it ruptured the tube, and now she was bleeding internally.

After the diagnosis, everything went into hyper-speed. Before we knew it, she was signing liability waivers, being counseled on the potential risks of blood transfusions, and then getting wheeled into the operating room. I remember her in a semiconscious state asking the on-call ob-gyn, "Will I be able to get pregnant again?" The doctor replied, "The next time you see me, I'll be delivering your baby." JLu half smiled and closed her eyes, and then they took her away.

After hours of me pacing in the waiting room, she was back. We drove home at 6:00 the next morning and took stock of the damage. We'd lost a baby, but thankfully we still had each other.

Never being one to take the easy route, she'd refused to let me carry the bulk of our gear on the trail, even though she was still recovering from surgery. At least I'd managed to convince her to let me carry all the water—and there were long stretches without water caches on the PCT. During thru-hiker season, local "trail angels" selflessly set out hundreds of gallons of water to make the Southern California desert sections slightly more hospitable. Otherwise, in drought years, thirty- to forty-mile stretches without a drop of water would be commonplace. So would bodies, probably.

As the mercury rose and heat waves rippled off the immediate horizon, my thoughts evaporated and drifted up and away from JLu. The desert too had its hard and soft parts, its own equilibrium. Scorching afternoon heat melted into cool, pink sunsets. The apparently lifeless landscape secretly teemed with radically adapted plants and animals. Back when I was an altar boy, I often heard people repeating the verse "The Lord giveth and the Lord taketh away." Back then, I understood it as a kind of observation.

But out here in the desert, it felt more like a law than an observation. Giving and taking. A rule of existence that people often failed to acknowledge except when out here in the marginal spaces, out where they're confronted by it. I welcomed the give-and-take of the desert. I welcomed what it required of me. Somewhere in between was balance, and nature always encouraged me to find that stability. What would water be without the arid desert floor, and what would lightness be without the weight? And maybe that's why JLu and I were out here; maybe we were trying to chase that balance through the desert.

I was free at that moment to contemplate the mysteries of the desert because we'd had a little flare-up a few miles back and I needed the space. The good thing about the desert and the PCT is there is plenty of open space and miles of trail to let things calm down. It all started when she asked me the age-old question "Where are you and where do you want to go?" Actually, it was more like "What are you doing with your life?" It escalated a bit after she provoked me with "I thought you retired; why do you keep saying you still have some races left? You always said you'd be done at forty, so why are you backpedaling? I'm tired of you spinning your wheels, saying you're going to train for this race and that race. You say you have the drive, but I don't see it."

So I made the mistake of going after her with "Well, what are you doing with *your* career? I don't see you being the next Coco Chanel. I don't see you winning *Project Runway*!" Of course she burst out laughing. What was I thinking, *Project Runway*? As if every designer's dream was to make it on a reality-TV show. I'm never a match for her in these blowouts.

She ate me alive the rest of the argument, and it ended in us screaming at each other in the middle of the solitude of the desert. It's not *all* peace and *wu wei*.

Part of the problem was that I knew what she meant. Maybe I was spinning my wheels. Maybe I'd convinced myself I wanted something I used to have. It's true that sometimes I felt washed up, and I vacillated between feeling content and feeling that I needed to do something more—or *be* something more. I didn't know how much of this was my own personal yearning and how much was, frankly, keeping up appearances. Everyone wants the champ to continue winning. We all want our heroes to be immortal; we don't want to watch them slow down or become weaker. It was hard for me to deal with the incessant questions: "What's next for you? So what race are you gearing up for?" As JLu nudged me in the desert, "Maybe it's time to transition from athlete to ambassador and let go of the glory days. I can't watch you fake another half-hearted effort. It's not the Jurker I know. Don't you want to be somebody?"

How was it that she could see me better than I could see myself?

And why did she have to drive me crazy in the process?

I was fuming because she was right. And she was asking the right questions, exactly the kind that made me flail around mentally. My sensation of enlightenment dried up and fell away like some molted snakeskin. Later, I would be grateful to her. She was doing the thing I loved her for: being a great partner, a challenging partner. She didn't just pat me on the back, stroke my ego, and tell me how amazing I was. JLu can give me tough love like no one else.

That's not to say that I rushed back down the trail to thank her. All in good time.

Besides, she really had kindled a line of thinking that was burning me up. Maybe racing and winning wasn't the challenge I needed right now, or ever again. If that was the case, I really didn't have a good answer to the question of what I wanted. What would come next?

More trail, for starters. We were a mere twenty miles through our planned hundred-and-fifty-mile section. I didn't want to finish. I just wanted to keep hiking toward forever. JLu made me realize I didn't know what I wanted next, but the desert reminded me what I wanted now. Give-and-take.

I have always been fascinated with multiday adventure runs and thru-hiking. As a kid in Minnesota, I never traveled beyond a handful of neighboring states, so I was in awe of people who rode their bikes along the shore of Lake Superior and of the cross-country cyclists I saw. Later, I heard stories about people walking and running across the country. The idea of powering myself across the country—an expanse I could barely conceive of—was overwhelming. I vowed that I would do it someday, somehow. Then the rhythm and patterns of life got in the way—school, summer jobs, internships, college, work, grad school, more work. When I got into ultramarathoning, I read about the great Trans American

Footrace and of records being set on long national scenic trails and on trails that crossed famous landmarks in national parks. But then my new focus on ultraracing took over, and I promised myself I would do the multiday and "really long stuff" toward the end of my career.

And then, in 2003 on a run on this same trail, twenty-two hundred miles north in the Cascade Mountains of Washington, I told my buddy David "Horty" Horton that I thought I was ready to tackle the speed record on the PCT. He said, "You were made for this, boy! But wait a little bit, do some more racing, you have time. Let me do it first, then you can break my record!" That's old Horty for you; he's always got some half-sage advice to offer with a little something in it for himself. He had already set a speed record on the Appalachian Trail earlier in his career, so he knew what he was talking about. I really didn't care when I did it, and he was probably right. I had plenty of time to blow away whatever slow record he set on the PCT. Back then, I always had plenty of time left.

I also couldn't forget what another veteran ultra buddy of mine, Rob "Hollywood" McNair, had told me when I was tempted to run the Trans American Footrace after listening to his stories. "Scotty, you run that race and that will be the last race you'll run!" he said. "Stick to fifty and hundred milers." Now I knew what he'd meant.

So maybe it was JLu that did it. Maybe it was her brutally honest reminder that my career was coming to a close. All of a sudden I didn't have much time left. There weren't years stretching out in front of me, far-off days where I could stick a dream and wait for time to bring me to it. The only thing that stretched before me now was the rock and dirt and brush of the Anza-Borrego.

We had a week out here, but I wanted more. We had only started scratching the surface of our big life questions. I wanted more miles and a firm answer to "So what's next?" One that didn't involve hemming and hawing and halfheartedness. I wanted to go back to those woods in Minnesota where I'd fallen in love with the idea of life-altering adventures and trails that went on forever.

Suddenly, I also wanted to get out of the heat.

It took only a few moments to piece together a plan. I would run one of the National Scenic Trails. There were three big ones, and we were on one of them, the PCT. We knew parts of it like the backs of our hands. The Continental Divide Trail, the longest, at thirty-one hundred miles, followed the Rockies right through our new home state of Colorado and seemed like a good choice. But something about it didn't feel right.

As soon as the idea came to me, it started to roll downhill and gather momentum: Why not try to beat the Appalachian Trail speed record? It was *perfect*. I wanted a completely new type of challenge, and I'd barely ever been on trails east of the Mississippi. JLu was right; ultramarathons weren't doing it for me anymore. After a hard twenty years of competing, that wasn't a surprise. But a speed record in the woods and mountains, a monthlong adventure to crack myself open once again? I'd lost the passion to push my body and bend my mind to chew up miles in ultraraces. But I still loved to run and explore my surroundings on foot. I loved being out here.

Even the unfamiliarity attracted me. I instantly loved the idea of running somewhere totally new, totally unexplored, and totally unplanned. As my grandfather liked to tell me as we rambled over his back forty acres in Wisconsin, "The best way to know your land is to walk through it." Every twist and turn of the trail, every vista and boulder, and every road crossing and trailhead, would be completely foreign to me. A new, undiscovered world around each corner.

Of course, I wouldn't be rambling. I'd be chasing the speed record. Horty had done it years ago. I knew I could. Maybe it's what I needed to rekindle the flame that JLu had noticed dying out.

Later on, I would work out the details, but my mind almost immediately started running through the calculations. I would run and hike an average of fifty miles or more a day for about forty-five days along one of the most rugged trails on the planet. I would cover 2,189 miles while climbing and descending a million vertical feet. Over the course of about six weeks, I would cover the entire length of the Appalachian Trail faster than anyone before me.

Well, I would *attempt* to.

And I knew that I couldn't even begin to attempt it on my own.

We'd preserved our postfight silence for miles when I stopped on a switchback and let out the guttural *kraa* of a raven. That's her trail name, Raven, like the color of her hair and the smartest birds around. JLu *kraa*ed back, and when she caught up, I blurted out my plan.

"I think I want to do the Appalachian Trail, go after the record. It has lots of road crossings for you to meet me so we can hang out throughout the day. We can have lunches together and you can run sections with me. It will be a vacation, a fun adventure for both of us!"

Maybe if I kept talking, she wouldn't get a chance to say no.

JLu stopped dead in her tracks with a look of dismay and a wince of confusion. She had heard me talk about speed records and thru-hiking, but that had been idle daydreaming. And there was a trail that was much closer to us than the Appalachian, a trail that we both loved. We'd lived in Seattle for years, so the Pacific Crest Trail felt like our backyard. I had covered most of the trail in the state of Washington and parts of it in Oregon, and I'd run races on sections of it in California. JLu loved playing "find the Pacific Crest Trail crossing" with me as we made weekend road trips when we lived in Southern California. The PCT had been my home course, and then it became ours.

"The Appalachian Trail..." JLu said with a look that I knew all too well. *"Why?"*

Then there was silence, a deafening silence that even the eternally still Anza-Borrego Desert couldn't match.

Because I'm stuck.

Because I'm forty and I need to feel what it's like to go to the edge again, and then go farther.

Because I'm so thankful for everything I have, and for just a little while I need to remember what it feels like to have none of it.

May 2015

Before I agreed to go on this trip, I made Jurker promise me that we would rehearse. Not for him—all he had to do was run—but for *me*. I was the one who was going to have to drive a van to remote meeting locations and serve as a roving aid station several times a day. Even though I had plenty of experience, I was worried. I had been running ultramarathons for thirteen years, including two one-hundred-mile mountain races, so I knew what kind of logistics were involved. But this wasn't a race or an event; it was more of a multiweek vision quest than anything else, and it was going to be much more complicated than anything either of us had done before. So I wanted to practice.

That didn't happen.

It wasn't really Jurker's fault—or anyone's fault, for that matter. I'd had my second miscarriage in April, right when we were supposed to be on a three-day trial run on the Arizona Trail, and then

D and C surgery on April 30, nine days before we were scheduled to pick up our cargo van in Chicago. We had hoped to buy the van a month earlier, but given the added medical bills, the refinancing on our house took longer than we'd anticipated. Setbacks, not deal-breakers, but they left us scrambling to put all the pieces in place and there was no time for a rehearsal. Our departure date grew closer, and we were not only way behind schedule but also way underprepared. Every Appalachian Trail record holder had hiked the entire trail or at least significant sections of it before starting his or her fastest-known-time (FKT) attempt. We'd never even been to half of the fourteen states it crossed. Nevertheless, I can't claim that we were complete AT newbies. A few years ago, Scott was speaking at a running event in Pennsylvania near an AT crossing, so we drove the rental car to the trail. We ran out three miles and back. Those three miles, 0.14 percent of the trail, were the entirety of my Appalachian Trail knowledge.

I was worried. Jurker…wasn't. He didn't seem to feel the pressure of our prep time running out. He wasn't cranking out spreadsheets or studying previous record holders' splits. He wasn't obsessively checking the blogs and trip reports of past attempts. Then again, even if he'd wanted to, he couldn't. The most recent supported attempts had all been southbound; we were going north. It would be a completely different run.

The extent of Scott's planning boiled down to this: He made one single-sided spreadsheet with approximate daily mileage, bought *The A.T. Guide: A Handbook for Hiking the Appalachian Trail, Northbound 2015,* and called it a day. I bit my tongue.

To be honest, our lack of logistical planning didn't worry me as much as Jurker's indifference to physical training did. He wasn't out running long back-to-back days in the mountains with a heavy pack like he'd said he would. He also hadn't hired a strength coach or done any overnights on the trail. But whenever I grilled him about training, he gave me the same answer.

"Twenty years of ultramarathon racing *is* my training."

I couldn't argue with that. My version of training is casual. I mostly run solo with my iPod full of hip-hop and electronic tunes; sometimes I run with friends, but always without a watch. Once, after missing a Boston Marathon qualifying time by two minutes, I asked Jurker in frustration, "Why can't I run fast?" He said, "You can, but you don't like to hurt." Which is absolutely true. I prefer to run with ease, and it means I've never dropped from a race, even if I've never won one. I'd seen Jurker drop (or nearly drop) from seven big ones over the past six years. He always gave the same reason, one that I didn't recognize: his heart wasn't in it.

Well, it had better be this time.

I wasn't going to give up my spring and summer for some half-hearted effort. And I knew what it looked like when he faked it. The Leadville Trail in 2013 was a perfect example. He'd convinced himself that this was going to be his big comeback, that he would win this race that was steeped in ultrarunning folklore, a race in which he'd finished second ten years prior. And he went through the motions. He looked the part, said the right things, did everything to a T—everything except the running. I'm not sure if he was banking on muscle memory or if he was planning to *will* himself to the podium, but he just didn't compete. Even I could tell that much. On race day, he looked like he was struggling just to stay in the top ten. And then, finally, when he had about twenty miles to go, I saw him give up. He didn't fake an injury; he didn't drop out. I just saw him *relax*. He stopped fighting; he was running like I do, running with ease. I guess he didn't want to hurt anymore.

With three miles to go, he was jogging it in. But when the finish line came in view, he perked up and yelled, "JLu! Run with me!

Let's run it in together!" I cringed. I was embarrassed for him, but how could I tell him that? Yes, I was proud of him for finishing, proud of him for cheering the runners who passed him, but I was sad for him too. I knew this wasn't what he was looking for. At the finish area, Jurker hung around and chatted with everybody, seemingly unfazed to take the L. Maybe he was getting used to losing, or maybe it no longer mattered to him. Jurker actually seemed happy.

I'm not as gracious or as nice as Jurker. I wanted to get out of there as soon as possible.

I've known Jurker for fifteen years and he's always been that way, extra-nice. I moved to Seattle on March 26, 2000. I remember the date because it was the day the Kingdome imploded and everybody was in a kind of civic mourning. I had never been into running, but since I didn't know a single soul in town, I started doing local 5K races in hopes of meeting people. Scott worked at my local running store, the Seattle Running Company, and even at the height of his career, he was so approachable that I didn't realize he was a celebrity in some circles. I remember seeing him after I finished my first half marathon; he congratulated me as if I'd run an Olympic qualifying time.

I caught the running bug and two years later ran my first 50K ultramarathon. My main training buddy was a guy named Charlie who was also a friend of Jurker's. In 2004 Charlie decided to run the Western States 100-Mile Endurance Run, and I volunteered to crew and pace him. Around thirty-eight miles before the finish line, we heard that Jurker had won the race and broken the course record. At the awards ceremony, people swarmed over Scott, and someone asked, "How long do you want to keep doing this?" It was his sixth consecutive win. He was on top of the world. To this day, I remember his answer; it was immediate and confident. He said, "There are still a few things I want to do but I won't be doing this forever. I'm going to retire by the time I turn forty."

Now, at forty-one, he wasn't so confident anymore. I heard it in his voice, saw it in his manner. When people asked him if he was done racing, he got defensive. Eleven years ago he was planning on hanging it up at this point, but now it seemed like he was having a hard time letting go. I got it; he'd built his whole career winning races around the world. But he'd always told me he looked forward to sleeping in, to slowing down and spending more time at home.

So what was he trying to prove on the Appalachian Trail?

I didn't have time to ponder that question. We had less than two weeks to convert our black cargo van, which we named Castle Black, into something we could live in, and then we had to load it up with everything we might need for 2,189 miles of running.

An electrician installed a 200-watt solar panel on the roof.

We made a bed frame and threw a twin-size foam mattress on it.

Scott made a small tabletop for the gas camping stove.

I sewed blackout curtains.

There was no time to install a fan or windows.

I cut out pieces of reflective bubble wrap and duct-taped them to the walls for insulation.

We bolted down six low-budget shelving racks for storage.

We transformed those sixty square feet of bare metal into a home on wheels...kind of.

To me, the sooner we left, the better. I had RSVP'd yes to a friend's wedding in South Carolina on May 23. Jurker had insisted we go—he knew how much it meant to me, and he promised we would make it on time. We worked on the van around the clock, and it seemed to rain around the clock. It was one of the wettest Mays on record in Boulder. We couldn't build our bed frame in the rain. The first time it let up was at 11:00 one night. I didn't want to wake the neighbors but time was running out, so we drilled and sanded into the wee hours of the next day.

The longer we stayed home, the more Jurker overpacked. Every day he dug up dusty old gear from our garage and loaded it in the van. "Should I pack these mosquito head nets? Better bring them just in case." Two minutes later: "Do we need this cast-iron griddle? What if you want to make me pancakes? Better bring it."

"Are you seriously packing twenty pairs of socks?" I asked.

"JLu! Do you understand that my feet are the most important thing out there? I have to keep them dry!"

I rolled my eyes and removed ten pairs when he wasn't looking.

The timing was stressful but the work was fun and it took my mind off the things I was looking forward to leaving behind in Boulder. The pain, the frustration, the needles, the doctors, the surgeries. Friends stopped by to help with the van build-out and we often stayed up until 2:00 in the morning getting everything dialed in.

One afternoon my phone rang but my hands were covered in duct tape so I didn't answer. My friend Timmy O'Neill left a message. "JLu, bad news from the Valley. Dean Potter died yesterday."

I crumpled to the floor. Dead? I had just talked to him ten days ago. We'd had plans to visit him in Yosemite in April but my miscarriage had gotten in the way. I was devastated. Dean had lived far out on the edge, so perhaps it seems naive that I was shocked by his death. He was a master of the dark arts, devoting almost three decades to a series of high-risk, all-or-nothing pursuits, like free-solo climbing, some of the most towering, difficult rock faces without a rope or partner. And wingsuit flying, where he leapt from those same overhanging walls and glided not only downward but also as close as possible to the rocks he aimed to avoid.

Contrary to having a death wish, he sought to push himself to and through the impossible. He was the most meticulously precise and calculated guy I'd ever known, even more than Jurker. Razor-focused with a bird's-eye detail for everything, Dean was the Dark Wizard—in tune with the wind, wildlife, and the trees, and the last person I'd expected to die.

Suddenly, our adventure made much more sense and I felt an urgency to disappear into the mountains. That's where Jurker and I go when we need to clear our heads, to reprioritize and reexamine our lives. I was still concerned about being underprepared, but now I couldn't wait to get in Castle Black and drive east.

We locked up the house and pulled out of our driveway at 1:20 a.m. on May 23. My friend was getting married in fifteen hours. I'd been giving Jurker the stink-eye for days. He knew we were late and offered to drive through the night on the off chance that we might make it there in time. I tried to act mad, but I was too excited. I queued up my power song, cranked the volume, and woke the neighbors one last time. We were finally on our way.

DEEP SOUTH

465 MILES

What is straight? A line can be straight, or a street,
but the human heart, oh, no, it's curved like a road
through mountains.
—Tennessee Williams, *A Streetcar Named Desire*

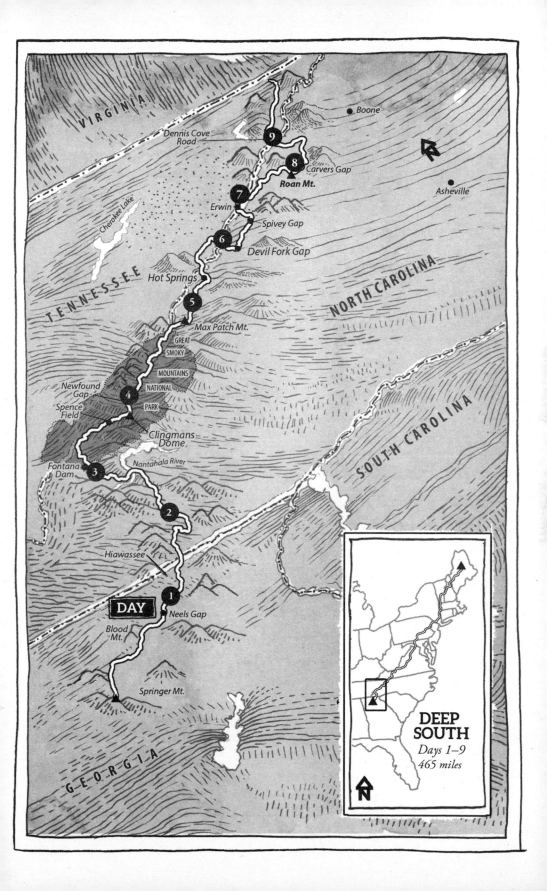

VIRGINIA

Boone

Dennis Cove
Road

9

8

Carvers Gap

Roan Mt.

7

Erwin

Asheville

Cherokee Lake

Spivey Gap

6

Devil Fork Gap

Hot Springs

NORTH CAROLINA

5

Max Patch Mt.

GREAT

SMOKY

MOUNTAINS

TENNESSEE

Newfound
Gap

NATIONAL

4

Spence
Field

PARK

SOUTH CAROLINA

Clingmans
Dome

Fontana
Dam

Nantahala River

3

2

Hiawassee

1

DAY

Neels Gap

Blood
Mt.

Springer Mt.

GEORGIA

**DEEP
SOUTH**

*Days 1–9
465 miles*

N

CHAPTER 2

LIVE WHAT YOU LOVE

May 24

VAST, OPEN PLAINS ripped by us at seventy miles an hour. As Boulder, home, and the Rockies sank into the horizon behind us, our worries and disappointments seemed to recede as well. We were finally on the road. And that road would eventually become a trail.

But first we had to drive across half of the United States.

Heading east from the center of the country is one long downhill ride. The Martian-looking sand dunes of eastern Colorado fade into the rolling fields of Kansas and then turn into the flatlands by the mighty Mississippi. It's land made for road trips. And I loved it— even though I was already exhausted.

In a bit of worrying foreshadowing, we'd hit the road a lot later than we'd wanted to. Actually, it was early. Very early. and after a couple of hours on I-70, we pulled over at a truck stop to sleep. Unfortunately, our undisciplined start time meant that we were going to miss our first goal. I had promised JLu that we'd make a detour to her friend's wedding in South Carolina. We were already too far behind schedule to do that. Besides, we probably would have fallen asleep during the ceremony. The past two weeks had been sleepless while we rushed to make sure the van was ready and to prepare for the drive.

So we were 0 for 1 on the goal list. However, we were still on track for our ultimate destination and schedule. And better yet, we were on the open road.

Sharing the American love affair for long unbroken stretches of pavement and mile markers, I loved seeing the country unfold and deepen as we headed east. I yearned for that feeling of being in-between: no longer rooted at home and not yet fastened to the destination. Both physically and spiritually loosened. Like Kerouac: "Nothing behind me, everything ahead of me, as is ever so on the road." I was in road-trippin' heaven.

Then the phone rang.

JLu glanced at my phone and said, "It's Speedgoat," not disguising the anxiety in her voice.

I didn't even need all the fingers of one hand to count the number of times Karl "Speedgoat" Meltzer had called me over the years. It was hard for me to imagine him using a phone or even owning a cell phone. It meant only one possible thing: He'd found out. *How had he found out?*

"I...better answer. Put him on speaker."

JLu fiddled with the phone and the new radio system we'd installed in the van, a concession I'd happily made for her entertainment on what would likely be long, lonely stretches of driving. And suddenly Karl was there with us.

"Duuuuude? *Why didn't you tell me?*"

I respect Karl. I admire him. We're longtime running buddies but also fierce competitors. I think the Speedgoat has been good for the sport, an old-school legend who isn't afraid to follow his own playbook. Nobody has won more hundred-milers than the Goat. But I was hesitant to hear his thoughts on my trail attempt. I focused on the road and let his question linger against the hum of the freeway.

"Okaaaaaay," he said. "First of all, you're going backward! Why the hell are you going *north?*"

Here we go. Karl had run the Appalachian Trail before—he'd taken two cracks at the speed record, to be precise—and been on countless missions to recon the twisted path. He knew it way better than I did; that was indisputable. But I didn't want to go in having studied the CliffsNotes. I didn't want to get schooled or steal unearned beta. I wanted challenge. I wanted adventure.

And—yeah, against my better judgment—I wanted to run north.

I didn't worry that the current record was set going south and that nearly all the other recent records and attempts were too. I knew I was running in an arguably slower direction. Karl was going to tell me I was doing it wrong, right from the beginning. And he wasn't incorrect. He had a lifetime of knowledge and experience with the trail. He'd have facts, figures, stories. The only rationale I could offer for running north was almost embarrassingly whimsical: I wanted to run with the spring. The way most thru-hikers do. The way the visionary Earl "the Crazy One" Shaffer did in 1948, becoming the first person to continuously hike the AT; he penned a memoir about it, *Walking with Spring*. I was worried that if I admitted that out loud, it might sound like I was attempting the FKT without 100 percent laser focus. Maybe aesthetic pleasure was not a sound rationale. Was I screwed before I'd even started?

Luckily Karl had other things to talk about. Namely, all things AT. He yapped on like an excited puppy. I loved that about the

Speedgoat. The AT was his baby. And pretty soon he was promising to come out in a couple of weeks and help Jenny crew in Virginia. He had an ulterior motive: He wanted to do some recon for his own record attempt next year, and he needed to drive his van out to the East Coast so it would be ready for a five-hundred-mile training run from Katahdin to Mount Washington. Southbound, of course.

JLu and I had set out on an adventure for the two of us. We had these romantic ideas about supporting each other, about hacking our way north without anyone else's help, rediscovering the very best in each other. But we were already behind schedule and taking on extras.

In Tennessee, we pulled over where the AT crossed I-40. We ran on it southbound, stretching our legs from the drive, knowing we would be retracing those steps in just a few days. I got back in the van and made one more phone call—to Jennifer Pharr Davis. When she set the current AT speed record in 2011, I was immensely impressed. I knew she was one of the strongest thru-hikers out there and she didn't run a single step during her attempt. I respected her record and I wanted her to know.

She left a voice mail in return, saying, "The Appalachian Trail is very different than a lot of other places," adding that she hoped we'd have a "really transformative experience out there" and wishing us all the best. I didn't ruminate on the way her voice hung on the words *different* and *transformative,* but I knew she'd been through the fire.

On May 25, we pulled into Georgia. The run was two days away.

And things hadn't yet stopped going wrong.

This time it wasn't my fault. The weather in Georgia was absolutely possessed—high winds and a drenching downpour. For some reason I had been imagining a sort of temperate, pleasant atmosphere in the South. As a Midwest kid, I assumed it was easier living in the southern part of the country. Instead, the forecasts were for tornadoes and flash floods on what was supposed to be day one.

The weather also meant that our good friend and adventure photographer Luis "El Coyote" Escobar was delayed getting in. Luis, who'd been running ultras since 1990, was joining us for the first few days; he'd be shooting pics while he ran and hiked with me for sections. He was flying in from California but his ETA kept getting pushed back due to flight delays and local Atlanta weather. Finally, he made it—kind of.

He arrived late at night, and JLu and I had to go pick him up at an ad hoc meeting location: a parking lot outside the Whole Foods in Duluth, Georgia. We drove in, and there, stepping out of a cab, was Luis. Utterly drenched already. And leaning into the gale at about forty-five degrees just to stay on his feet.

He was lugging a backpack that looked like it was fit for an Everest attempt. I wondered if he knew something we didn't. Wind-lashed and soaked to the bone, Luis looked defeated. Yet he was totally unfazed. Typical El Coyote.

"Amigo, I wasn't going to miss this! Whenever you call, man, I know it's going to be something good and crazy." He was game for anything. In his early fifties, he had a youthfulness that could rival the high-schoolers he coached and the twenty-somethings he hung out with. He always said that ultrarunning kept him young. That, and his spunky wife of thirty-plus years. As he says, "I'm the gas, she's the brakes," and from what I've seen, she doesn't pump them too often.

I invited him down to the Copper Canyon with me in 2006 to chase the legendary Tarahumaran runners. Whenever we traveled internationally together, we had to allow for extra airport time because his last name, one shared with a certain Colombian drug lord, always seemed to trigger additional security screening. But this time, we were taking a bus. On our twelve-hour ride back to El Paso, Texas, the bus broke down and we had to pile into another dilapidated bus that was already full. I sat on the floor between the seats with the rest of our group, but El Coyote climbed into the grimy overhead luggage rack and stretched out. For the next six hours. Luis knew how to take a beat-down. He was tough as nails but he knew something that was more important. El Coyote had the ability to laugh when he wanted to cry, the secret to longevity in ultrarunning.

He had brought his own camping gear but the rain was still relentless when we finally got back to the campground, so we invited him to spend the night inside the van—if he could fit. He found a way.

We had planned to make the twenty-four hours before day one a total rest day, a time for sleeping as much as possible, but that night, Jenny and I huddled together in our little mobile headquarters next to poor El Coyote, who lay crammed and contorted between cans of vegan chili, resting his head on a pillow of powdered coconut milk.

Castle Black hardly felt like a fortress as it shook in the gale. Rain slashed across the roof, branches scratched at the sides, the night stretched on…

…And we decided to postpone day one.

When we woke up the next morning, we knew it had been the right decision. The skies were still dark, the wind was still Wizard of Oz–ing around, and conditions were discouraging.

We hunted down a place where we could fill our brand-new mini–propane tank. We'd rely on that to make warm meals, and if the weather was going to stay like this, I was going to crave comforts at the end of each long, wet day. We checked out the AT southern-terminus trailhead, hiked a mile to Springer Mountain, and sampled some Southern culture in the form of boiled peanuts purchased at a roadside stand. My spirits were rising. I liked the South already and regretted that I wouldn't get to experience more of it.

We decided to have a last supper together with Luis and an independent film crew that was going to follow us for a few days to shoot a documentary about vegan athletes. We all met in the lobby of the lodge at Amicalola Falls State Park, and I found myself standing beneath a giant wall map of the Appalachian Trail. A bit of regional décor. The lodge held the last modern amenities that giddy thru-hikers would see before setting off on their two-thousand-mile journey.

That map made me both nervous and excited at the same time. I tried to catch JLu's eye but she was staring up at it, her neck craned to take in the whole *thirty feet* of the map. I could tell she was a little freaked out too. It looked like a map of the world or of Middle Earth. It looked *huge*.

I wondered if the lodge staff was trying to have some fun with the eager thru-hikers, giving them a little "Abandon Hope, All Ye Who Enter Here" thrill. What it did to JLu and me was make us actually come to terms with the sheer scale of what we were about to do. From our perch in Boulder—scribbling notes, looking at maps online, reading books—it had been easy for us to miniaturize and modelize the attempt. No longer. We were really here. And as I looked up at that map, in some way, it *put fear in my bones*.

Nothing about the map—or the Appalachian Trail itself—invited even the *contemplation* of speed. For starters, there's the magnitude of it. Say you started your journey at the northernmost point of the trail, the summit of Katahdin, Maine, and in a stroke of spectacular miscalculation, you tacked northeast instead of following the white blazes south. If you traveled the same distance as the Appalachian Trail spans, you would find yourself on the outskirts of Reykjavik. The AT is 2,189 miles long—the distance from Los Angeles to Atlanta. It would wind halfway around Pluto. And of those intimidating 2,189 miles, I had been on a mere twenty of them, a handful of miles in Vermont, Virginia, and Pennsylvania, less than 1 percent of the entire trail. Even with my vast experience running roads and trails around the world, the data was daunting.

Imagine running eighty-four marathons. Consecutively. Over the gnarliest and oldest mountains in the world. The AT follows the spine of the Appalachians, peaks once rivaling the towering summits of the Himalayas, now ground down by geologic millennia.

The Pacific Crest Trail, at 2,650 miles, is longer than the AT, and the Continental Divide Trail, at 3,100, is longer still. And while a lot of Westerners boast about the snowpacks and deserts, the granite outcroppings, the alpine meadows, and the oxygen-sucking heights, the fact is that if you're fit, it's a comparatively smooth ride. The western trails have their frozen passes and jagged peaks, but most miles were graded for horseback travel, and their switchbacks rarely climb at anything steeper than a 10 percent grade. As a foot-travel-only path, the AT is much sneakier and more devilish. It dives directly into ravines. It snakes into foggy river bottoms and then shoots straight up hills so dense with undergrowth that even deer have trouble climbing them. It is almost hard to describe it until you actually set foot on the AT's potpourri of rocks and roots. The tread and grade are like tentacles that grab at you from different directions when you least expect it, making forward progress a tedious and tense battle. On top of that twisted floor are walls of woods and a ceiling of tree limbs that are challenging in their own right. The Appalachian Trail is so wooded and thick, so dense and enclosed, that it is known as the Green Tunnel.

Which hadn't sounded so bad back when we were first toying with the idea at home. A tunnel sounded nice. An escape from miscarriages and the failure to start a family. A chance to focus on just one thing, to do something hard, to get away from a warm bed and pancake Sundays and a life that I loved but that had ceased to be enough for me. I think we all assume that we'll chafe against conformity and settling in our lives, but settling isn't dangerous because it's unpleasant. The real danger was that I was beginning to like it.

JLu saw it too. She knew how comfortable I had become. She wanted a new challenge for both of us. Still, standing under a three-story map of the AT labyrinth as wind and rain howled outside, we couldn't help wondering if we'd been a little hasty in picking this particular challenge.

The next morning, May 27, 2015, the alarm startled me. Not because it was loud but because I was surprised I had actually fallen asleep the night before. The rain had been pounding the van incessantly, and because we didn't have time to properly insulate the roof before we left Boulder, each drop seemed to land like an open-handed slap across the thin sheet of metal three feet above my face. It wasn't just noisy in there; it was cramped too. JLu and I were used to tight fits, but somehow the twin bed that we shared—normally without issue—seemed to shrink in the humidity.

Then there was Luis. He was curled up on the five-foot patch of floor we'd cleared for him. If he hadn't been snoring, I might have squished him when I hopped out of bed. El Coyote stacked a few boxes of coconut milk to make a chair, and the three of us drove to the trailhead in the dark. It was silent in the van. The winding road seemed endless in the rain and we were all tired and nervous. There were still so many unknowns.

Sometimes you have to go backward to go forward. We stepped onto the trail and hiked *southbound* to Springer Mountain, the shortest way to access the Southern Terminus. Fog was swirling around the viewless summit, and rocks were greasy with a mixture of rain, mud, and humidity, but there was no more postponing. And I knew that I could expect to see plenty more of this kind of weather over the next forty-odd days. We couldn't wait for perfect conditions. From the very beginning, JLu and I had been moving forward only semi-prepared.

No reason to start being cautious now. It was time.

We turned on our headlamps and signed the summit logbook.

I wrote, *On one of the biggest adventures of my life. Georgia to Maine!—Scott "El Venado" Jurek.*

And JLu wrote, *Live what you LOVE! Jenny "Raven" Jurek.*

I made a few last-minute adjustments; I tinkered with the GPS tracker and my watch. We firmed up plans to meet Luis, who would drive the van that morning so I could run with JLu; we hugged each other, and then I said, "Well, let's go to Maine!" At 5:56 a.m. our odyssey began.

We were putting everything on hold for two months. This insane Green Tunnel and the landscape surrounding it was going to be my life, our lives, for the foreseeable future. We would be eating, sleeping, thinking, dreaming out here. The planning was done, our doubts were irrelevant.

And contrary to what I'd feared, my body felt ready too. I had never run more than two hundred miles in a week, and, as a physical therapist, I knew the risks involved in logging three hundred and fifty miles a week. But I also knew how to listen to my body. I'm far from symmetrical, nor do I have the perfect physique for running, but with careful preparation and prevention, I'd never been sidelined due to an injury for more than a few weeks over two decades of racing hard.

Injuries and problems were inevitable; that was the point. We were used to problems. That's what all this was: a two-thousand-mile problem that JLu and I would get to solve on our own terms, together. Hidden in them were opportunities for growth, but we hoped there wouldn't be *too* many.

I can't remember what we talked about, or if we talked about anything. All I remember is tuning into our new surroundings and surrendering to the pull of the white blazes, each one a rectangle of white paint, two inches by six inches. It used to be said that no matter where you were on the trail, if you looked north or south, you could always see a white blaze. Despite being so rugged, the Appalachian Trail is one of the most well-marked trails in the world. That white rectangle gave hikers the extra confidence they were on the trail, and I had already found comfort following them in the first few miles.

I hadn't even begun to think of the run as an attempt, as *the* attempt, the FKT. I was enjoying the simplicity of connecting these dots, feeling more like a playful, exploratory kid, the type who dreams of someday embarking on a grown-up wilderness quest. That day had arrived.

At one point, JLu mentioned that we were making good time. I checked my watch, did a couple of calculations, and told her this was the pace I'd have to keep for the next forty-six days. She blanched (she's always been pretty bad at hiding her concerns). Four miles per hour—consistent, efficient, and metronomic. It was just numbers. I knew I could outrun numbers.

Luis joined me eight miles in at a forest-road crossing called Hightower Gap, where JLu reclaimed Castle Black.

That first day, I felt myself slipping into a rhythm I would later try to remember and replicate during more challenging days. The tunnel swallowed me, then spat me out, then swallowed me again. The rain stopped, then started, then stopped. Notions of unpaid bills and house projects evaporated. Like it had during our cross-country car trip, my mind loosened a bit as I dispassionately examined things I'd normally taken for granted. We traded the four walls of our predictable domestic existence for the four wheels of life on the road. And for me, my two feet running and moving over thousands of miles of forest-covered mountains.

That was a feeling I would chase for forty or more days. Those first few miles were the template. I didn't know what was next, and that was okay. That was more than okay. With each step, I felt as if I were being pulled forward. The reasons for the journey would come into clear focus, then blur, then sharpen again many times in the coming weeks. But my direction would never waver. After so many years of running, of winning, and then going nowhere fast, I was headed somewhere. For the first time in a while, I *had* a direction. North.

When Luis and I were on the trail together, he sometimes ran ahead doing his own thing, which left me alone for long stretches.

My mind ate up the silence, as it has done my whole life. I thought about JLu. And what we were doing, and what we had been through. I thought about our friend Dean. And I thought of my mother. She had been denied so much pleasure due to her struggles with MS, it made me not want to miss any. And I thought of my father, how discipline and control had been the pillars on which he built his life, even more so after my mother died. I remembered her stoic endurance of pain, and I remembered how my father's demands helped forge me into the person I am. As I turned these familiar memories and feelings over in my mind, I felt them begin to change shape. My roots are the calculus of who I am, but they are not *only* who I am. I was in a new place, at the beginning of a vast journey, and I felt myself grow lighter.

When Luis rejoined me, I was well on the way to Big Cedar Mountain, twenty miles in and thirty to go. We ran through the grasses and ferns of Blood Mountain Wilderness before climbing again. I had started before dawn at 3,700 feet, spent much of the day plunging through small valleys and pushing through the mud and woods that guarded them, and now we were back at 3,700 feet. We took a moment to take in the view. The vista was obscured by thunderheads and dense clouds, but I could still see distant ridges, a reminder that Georgia was nowhere close to a flat state.

I remembered from the little preparation I *did* do that the name of Blood Mountain Wilderness came from war. Cherokee and Creek tribes loved this stretch of Georgia so much that they fought a battle for it. During the definitive encounter, Slaughter Creek ran red. The victorious Cherokee named the land Blood Mountain.

The memory injected a forbidding quality into the beauty of the landscape. It felt like a wild place, a place suffused with lives and deaths. A place dense and crisscrossed with more history than anywhere out west. It made me ponder my own memories of life and death.

I finished that first day wet and tired. I would remain mostly wet and tired for the next several days. But I was *fluid* now. I had tapped into the old El Venado spirit, the one who sensed all the trail rhythms. I had been waiting for this and wanting it more than I'd even realized. I remembered what Jenny said to me during that argument in the blistering sun of the Anza-Borrego Desert.

"I want to see the *old* Jurker. I want to see you *care*, I want to see you *win!*"

I felt that "old Jurker" flickering inside of me; the fire was beginning to spark and burn a bit brighter. Horty had said, "You were made for this, boy!" and I was finally feeling it again.

I'd crewed a ton of Jurker's races, but this was total immersion, and it meant I was picking up duties I didn't have much experience with. Or, in some cases, aptitude for. Everyone who knew me was shocked and horrified to learn that I would be in charge of all the cooking. I admit it—it's not my strong suit. Climb, run, slack-line, design, sew, knit—yes! But cook? If I hadn't married Scott, I'd still be eating cold cereal and almond milk for dinner five nights a week. The other two nights would be toast with crunchy peanut butter.

Jurker was obsessed with food; it was his love language. Me? *No comprende.* It was one of the many differences between us that made us fit together. He practiced discipline and detailed precision, while I embraced wabi sabi. At home, I pursued my design career and Scott did his running/speaking/writing thing. We ran together as often as we could, but then I went climbing with my guy friends while he cooked with their girlfriends. I planned our social calendar and he handled our day-to-day lives: paid the bills; took out the garbage, compost, and recycling; trimmed the bushes; shoveled the snow; raked the leaves; planned the meals; did the dishes. It was true, I was going to be like Jurker's personal assistant out on the trail. But I didn't mind. He was my cabana boy back home. Swapping roles for a few weeks couldn't hurt.

It was never all about him, I enjoyed being out on the trail as much as he did and was having daily revelations of my own. At

Neels Gap, where I waited for Scott at mile thirty-one, I parked the van in front of an old stone building that had been converted into a store called Mountain Crossings. I started making sandwiches for Scott while Luis went inside to look for coffee. He finally came out half an hour later and said, "Hey, kid, you gotta check this place out, it's a trip."

I went in. He was right. The store sold everything from dehydrated meals and water filters to AT souvenirs like bumper stickers and T-shirts that said I HIKED THE ENTIRE WIDTH OF THE APPALACHIAN TRAIL. Hanging from the ceiling were dusty, beat-up vintage hiking boots. Outside, a tree was hung with modern boots that had been left by hikers who'd abandoned their thru-hikes here, a mere thirty-one miles in. The place had an undeniable religious feeling. It was saturated with memory and history, like it was the last piece of civilization for pilgrims before their long, treacherous journey. When I'd stood beneath that giant map in the lodge the day before we started the trip, I'd been awed by the size of the task we were attempting. It felt alien and scary. But here, beneath a pair of worn-out boots from some anonymous hiker, I finally understood the magnetism that had reached out and touched Scott—and so many others. I could feel the communal devotion, the reverence that so many felt for the trail.

My reverie was cut short by a familiar sound from outside: the signature Jurker whoop. I rushed out—and saw no one. Just thick walls of leaves all around. I was already getting used to the way the Appalachian Trail seemed to hide its inhabitants. He was out there, and he was getting closer.

Finally he whooped and came into view. It was only the first day of our journey, but I realized right away that he was genuinely having fun.

The morning of our second day started early, in the pitch-black predawn hours. We had parked on the side of the road the night before. Luis quickly packed up his tent while Scott got ready for the day's first eleven-mile section. After I watched his headlamp disappear up the trail, the darkness and silence made me realize how much I really did like having Luis around. He was half asleep but he still had that El Coyote energy. With bags under his eyes, he told me he wanted to find his three essentials—coffee, WiFi, and a toilet. These turned out to be at the McDonald's in a nearby town called Hiawassee.

We both checked our e-mail and looked at social media. I was surprised by how many people were already following and commenting on Scott's posts; once again I realized how I had underestimated the draw of the AT. The overall chatter was encouraging and supportive, but there were, of course, some critics. They didn't bother me, but Luis seemed disturbed. There was some predictable lecturing: *The AT is for hiking, do your racing on the track* and *Don't forget to stop and smell the roses*. Other stuff was more personal: *He's washed up* and *He has no multiday experience*. There was some truth to those armchair critics' comments; this was slightly out of his wheelhouse. But let's be honest—he had a pretty decent résumé.

CHAPTER 3

WABI SABI MASTERPIECE

Day Four

I HAD NEVER been where I was standing now, never even been near it. Spence Field was just one more pretty little spot deep in the hushed heart of the Great Smoky Mountains National Park. It was high on a breezy ridge in the middle of my own little terra incognita—and exactly where I needed to be.

An entire world away from my life back home. Here at my feet, an Appalachian Trail anomaly: a grassy meadow, soft as a dream. And above me: a lone oak of rustling green and yellow. Nothing around me that even remotely resembled an obligation or a routine or a phone call or an e-mail or a presentation... just the trail, and *miles*.

I'd run a marathon already and I had twenty-five miles to go to-day. I was only halfway through. Then I would meet up with JLu, sit on the edge of Castle Black's sliding doorway, remove my muddy shoes, and rinse off with a portable camp shower. We wouldn't be answering any calls from the doctor or following up on any tests or appointments. After I cleaned up, we'd climb into our van and enjoy a meal of canned Thai coconut curry over rice noodles. Out here it was very easy to appreciate the few things we had with us. It was better than lamenting what we had lost.

I was in good shape physically. I was breathing steadily, and I felt my skin cooling as I took a moment to take in the view. I was tired, of course, but the ache in my muscles felt good; I was alive, doing what I did best, and pushing myself to do more. That was the reason I was out here.

I was still in my own little honeymoon phase. We had just entered the Smokies, and a handful of excited runners were venturing out to find us. There was a buzz in the air from the locals and the AT enthusiasts online. Just that morning, a gentleman had met me outside the van at five thirty. He'd driven six hours from Louisville just to run a few miles with me. I felt bad when I had to tell him that JLu and I had planned to start that day alone. But I invited him to join me after the first six miles. He did—and so did my one-eyed buddy adventure zealot Mikey Ray and his Macho Beach Running Club friends from Charleston, including a young runner named Victor.

Victor came with a very specific goal in mind: he wanted to join me for the remote, no-road-crossings, thirty-two-mile section of trail that connected Fontana Dam to Clingmans Dome in Great Smoky Mountains National Park. I was happy to let him. We ran together for six hours or so until he told me he was going to scramble down the ridge to Spence Field Shelter and make a water run. I decided I would treat myself to a nap, the very first of the trip, while he was gone. I was making good time, and I was in good spirits, but I was so sleepy. The long trail days were taking a toll and I'd caught a case of the midday nods. Before Victor left, I told him to wake me up in twenty minutes. No matter what.

44

I arranged my hydration pack behind my head, stretched out, pulled my lightweight jacket over my chest, and let myself sink into the ground. I did some low-intensity calculations as I settled in. I was on a good pace. If I kept up what I'd been doing over the past three and a half days—difficult but doable—I'd be on track to set a new fastest-known time. Everything so far was going according to plan. Better than the plan, really. But then, as all the fatigue and sleepiness set in, doubts began to play with my brain. What had I gotten us into? Could I really do this for another forty days? What the hell had I been thinking?

Fat, majestic clouds drifted slowly across the sky, and the foliage of the Smoky Mountains forest whispered me to sleep.

I closed my eyes. And waited.

And waited.

My brain and body were not on the same page. I managed to steal a few minutes of rest for my legs, but my mind took up the slack. My thoughts were doing the racing now.

I thought back, with a pang of embarrassment, to two nights earlier when a magazine writer had called to talk about my attempt. I'd tried to express how important it was to me, how it differed from my hundred-mile-trail wins and the twenty-four-hour American road record, but I was reaching for feelings and ideas that were still incipient, even though I'd finally put my feet down on the trail. So what came out of my mouth was...less than articulate. I said something like "This is going to be my masterpiece." I was trying to sound confident, but instead I sounded full of myself. The truth is that I was afraid to say *I really don't know why I'm out here. Hopefully I figure it out over the next two thousand miles.*

This haphazard approach was new to me; it was more JLu-style wabi sabi than the calculation of my past records. But maybe I needed to fuse the dreaming artist and the scheming tactician and become a different animal. I didn't have time to ponder; my twenty minutes were half up. Victor would be back very soon bearing water. I'd missed my nap opportunity.

I focused on recovering a positive mind-set and let my thoughts drift to the day before. It had been a perfect morning; the sun had been out and the birds were whistling their little beaks off. JLu and I were entranced. We couldn't believe how loud and melodic they all were—the wrens, sparrows, and warblers especially—as we ran through a forested ridge under a canopy pierced by dawn beams. We had decided to try to run together, alone, every morning—and *not* to talk about logistics or strategy or anything "important." We would just enjoy the trail until JLu reclaimed the van.

Later, right in the middle of another thunderstorm, I ran into two women well into their sixties. We all stopped to chat, and I asked how far they were planning to go. I was expecting to hear about a day trip, maybe an adventurous overnight, maybe a drop-off and pickup somewhere on the other side of the forest. They smiled and said, "Katahdin!" Their spirit sustained me through the rest of the day. It began to rain harder as we conversed, but it didn't matter. I hoped to be just like them one day: older, vibrant, and on the trail.

Then I met JLu for lunch and submerged myself in the icy waters of the Nantahala River. I was feeling confident so I declined to pack my headlamp for the last stretch of the day, certain I would finish my miles before dark. But by the time I had climbed and descended a notorious stretch of trail named Jacob's Ladder, the sun had set. I ended up having to use my phone as a flashlight. But my mistake led to a small piece of grace, a hallmark of the trail, I would come to discover—the dense darkness of my final mile or so sparkled with thousands of fireflies, making me feel less like I was in North Carolina and more like I was in outer space. It reminded me of my childhood in Minnesota, when endless summer days finally phased into a darkness I ignored, and my mom, unafflicted by disease then, would continue tossing the baseball to me in the firefly light. I was overcome with a mix of joy and sadness that could only be explained by nature's hard and soft edges. Until yesterday, JLu had never seen a firefly. When I met her later that night, she was wide-eyed with wonder—and I forgot my sadness.

I reluctantly rose to my feet before Victor came back. I would spare him the bother of getting me up. It was time to get going again. I hadn't gotten any sleep, but I had spent some time remembering why I was out here in the first place, and that was just as good. Better, probably. It was probably okay that the off-the-cuff interview happened early in the trip, because I had to handle it. I had to accept that I would have doubts and not let those doubts derail my plans. I told myself that what-the-hell moment in Spence Field was a gift.

I knew even then that I was going to need to store up the good times. It was only day four. Day forty-four wasn't going to be cool rivers and fireflies.

Victor came back, and we set off for Clingmans Dome, where JLu would be waiting with a smoothie. Back in our planning stages, we'd barely even considered going after the self-supported FKT. Self-supporting was impressive, but it didn't fit my life right now. It involved mail drops and hiking off trail for resupplies, having the flexibility of crashing wherever the day ended, and not seeing your best friend the entire trip. The aesthetics and ideals appealed to me, but this time I wanted to share the experience with JLu.

The people along the way, like those two women I met and like Victor, were part of what kept my spirits up, even during those first few days.

At the same time, I began to realize I was becoming a flash point in an all-too-predictable controversy, one stoked by hikers and run-ners who crossed my path. The sad thing was that I was more sympathetic to the naysayers—the people who were using me as an example of the counter AT mind-set.

The controversy was perfectly summed up by a day hiker who shouted out, "Hey, what's your hurry?" as I ran down a ridge to Buckeye Gap right on the border of North Carolina and Tennessee. I didn't answer right away. I knew what he was really saying.

For some people—many of whom announce their views loudly online—the Appalachian Trail is an opportunity for unplugging, for connecting to subtler rhythms of nature, for letting go of tech-nology and submitting to forces beyond one's control. In the par-lance of the decade, it's an invitation to be mindful. And mindful-ness, for these people, must be uncoupled from ambition. When they saw me and countless others—professionals and amateurs alike—lacing up our running shoes, carrying small packs with min-imal gear, and actually running on the trail, they saw a bunch of pretentious heretics. When Jenny told me about the reverential store near the trailhead down in Georgia, with the sacred pair of beat-up boots, I smiled. But I quickly realized that there really were people who saw the AT as a kind of church. And if you were to visit any historic church anywhere in the world, you'd follow the rules and keep quiet. You wouldn't race around the pews. So in that re-spect, I couldn't blame my detractors.

And I largely agreed with their outlook. It was something I struggled with. The most joyous moments out here were those of natural serendipity and grace; the slow moments, the moments of stillness and smallness. I agreed with those who saw the AT as a place of worship.

I also wanted to beat the record and push the edges of my capa-bilities. I thought I could do both. So far, I had.

The hiker at Buckeye Gap probably wouldn't agree that you could revel in beauty while *also* struggling in pain. I didn't feel like lecturing him, but I had a bit of experience with doing exactly that. He also probably didn't know that I was moving at three miles an hour, no faster than a strong thru-hiker, not at the ten-mile-an-hour pace he likely imagined runners kept. Would he have understood if I'd told him that, though man's soul finds solace in natural beauty, it is forged in the fire of pain? That if I wanted to find real peace, I had to pass through the crucible of fifty-mile days? Probably not. Would he comprehend that there was joy in speed, and that *speed* is a relative concept in any case? Perhaps I should have told him that, even though I was covering more miles a day than most, I was also spending far more hours awake on the trail than most, so I was able to enjoy the trail and its inhabitants when it was blanketed in darkness as well as during the daylight.

I decided there was a time to discuss the meaning of life and there was a time to offer a simpler, less confrontational answer. As I went by, I kept it short.

"Gotta catch a bus."

The smoky haze blanketing the endless layers of ridges and valleys had disappeared into the thin mountain air hours ago. The sun beamed brightly and rewarded me when I came to a rare opening in the dense canopy of trees. I had been looking forward to reaching the Great Smoky Mountains even though I knew they would make me earn every mile.

To the Cherokee, these mountains were sacred. They called the area Shaconage (pronounced "sha-kon-oh-hey"), meaning "land of the blue smoke." Modern scientists learned that this sacred and mysterious blue smoke is actually fog created by the local plant life. The same biological processes and products that create that freshly mowed–lawn smell after you cut the grass are at work behind the smoke of the Smokies. Only multiplied about a billion times. It's almost like the earth itself is exhaling.

I was adding to that great communal exhalation with my own breath as the AT dragged me up and onward. Down twenty flights of stairs, then up thirty; down ten flights then back up twenty. That's what following an ascending ridge is like. A hundred feet here, fifty feet there, and on and on it went. Going nowhere fast. The trail cut a rocky path straight up, then straight down, then up and down again. I climbed two thousand feet, then descended five hundred, then climbed another thousand. By the numbers, the elevation change from Fontana Dam to Clingmans Dome is a modest forty-four hundred feet. In reality, I had to go up and down three times that, climbing more than twelve thousand feet in the span of thirty-three miles.

When pondering elevation gain and mountains along the Appalachian Trail, most people think of the high peaks of New England: the Green Mountains of Vermont, the White Mountains of New Hampshire, and the Mahoosuc Range in Maine. However, the highest mountains are actually in the South. In fact, seven of the ten highest peaks on the AT are south of Virginia, and four of them are in Great Smoky Mountains National Park; three of those are over six thousand feet high.

When Victor and I finally reached the highest peak on the entire trail, Clingmans Dome, we were greeted by a small group of runners who had driven three hours to catch me on the roof of the AT. I was hours behind schedule and I felt bad that I'd made them wait. I chatted with them a bit before starting up the spiraling concrete ramp to the lookout tower. It was a detour, but I wanted to enjoy the view. Groups of tourists leaned far over the railing with their cameras, and a small group from Alabama was shocked when they heard I was doing the whole AT. A heavyset young man seemed intrigued, and I told him he should hike the entire trail. He told me that someday he would, and I hoped he might.

We looked back out over the dense, thicketed ridges that shrouded the Georgia–North Carolina border. From the ground, those mountains looked like densely forested humps, nothing more. But the southern courtliness with which those ridges hid their hazards didn't fool me anymore. I wasn't alone in viewing that stretch of the AT with respect. The great long-distance hiker Daniel Boone described these particular mountains as being "so wild and horrid that it is impossible to behold them without terror."

That reputation had lasted, but somehow the terror of the Smokies brought me delight minutes later as I ambled beneath firs and spruces pierced by the orange beams of the sunset. Root-balls the size of dump trucks were strewn along the trail, reminding me of my insignificance in the face of Mother Nature's might. My first day in the Smokies was a long, strenuous one, but I felt alive and content as it wound to a close.

When I reached the van after 11:00 that night, all I wanted to do was lie down on the bed. But JLu insisted I rinse off with the camping shower, knowing I would sleep better without the trail grime on me. Reluctantly, I jumped out of the van and bathed with cold water in the wind and fog. As I finished up, headlights approached, and I thought a ranger was about to pop out of the vehicle and tell us we couldn't park here for the night. Instead, I heard a loud, excited voice cut through the gusts. "Hey, do you know when Scott Jurek is going to arrive?"

I knew what Jenny was thinking as she was warming up dinner inside the van—*Just tell him Scott Jurek came through hours ago!* I knew because I was thinking the same thing. Still, I couldn't help myself. JLu knew I couldn't say no to fans. So, half naked, shivering in the wind, I said, "Uh...I'm Scott Jurek."

"Oh my God! Son, get out here! I can't believe it—we found him! What luck; Scott Jurek is here! We've been driving for hours and we're big fans. My son is eleven and we run ultras together. Can we get a photo with you?"

Maybe because it was dark, they couldn't tell I was wearing only goose bumps and a camp towel. I told them I needed to put some clothes on but that I'd come back out. Jenny didn't even look at me when she tossed me some shorts. I knew she just wanted me to put my feet up and eat. And I did, but only after I posed for a few photos and encouraged the young boy to keep doing what he loves. I've met so many people at races and my events, and I've found that it's their stories that keep me going. Many athletes have inspired me throughout my career, and I feel like it's my duty to pass on inspiration in that giant circle of motivation.

As I stepped back into the van, JLu and I broke into laughter. The father and son almost saw more of me than they would've cared to.

On the morning of the fourth day, in the gray, predawn light, a white sedan pulled up and parked near our van. It was eerie to see another car out here this early, but I figured somebody had just gotten lost and spotted the light from our van. Jurker and I were getting ready to start our day the same way we'd started the previous two—by running the first section of the trail together, just us. It was by far my favorite part of each day.

But as we stepped out of the van and turned on our headlamps, the driver emerged, and he looked anything but lost. In fact, he was wearing a running pack.

He had driven six hours through the night from Louisville just to meet Jurker. I had to hand it to him for finding us—our tracker hadn't been working consistently—but it was too early for company. Friends are one thing, but complete strangers require a whole different level of presence. Also, I'm not particularly good at social niceties. Jurker, however, is a master. It's a Minnesota thing. At home, he chats up all our neighbors as I try to avoid eye contact and make up excuses to go inside. Normally I admired his friendly demeanor, but right then I wanted to slip into the trees and listen to the birdsong.

Now that I knew we would have a visitor with us, I started up the trail by myself to have some quiet moments alone. I'd barely taken a few steps off the road before it got dark again in the tunnel. In the South, night lingered past dawn in the thick woods of the trail. Wet cobwebs hit my face as I hiked forward. I quickly emulated Jurker and began speed-walking, with my poles up in a big X in front of me. On the other side of the spider neighborhood, I passed a shelter where two hikers were sleeping. It looked nice, peaceful. I missed our days on the PCT when we would sleep in and be the last hikers to leave each morning but still catch up to the pack before dusk. Pretty soon, I turned and saw the beam of a headlamp gaining on me. I was grateful to see only one.

"What happened to your new friend?"

"I told him that I wanted to run alone with you, told him he could meet me after the dam."

So we made our morning run with just the two of us after all, and it turned out to be one of the most spectacular sections of the whole trail. I'd read about the Fontana Dam in the guidebook, but the description didn't come close to doing it justice. Its scale is breathtaking, and from halfway across it, we could look out over the basin of the Little Tennessee River and see the whole world around us: the hills, the horizon, the little white riverbanks. I've traveled all over the globe and run in a lot of fantastic places, but running across that mighty dam that morning was among the most magnificent experiences of my life. It felt momentous, as if we were running to another place in our lives. It reminded me of a story Luis loves to tell about the Copper Canyon.

When he and Jurker were exploring the canyon trails outside of Batopilas with their guide, Caballo Blanco, they approached an old suspension bridge. Caballo made them stop before the bridge and said ominously, "There is adventure on the other side of this bridge. When we cross this bridge, there will be no turning back. Now, raise your right hand and repeat after me: 'If I get hurt, lost, or die, it's my own damn fault.'"

Scott and I were making tangible progress on this journey north and there was no going back. On the other side of the dam, a sign welcomed us to the next phase of the trail: Great Smoky Mountains National Park.

Standing next to that sign was the eager runner from this morning as well as a few others.

But this time I didn't mind. I had been nervous about Scott running in the Smokies alone. Road access and cell service were limited out there, and bear sightings were frequent. The additional company was welcome; he'd be doing the next thirty-two miles unsupported because the AT was blanketed by wilderness for that entire stretch.

Once Jurker and the runners took off, I hopped in the van with Luis and we drove back to a little oasis called the Nantahala Outdoor Center that we'd discovered the day before. Luis wanted to do a load of laundry. I couldn't believe it—we'd been out on the trail for only four days, Luis would be leaving in two, and he wanted to do laundry already! The van life is not for everyone.

He chucked his clothes into an ancient washing machine that was caked with dirt and hoped for the best, and while I waited for him, I went to a restaurant overlooking the Nantahala River and checked my e-mail. I had a reminder from my doctor that I needed to get my blood drawn today so we could make sure my HCG level was back down to zero after the miscarriage. *Shoot.* I had completely forgotten about that. All of it. I hadn't thought about any of it since we'd arrived in Georgia. It was nice to forget after so many months of rumination, to get out from under the dark cloud of sadness and frustration. Nonetheless, I really did need to get my blood drawn. I found a little medical clinic thirty minutes away, and Luis waited in the van while I got the test I needed so I could put that chapter of my health to bed. I hoped. When I left, I felt lighter (and a little light-headed).

This whole journey had been a direct result of another journey we had started three years ago: we were trying to have a baby. It turned out to be the most difficult thing I'd ever done. I couldn't understand why. Wasn't it my maternal right to have a baby? Everything else in my life had been attainable with a little hard work, but after doing all the diagnostics, seeing different specialists, and drawing on traditions both Eastern and Western, we had zero answers. We fell into the vague category of "unexplained infertility." And we'd had two disappointments. The first one nearly killed me. In the past, every time life had told me no, I'd put my head down, silently screamed, *Yes,* and kept marching forward. I wasn't done dreaming.

I got back to the van and discovered El Coyote fast asleep, slumped over the steering wheel. The van was idling. I would have scolded him for it, but he was exhausted, and I got it. Crewing for four days had been more tiring than we'd expected. We both needed rest, but we had a list of errands to do before we made our way to our next meeting location with Scott.

The long hours and uncertainty weren't the only tiring parts of the trip. After we left the clinic, we drove to a grocery store, a gas station, and then a rest stop where we could wash some dishes. Luis hopped out of the van wearing his running tights (so tight I referred to them as his plum smugglers), a ceramic medallion around his neck, and huarache sandals. Typical El Coyote. Nothing out of the ordinary. Then I came out in my fluorescent running shorts and a polka-dot tank top. Boulder-chic, in my opinion.

But a group of about a dozen guys lined up on motorcycles next to us in the parking lot had a different opinion. They were all in full leathers and made no effort to hide their fascination with us. As we went about our business, one of them was moved to comment, "Good Lord." Perhaps it was the clothes, or perhaps it was the image of a Hispanic and an Asian driving around in a big black van with images of Clif Bars and the words *Run Happy* plastered on its side. Regardless, after we got back in the van, we dissolved into laughter.

But only *after* we got back in the van. There were plenty of Confederate flags around. And I had my doubts about Luis and his plums if it came to a fight.

CHAPTER 4

THIS IS WHO I AM, THIS IS WHAT I DO

Day Five

IT WASN'T JUST strangers who were finding me on the trail. It was old friends too.

He was the embodiment of a crotchety prophet, that homespun coach who boosts your progress by cutting you off at the knees, and he became one of my first type 2 friends, someone who could be difficult to be around but whom I sorely missed once gone. He was my Southern Yoda.

His name was David Horton, but some called him Horty, which he didn't particularly like. A student of his—one of his many disciples of trail-running pain—had bestowed the name on him. It probably sounded better in the original South Carolinian twang, but JLu and I couldn't imagine calling him anything else. We certainly couldn't call him by his given name; he just wasn't a David. But he was most definitely a Horty. He preferred, even demanded, that people refer to him with titles of respect: Dr. Horton or even King D-Ho.

Horty and I went way back. We'd met in Lynchburg, Virginia, at the pre-race briefing of the 1998 Mountain Masochist Trail Run fifty-miler. I had placed second in my first hundred-miler, the Angeles Crest 100 Mile Endurance Run, a month earlier that year; I'd won three fifty-mile races and finished in the top three in three others. I was twenty-four years old and wore my hair down to my shoulders. I was just starting to expand my ultramarathon career, and that's why I was in Lynchburg, in the Blue Ridge Mountains. It was time to test myself against the competition east of the Mississippi. I stood out, and the race director who was presiding over the briefing that Friday evening looked me up and down, glanced at the stainless-steel bowl that held my dinner of quinoa and black beans, and then smirked. He was lanky and sinewy. Not old enough to be grizzled, but well on his way. His white polo shirt and fresh crew cut told me that my long-hair-don't-care West Coast vibe didn't belong in these parts.

"Hey, Jurek," he said in a deep drawl I would come to know well, "you're lookin' *reeeeal* good. *Girl!* What ya got in that bowl? Looks like dog barf!"

The first words spoken to me by Horty. (Much later, Jenny would have a similarly droll introduction.) Then he laid into me, Horty-style.

"Ya think you're gonna run *faaast* on these Appalachian Mountains, *don't* ya, Mr. Jurek? We grow 'em tougher out east here!"

I liked to think I wasn't one to judge someone by his or her reputation, but his reputation preceded him. Maybe this was just prickly Southern humor and his way of messing with me. In any case, I knew this seemingly straight-edged Southerner was a wild man in disguise. Despite being polar opposites, we became running buddies, meeting up for mountainous adventures.

He held a PhD in education and was a professor of exercise physiology at Liberty University, the college founded by evangelist Jerry Falwell. Along with academic courses in exercise science, he taught a running class, which consisted of a semester of students getting muddy and bloody on the trails he had built around Liberty. In classic Horty fashion, running an ultramarathon earned students an improvement in their final grade.

It was common for Horty to place signs on long uphills of his racecourses with slogans like "Fat is the enemy of speed." He founded and race-directed five ultraraces a year for fifteen-plus years. He loved trail running and the community it nurtured possibly more than anyone I knew. Most ultrarunners feared King D-Ho. Or revered him. Or avoided him. Or all three.

He loved to try to big-time me. He was one of the few people who plausibly could, at least in terms of sheer experience. He had won twenty-five ultras, including some of the most notorious and maniacal endurance races on the planet. He had owned the third-fastest transcontinental run in history, covering America in sixty-five days, running an average of forty-five miles per day, or nine minutes and fifteen seconds per mile—not bad at all when you factor in the Sierra Nevada Mountains, the Great Plains, the Rockies, the Appalachians, and the rest of the 3,067 miles of this country. In 1991 he set an AT speed record. In 2005, late in his career, he went on to set an FKT on the 2,650-mile Pacific Crest Trail, completing what he likened to a giant "*H* for Horton" across the United States: both north–south national scenic trails and the transcontinental run through the middle of the country.

Horty may not have been the most prominent champion in the sport, but he prided himself on being one of the toughest. He'd twice won the Hardrock Hundred, which, in reputation and reality, is the most grueling hundred-mile race in North America. The course, which starts and finishes in Silverton, Colorado, in the heart of the San Juan Mountains, takes runners over a fourteen-thousand-foot peak, across six snow-covered passes above thirteen thousand feet, through fast-running icy rivers, and into the heart of scree slopes so loose and steep that even runners scrambling on all fours still manage to spin in place and slide down instead of climbing up. The course ascends a total of thirty-three thousand feet and descends the same distance; as the race handouts say, it's like running up Mount Everest and back down.

The Hardrock victories weren't what made Horty resilient, though. It was how he'd won them.

In 1998, as he was ascending Grant Swamp Pass, a melon-size rock dislodged by a runner above struck his right hand. "A little later," Horty, then fifty-one, wrote in his account of that race, "I noticed that my glove was soaked through with blood." Afterward, he learned that he had a compound fracture. In 2001, he and Blake Wood became two of only three people in the world to finish the Barkley Marathons, a race designed to make finishing impossible. Its slogan was "the race that eats its young."

I'm not sure if one would call it toughness, stupidity, or that wildman spirit, but in 2011 Horty somehow convinced his cardiologist to postpone his open-heart surgery by three days so he could race-direct the Hellgate 100K. Like a cat with nine lives, he survived race weekend and was on the operating table Monday for septuple-bypass surgery. Of course he blamed the need for it on genetics and not his gas-station-fare diet.

I hadn't seen Horty since the 2014 Hardrock, shortly after he'd had his left knee replaced, when he rode around aid stations on a mountain bike. He hadn't mellowed much since then.

"*Reeeal* purty up here, eh, boy?" A hidden voice emanated from the fresh darkness.

He found me late in the evening of day five like the AT bloodhound that he was, and surprised me at the grassy summit of the 4,629-foot Max Patch. From there, we looked out over the multilayered North Carolina valleys, bathed in mellow moonlight. It would have been an exquisite moment for anyone. Even for me, after a day slogging in the rain-drenched Green Tunnel, after forty-five punishing miles through the saw-toothed ridges of the Smokies, it was still sublime. A high, lonesome Eden stretched out beneath us, its every hard edge and angle smoothed by occasional diffuse lunar light, broken up only by pockets of phosphorescent bluish-green from fox fire, a fungus that causes decaying wood to glow.

Horty loved the AT and he loved being in the mountains, but he preferred to take quick hits off the scenery-and-ambience joint. No long drags for old Horty. He had places to go and people to see. And that go-go-go mentality wasn't just for the trail; it was how he lived all aspects of his life.

I quickly realized that Horty and I had very different approaches out on the AT. We both wanted me to get the FKT, but we had different visions of what exactly that might look like. He'd shown up just in time to share a summit in Appalachia that was especially beautiful after sunset. The soft, pulsing colors, the silence and cool evening air, and the surge of dopamine coursing through my body made me want to soak in the ache of nighttime for hours, to bathe in the flush of hard-earned endorphins. Horty didn't soak. Horty didn't luxuriate. I don't think he ever had. He *was* one for offering advice, though. He told me I should get this day finished up and get on over to Lemon Gap. He said I had to be more efficient if I wanted even a hope of owning the FKT. He told me I needed to get to sleep earlier so I wouldn't have to run through the dark at night. Then he took off south, back the way he had come, down to the trailhead and his Honda Element. He shouted at me as I turned away from the fox-fire-lit valley and faced north.

"Now, boy, watch for them trail markers! Gets *reeeeal* tricky down below!"

He was right; it got *real* tricky down below. As I negotiated the wet, rock-strewn trail, my lower joints were frequently and unavoidably torqued. I felt an intensifying twinge in my right knee as I descended. And the repeated stress to my ankles and shins was throwing me off and destabilizing my gait like a shaky foundation. Whatever caused it, the knee pain had first visited me earlier in the day, on the thirty-mile descent out of the national park and along the ten-mile section where JLu joined me. I knew something was up when she kept pulling away from me on the downhills. She never drops me on downhills, not even when I have thirty miles on my legs. We laughed it off, running happily in an afternoon thunderstorm, and then I gobbled down soggy vegan cheesy potato chips. Later, JLu tried to cheer me up and mock me at the same time by blasting the *Rocky* theme song from her phone as I clearly struggled to catch up. It was in those little spaces of laughter amid the seemingly infinite muddy miles together that Jenny and I knew we were in the right place. And that sharp knee pain? It wasn't going to ruin our party. Like all seasoned runners, I tried not to think about it as I approached the day's end at Lemon Gap; I hoped it would just disappear overnight.

It didn't.

The next morning, my knee was swollen, sore, and achy. As a physical therapist, I knew enough to suspect I had irritated the cartilage beneath my kneecap. The condition is so common among runners that it has a spectacularly obvious name: Runner's Knee.

It was irritating and painful, but not fatal to my chances; it wasn't going to stop me. I had known ultrarunners to finish races as their kidneys were shutting down and they were losing control of their bowels. One veteran mountain runner, Joel Zucker, gutted out the last twenty miles or so of the 1998 Hardrock Hundred while suffering a near-crippling headache. After the race, on his drive to the airport to catch a flight to his home in Upstate New York, he died of a brain aneurysm. Runner's Knee wasn't even near the worst thing someone could have. We all kept going.

In the first eight miles of June 1, day six, I climbed five hundred feet, then dropped twelve hundred, then ascended again, then dropped again. I took some pleasure in the fact that the rain had finally stopped, and after a few miles my knee loosened up and seemed to remember its job: hiking and running fifty miles a day. That's the interesting thing about Runner's Knee (or Patellofemoral Pain Syndrome, as it is more formally known among medical professionals)—it can often feel better if you're moving, as long as the stress to the cartilage on the underside of the kneecap is minimized. Like a fresh blister that's being pressed, inflamed and angry patellar cartilage doesn't like to be poked and prodded. If you run too fast, go downhill too often, or log too many miles, there's little likelihood of recovery. Avoiding too many miles was out of the question for me, so I gambled that I could ease the burden on my right knee by putting just a bit more weight on my left leg. The bet seemed to pay off, and the morning's reprieve from pain was encouraging.

By the time I got to North Carolina Highway 212, I was late and in significant pain. I had an ice pack wrapped around my right knee and wasn't so much running as hobble-hiking. And I was only 310 miles into the journey.

I was soaking in the spirit of the trail, though. A few miles back, I had passed the Shelton gravesite, where the Union-supporting Shelton brothers were laid to rest after they and thirteen other alleged Union sympathizers, including women and children, were ambushed and brutally killed by Confederate troops. (The Shelton Laurel massacre was the basis for a scene in *Cold Mountain*.)

Next, an endless ridge before the two-thousand-foot plunge down to Devil Fork Gap to meet JLu. I'd already managed to run fifty miles, and the sun was going down. Given the century-old tombstones, the fog, the rain, and the darkness, the mood was spooky—straight out of a horror film. To top it off, when I got down to JLu and the van, Horty told us that this area was known for locals hostile toward the AT and thru-hikers. Their resentment dates back to a land-grab the U.S. government made to forge a right-of-way for the newly created National Scenic Trail. During Horty's 1991 AT record, this area was littered with booby traps: barbed fishhooks were hung across the trail on monofilament fishing line to rip through the flesh of thru-hikers. Next to the road crossing where she parked, JLu saw a handwritten sign to all the *hickers*, as it was spelled, blaming them for the death of a dog that had followed them and gotten run over by a car. It became a meme among this year's thru-hikers; they started calling themselves "hickers" and "hicker trash," as if they were a bunch of outlaws and misfits feuding with the Southern locals.

I hobbled into Castle Black while dodging imagined fishhooks. It was becoming clear that I had lost the bet with my right knee, and now there was another problem: a jabbing pain in my left thigh. I was fairly certain that I had been favoring my right knee so much that the fatigued and overused muscle in my left thigh had ripped. My quick diagnosis: a laterally torn quadriceps.

Luckily, I knew the recommended treatment. Unluckily, I knew the recommended treatment: Rest, ice, compression, and elevation, or RICE, an acronym that might as well have been SCREWED. Mild strains usually heal in about ten days, but moderate ones can take up to four weeks. A severely torn quad can keep someone out of full action for a couple months.

Time was not on my side. I lay in bed in the van with ice water dripping down my legs, one hand clutching a pot of olive-oil-drenched whole-grain pasta and the other an AT guidebook. Just twenty-four hours after the pain started in my right knee, I appeared to have injured my *other* leg to balance out my extremities. In the FKT gambling game, I needed to win more than time; I needed to score a new set of legs.

As I finally drifted off to sleep, I thought about Horty's encouraging "You were made for this, boy!" way back on the Washington PCT twelve years earlier. Then I thought about last night's hike with Horty. I wished I'd stayed up there in the moonlight.

The previous two days had brought more miles, more rain, more pain, and more doubts. The honeymoon period was definitely long gone. By the end of day six, I'd hit a seemingly insurmountable wall, built right across the Green Tunnel.

That wall grew taller each day.

I hit the trail early and alone, hobbling and grimacing, but making steady progress, until…

I blinked and tilted my head slightly upward.

I heard it before I could see it.

Far above the ceiling of oak branches, beyond the emerald tunnel that had become my entire world, the sky was cracking wide open with a thunderous roar. I'd been on the trail for only a week, but I already knew that the AT ceiling was not actually going to keep me dry.

Sure enough, as the rain intensified, it found more and more holes in the lattice of foliage overhead. Within moments, the trail was transformed into a slow-moving river of mud, and I was soaked to the bone. The soft roar of the rain smothered every other sound: my breath, my heartbeat, the splashing of my footfalls as they landed in one puddle after another. Even the songbirds had grown silent, which they never otherwise did. I was alone. I was wet. Again.

There were times when the endless trail stretching forever north felt as comforting as a shelter, and there were times when it felt like a dark, isolating cave. And every once in a while, I felt like slowly falling toward a distant something. I didn't know exactly what was pulling me on.

This was one of *those* times. It had been only three days since I stood in that high clearing in the Smokies and felt a surge of doubt and self-pity about the adventure I was finally on. But, as I was going to discover over and over again during my FKT, three days was more than enough time to go from a peak to a valley.

I was stumbling over mud and rocks and roots, making my way forward on a ribbonlike trail that rose and fell to the rhythm of the unknowably ancient geology in this part of the country. I was falling north.

Not to suggest there wasn't any variety. I don't want to give the impression that following the Appalachian Trail in North Carolina was a constant, undifferentiated stretch of suffering and pain. There was poetry and, of course, novelty. For instance, my right and left legs were experiencing entirely different injuries.

Hobble. Limp. Hobble. Limp.

Jolt. Burn. Jolt. *Searing burn.*

I was just seven days into my run, and my left leg had a severely torn quadriceps muscle and my right had a raging kneecap inflammation. With one step, I would get an electrifying jolt, as though a dentist was drilling through my right kneecap, and my next step would ignite a searing pain through my left thigh. With every other stride, I imagined someone slicing through my left thigh muscle with a butter knife.

I'd spent a lifetime pushing my body right up to its breaking point. I'd had injuries that invited me to make comparisons to all kinds of medieval tortures. I'd suffered. Twice I'd run 135 miles through Death Valley on days that hit 125 degrees. The Appalachian Trail was downright bucolic compared to the Mojave Desert.

All of that was true, and at the same time, none of it mattered.

I had never been in this much pain, ever. I'd been injured before, demoralized and beaten down. But this was different.

Seven days into my speed-run attempt on the Appalachian Trail, I was beginning to realize that there were two types of pain. There was the kind that I'd known for decades: the catalyzing kind, pain that's fierce and angry, that kicks you in the ribs as you're scrambling forward and slaps you across the face as you get to your feet. The kind that starts screaming at you as you approach the impossible—and makes you want to scream back. That pain fills you up. It weighs on you. It makes you big.

And then there's the pain that does the opposite.

This pain was *taking* from me. I was emptying. I felt like I was leaving pieces of myself on the trail. I was *disintegrating*. Very simply, I was failing, fast.

For more than twenty years, my legs have been my second-greatest asset, propelling me over thousands of miles and on runs throughout the world. They had never failed me. But my greatest asset—which I've only occasionally lost—has been my mind.

Well, it *had* been my mind.

But on that day, as my legs were indisputably failing, as the rain picked up, as the doubts started to ring louder in my ears, I understood that despite all my conditioning, despite all my attention to diet, I'd been neglecting to work on my *why*. As in: Why was I even out here in the first place?

I've experienced my fair share of success. And I know this: You rarely ask *why* when you win. It's a word you can outrun and out-perform. Applause makes it hard to hear yourself. But just because you ignore it doesn't mean it's not there. And *why* doesn't get old and tired. It catches up, and it gets louder. It churns up thoughts that are best kept down in the dark.

Maybe I'm too old for this.

Broken and very much alone, I checked my watch and limped on north.

Even if everything went according to plan, I still had *at least* thirty-five more days on the trail. Thirty-five days to chase the record and outrun the ghosts of hikers and runners who had already proven themselves. On paper, I was a strong candidate to set a long trail record. I'd endured mountains, deserts, roads, and trails filled with adversity.

And I wasn't alone, not really.

I knew that JLu was somewhere waiting, wondering, and probably feeling every bit as alone as I was. Although we were doing this together, she had her own obligations and a very different set of challenges. This trail adventure wasn't just mine; it was hers too. It was ours. It had been my idea at the start and she jumped on board quickly, a collaboration stemming all the way back to that argument in the Mojave.

I was forty-one years old and blazing my way into midlife. Some paths I'd traveled had been smooth and obstacle-free, but others had involved some hasty bushwhacking. My mother's passing, a divorce, multiple jobs, and unrealized plans to start a family had recently, rapidly, accumulated. I'd been in and out of debt, and now I was carrying a mortgage (for the first time in my life), car payments, and medical bills, financial worries that felt like a nagging injury that I just couldn't shake.

But I had plenty of experience with pain, and I was managing. Actually, I was more than managing. I was content. Endurance itself brought its own deep-seated warmth; I'd achieved a lot, and the rugged path of my life had shaped me into the person I was. And there was that paradoxical peace of mind that emerged with middle age: As I accumulated more and more memories—good and bad—the pain of each individual bad one was blunted. What's one more mile when you've already run forty-nine?

But more than that, I had so much to be grateful for. Most of all, my best friend and wife, JLu, and her willingness to let me entertain the *why*.

Way back in the desert, the *why* had seemed so obvious—first to me, then to JLu too. It felt like fate that the Appalachian Trail and I would meet for a battle of wills.

But like execution and adaptability, will is just another ingredient in the recipe for success. You can buy the ingredients for a dish, but putting them together for the perfect meal is a whole different story. Anything can happen over two thousand miles. It's a span that resists the influence of planning. In the early stages, I'd considered that a positive. I knew that my prior experiences in dealing with unforeseen adversity would be a secret weapon. I'd gotten through a lot of tough spots in my life, and I knew I would be fully capable of tapping into my best self once again to meet whatever challenges inevitably cropped up over six weeks.

I just needed to find that best self. Quickly.

Because I was beginning to realize that there was a contradiction at the heart of my journey north. Those two big reasons that had been so clear were starting to wash out and bleed away in the rain. Worse than that, they were starting to seem *antagonistic*.

Was I here for adventure—to test myself, improvise, discover, and refill myself so I could meet midlife with an open heart and mind?

Or was I here to win?

Thunder rolled above and brought me back to earth. The trail didn't care why I was here. But with, at the minimum, thirty-five days to go, I realized that everything depended on whether I did.

The rain, the muck, the rocks, and all those doubts that could trip me up worse than a gnarled root were reminders of how ruthless and sinister the trail could become. But, damn, it could be beautiful too.

Earlier in the day, at a place called Sams Gap where I-25 slices through the belly of the North Carolina Smokies, I'd been joined by an old ultrarunning buddy, Will Harlan. The trail tracks the North Carolina–Tennessee border for many miles, and Will knew these mountains like the back of his hand. He lived near Asheville, North Carolina, so this was basically his backyard. As we ran, he told me about the area's natural history, the flora and fauna, the stories about the indigenous people who first roamed these mountains and the mysterious prairie summits we were climbing. We climbed over fifty-five-hundred-foot Big Bald and fifty-two-hundred-foot Little Bald into open fields of grass.

"These balds are an ecological enigma and a conservation dilemma. Scientists still can't figure out why they exist," Will said as my crippled body struggled to keep up with my sightseeing tour.

He gave me a primer on the little crimson newts—officially called red efts—that crossed the trail and explained that this small area of the Appalachians was home to several species of amphibians found nowhere else in the world. Will's natural-history lesson was taking my mind off the pain, but throughout the morning, the muscle tear in my left quad continued to worsen. The pain must have been affecting my ability to hold a conversation because Will kept reminding me that if anyone could get through this, it was me.

That sounded right, and I appreciated it, but right then it didn't *feel* right.

During those moments of quiet, my mind snapped back from newts and grassy balds and homed back in on the pain. To try to take command of my ruminations, I started repeating my tried and true mantras: *Sometimes you just do things. This is what you came for.* I'd chosen this path, and I'd chosen to push myself to the limits of my body and mind. I knew that adversity bred transformation, that there would be an enlightening ease at the other end of this struggle. The sweetest reward lay in that ease, and it was a feeling that neither money nor power—nor a healthy quadriceps—could guarantee. And it existed in each one of us. *Stay the course; keep pressing forward*, I told myself, but part of me—a lot of me—kept questioning the choices I'd made that had gotten us out here.

The schedule and logic of the FKT made my predicament worse. It was hard to imagine that I had hit this low of despair and self-pity so quickly. *Just one week in.* And we had started so well. Before the injuries, I'd felt like I was getting into a groove, like JLu and I were working out the kinks in our take-things-as-they-come adventure.

I kind of blamed the Smokies and their long, steep descents. And I blamed Horty, wherever he was. I should have just stayed up on top of Max Patch and watched the fox fire.

I was still waiting for those new legs to materialize. Will and I were now a couple of miles from the next road crossing at Spivey Gap, where JLu would meet us. Noticing my hobbling and slowing pace, he decided to run ahead to see if he could find a hiker who might have some ibuprofen. He was shocked that I didn't have any on me, but I never use it.

My thoughts dried up and I started to feel the rain again. I wished I could enjoy the calming sound of its pitter-patter on the canopy of leaves above me. Back in Seattle, the rushing sound of water and tapping of raindrops was something I'd grown to love. But back in Seattle, the rain didn't feel like a wet and inconvenient metaphor for my world crashing around me and flowing down a flooded trail.

When things got really bad, I instinctively thought of Jenny. I thought about how she might be even more disappointed than me if I had to stop. I had told her I was doing this one for her. I knew almost down to the word what she'd say if I told her I was thinking of pulling the plug, and the thought of that conversation crushed me even more.

Hobble. Limp. Hobble. Limp.

Creak. Thump. Electrifying jolt. Thud.

And of course—

Searing burn.

I was at the lowest of lows and couldn't imagine things getting any worse. And then I heard that voice.

"There's that runner! How ya doin', boy?"

Good old Horty was back in his usual form.

Quite frankly, I wasn't in the mood for Horty or for his boundless energy. I'm not sure what I *was* in the mood for, but whatever it was, it wasn't Horty. But he knew this trail, and twenty-five years ago, nearly to the day, he had been chasing the same speed record. Now, at sixty-six years old, he had a wealth of experience and wisdom—and, unfortunately, he knew that.

"What's da matter? You lookin' like an ol' man," Horty hollered for the entire forest to hear.

I shook my head, wincing in pain and signaling my mood. *Don't even start with me,* I thought. "It's bad. Real bad," I said. "I've never had a muscle tear like this, right in the belly of my quad. I can barely hobble. It's taken me two hours to go the last two miles and I'm getting slower and slower."

Horty knew where I was at, physically and mentally, and, to his credit, he used the opportunity to be helpful rather than just loud and obnoxious.

Fortunately, we weren't far from the crossing.

"Let's get down to the van. Jenny's made you some sandwiches and she'll get ya some dry clothes. Will found some ibuprofen. Got a real nice, long climb ahead. It'll get you feelin' better. Those eccentric contractions are the worst for that quad and knee. These downhills are *naaasty!*"

I let out a big sigh of frustration and said, "Horty, I don't know what I'm going to do."

He started off, and hobbling down the trail behind him, I tried to put on my game face, but dark emotions were running through my veins. I sensed the tears welling up deep behind my eyes. Just when I felt like I couldn't hold them back a moment longer, Horty spun around and looked straight into my soul.

"Remember this, boy: *This is who I am, and this is what I do.*"

He was still crazy old Horty, and on any other day, that would have sounded like nonsense. But in that moment, it felt like an answer to that question I couldn't shake.

Why?

This is who I am.

This is what I do.

I leaned over, grabbed the atlas sitting on the passenger seat, and traced my index finger over the red dotted line that signified the Appalachian Trail. I'd been driving up the seam that connects Tennessee and North Carolina for the past two days. I didn't know which state I was technically in at the moment, but the nearest town was Erwin, Tennessee.

I'd last seen Jurker at Sams Gap, and I'd left him there right when it started to pour. It came down so quick and hard it almost looked fake, like those cheesy sheets of rain you see in old movies. The Jureks in *Jurassic Park*. He was wearing a tank top and shorts and I could see the bright red bumpy rash that had appeared overnight and crawled over his entire torso. Along with that rash, there was the poison ivy that he'd picked up before we left home. And the humidity meant that his skin was constantly chafed by his wet clothes. Everything got—and stayed—wet. In Colorado, we were used to clothes drying out nearly instantly. We weren't in Boulder anymore.

Having lived in the Northwest for years, I was used to the rain. In fact, I'd grown to love the rain, especially running in it. But out here, you got soaked even when you had a roof over your head. The humidity made sure that beads of sweat constantly rolled down my legs from the back of my knees, and I wasn't even the one running fifty miles a day. Nothing escaped the wet. Even everything *inside* our van got damp. The bag of Scott's dirty clothes reeked of wet dog; loaves of bread got moldy within twenty-four hours, and fruit went bad nearly as quickly, all of which added to the odors of the sixty square feet I called home.

But I wouldn't have traded places with Jurker.

Wherever he was.

When you crew for someone at a race, you rush to the next aid station, get everything ready, and spend the rest of your time checking your watch and craning your neck to look for signs of movement on the trail. They say it's the hurry-up-to-wait game. Every time I checked my watch, more worry set in. I was scared I'd somehow missed him, but that wasn't likely. He couldn't have already passed through—or could he really be moving that fast? The majority of the time, I was waiting at trailheads that didn't have cell service, so I couldn't check the GPS tracker like we had planned on being able to do. The irony was that all the people following along on their computers at work or home had a better idea of where he was than I did.

All I knew for sure was that a guy I'd never met before, Will Harlan, was running with Jurker. Jurker hadn't told many people about the trip before we left, but once he'd posted a picture of a white blaze on social media, people started asking if they could help.

Help can be a complicated word.

It all came from a good place, I knew, but I wasn't as chatty or as patient as Jurker. The last thing I needed was a bunch of friends, runners, and strangers trying to coordinate plans with me, especially out here where it was hard to communicate with anyone beyond shouting distance.

It's almost impossible to get lost on the Appalachian Trail, but driving around and finding all the rural backroads that intersect the trail is another thing. So far it seemed that for every ten miles Jurker ran, I had to drive thirty miles. And whenever I thought I was getting close to the trail, I'd have to slow down to a crawl and try to catch a glimpse of that white paint through an opening in the trees.

I drove a little farther, around another curve in the narrow road, and that's when I saw Horty's unmistakable bright orange Honda Element parked at the trail crossing. I felt my shoulders relax. I knew I'd found the right place.

I'll admit it: I cringed when I first heard Horty was going to meet us on the trail. My only prior experiences with him were from years ago, back in 2003, when he'd made fun of my high-pitched voice at the start of my first fifty-mile trail race. I'd started running only two years before that, so I was nervous, and here was this revered ultrarunner David Horton mocking me. "Ginnnny!" he said, imitating my voice. "Ginnnnnnnny, are you gonna run this race? This is a *man's* race, Ginny!" I walked away and thought, *How in the world does this flagrant heckler teach at a Christian university?* When I crossed the finish line (only fifteen places behind Horty, just for the record) and saw him lying down in the medical tent, I realized that the old dog was all bark and no bite. I'd come to realize that taunting was his love language. If you could take it and, better yet, dish it out, then you were A-OK in his eyes. So despite his bullying, Horty turned out to be really helpful.

As I parked Castle Black behind his car, I could see Horty hunched over in the driver's seat studying his AT data book and scribbling notes. I figured he was reflecting on his own AT FKT run, and I hoped he was remembering something useful.

While Horty was hatching plans, I started making sandwiches for Jurker and getting his supplies ready. The rain pounding on the van was lulling me to sleep, but I had to stay awake, so I cranked up some music and almost forgot about worrying until I saw somebody running toward me.

"Hey, Scott's a few minutes back," Will said. "He's hurting. He can't put weight on his left leg and his right is messed up too."

About five minutes later, Jurker staggered out of the woods, using his trekking poles like crutches to support his body. I wanted him to stop, sit down, and tell me what was going on, but Horty was taking charge.

"When I was on this section of the AT, my shins were killing me, but I just walked and got the miles in anyway."

Jurker, wait. Talk to me. Don't just keep going because Horty wants you to was what I wanted to say. But I swallowed my words. Horty knew the AT. But I knew *Jurker,* and I knew he wanted to stop. He ducked into the van and sat in the passenger seat. He stared blankly out the windshield, through the rills of water and raindrops.

Horty rapped on the passenger window. He had a plan. He would leave his car here and walk the next ten-mile section with Jurker. This sounded like a terrible idea to me. I knew that Horty had had knee-replacement surgery just last summer and hadn't walked farther than five miles since then, but again I bit my tongue. Maybe having Horty out there would be a kind of balm. Or maybe I was about to be responsible for two gimps out there on the trail.

No time to wonder. They set off. The two old friends crossed the road and immediately disappeared back into the green. I could hear their voices long after I could no longer see them.

Horty left me a list of instructions cribbed from his notes.

I drove to Erwin and booked a room at the hotel closest to the trail, the Mountain Inn and Suites. I didn't want to end the day there; that would put us behind our schedule. However, the idea of a hot shower—the first in almost a week—and the prospect of drying out our clothes sounded nice. Next, I went to Walgreens to buy the strongest anti-inflammatory painkillers I could get. That's when I knew things were *really* bad. Jurker never took pills or any meds at all, ever. In the suddenly foreign, fluorescent-lit cleanliness of Walgreens, I started to think our trip was over. *Well, that was a bust. How's he gonna explain this to the internet?* I wondered. Perhaps: *I blew my wad early...the end.* Or maybe: *I'll get it next time; this was just a rehearsal run.*

No, there would be no next time. We were one and done.

After my errands, I drove out to the trail crossing near Uncle Johnny's Hostel and got a text from Horty saying that they were closer to the road than I'd expected. Somehow, some way, they were moving steadily. I texted back, Excellent! I have two wheelchairs and some Geritol on ice ready for you guys!

I hiked up the trail to meet them and crossed their path right when there was a break in the rain. Horty was playing tour guide, pointing out where the old AT trail used to come down, and when we got a view of Erwin proper, Horty yelled, "Heeeeyyyy," at the top of his lungs and the valley answered back. Jurker was still in pain, but for a moment I forgot about the impossibility of what we were doing and I remembered that feeling we'd both had when we were crossing the country to get here. We really were on an adventure. A little rougher than we'd imagined, but an adventure nonetheless.

They had caught up to a thru-hiker nicknamed No Poles who was keeping a similar gimpy pace because his boots were so uncomfortable. When the four of us reached the van, Jurker pulled out his brand-new size 12 Brooks Cascadia trail-running shoes. (Scott wore an 11½ but he'd brought a size 12 just in case his feet swelled). He and Horty each autographed a shoe and gave them both to No Poles. If our trip was over, Jurker wasn't going to need them for the drive home.

I shuttled Horty back to his car and then the three of us went back to the hotel room. I made dinner, fusilli pasta with red sauce with vegan-sausage bites. Horty was too tired to make fun of my cooking and even asked for seconds.

The two trail-worn men lay down in separate beds with an old lamp on a nightstand between them while I cleaned up and got things ready for an early start the next day. But then Jurker, who had been more quiet than usual, came clean. "I just don't see how I can do even forty miles tomorrow with two bad legs." I stayed quiet. I didn't want it to be over, but I knew it didn't matter what I wanted.

Jurker took out the anti-inflammatory pills, and Horty leaned over, stretched an arm across the gap, and said, "Hey, pass me some of those, boy."

It was nothing, a moment of shared pain and resignation, a little bit of humility between two crazy runners, but I started laughing. We had hit rock bottom.

Before he fell asleep, Horty said with authority, "Your body will find a way to heal itself. It has a memory." He turned off the lamp. "Your body will remember."

CHAPTER 5

NEVER BET AGAINST
THE CHAMP

Day Eight

HORTY SAID MY body would remember.

But Horty didn't say *what* my body would remember. I think he meant it would recall the glories of my past victories and that it would rise for one final victory, like a battle-scarred veteran. The long-term memory of a lifetime of triumph. But when I woke up in that hotel, my body had only a short-term memory: the reverberation of every single footfall from the past eight days. Every step and misstep, every root, every rock. And the memories concentrated like clots in my right knee and left thigh.

My injuries were bad. I knew it, and Horty did too. And JLu, who wanted this record as badly as I did, was worried because I was resorting to pain relievers. But truthfully, I could have skipped them altogether. In fact, I stopped taking them after a day because they weren't helping.

But just to be sure, just to confirm that my mind wasn't concocting some excuse to quit so I could give myself an easy out, I got out of bed and took a step…and clenched my teeth in agony. I lay back down and took some comfort in the fact that this time no one could say I had given up. My body had given up on me.

And then, the voice of cruel reality.

"Just get to Roan Mountain and Carvers Gap," said Horty. "Roan's the key. It'll be a nice climb, make you feel good, and the uphill will be easier on those injuries. It'll remind you of the Pacific Northwest up there. Big ol' pine trees, and it's foggy. Jenny, when you get to Carvers Gap, drive up toward the summit and walk on up to the lookout. Bee-you-tiful! It's a little hike, but, man, is it worth it!"

Horty was all rambling optimism this morning. He was saying some nonsense about…getting out of bed and getting back on the trail. I let his Southern-drawled comments pass without reply. Instead, I reflected on several things, ranked in order of pertinence. One: I could barely walk. Two: Roan Mountain was a crushing thirty miles and forty-five hundred feet of elevation from where I lay at that moment, looking up at the hotel ceiling. Three: Because of the pitiful thirty-three miles I'd covered yesterday, I now needed to average *over* fifty miles a day just to stay on record pace. Four: I would be lucky just to make the thirty-six miles to Carvers Gap today. Five: I risked further injury if I pushed myself too far. Six: Horty would be leaving this morning, Luis had left two days ago, and I did not like the idea of JLu alone on the rutted dirt roads of the Deep South while her crippled husband hobbled along somewhere too far away to help her. Seven (and possibly most important): Horty was a crazy old man.

I ran down this list with JLu. She understood how I felt, she said, but disagreed with two of the points. She said that I wouldn't do any permanent damage, that I knew my body well enough to pace myself. And as for my concern about her well-being in Dixie, she gave me one of her give-me-some-freaking-credit-Jurker looks. I got the impression that if I stayed in that motel room, she would knock out the five remaining points as well.

So on June 3, at 6:30 a.m., after downing a banana, a Nuts and Seeds Clif Bar, and a room-temp coconut-milk latte, I put on damp shoes, wrapped my knee and quad, kissed my warrior wife good-bye, and started limping toward sixty-two-hundred-foot Roan Mountain, a towering pile of mossy rocks and conifers in eastern Tennessee and the highest peak before the AT dipped into Virginia. I was outnumbered in that motel room. Horty and JLu weren't going to let me stop.

Anyone following my progress on the GPS tracker thought I was on day eight of my courageous attempt at the FKT. To me, though, it was day one of the second phase of an impossible goal. I was crawling up from the bottom of a seemingly bottomless abyss. I had lain in bed and given up, and if it weren't for the grit of my wife and the wanton disregard for my health that came naturally to Horty, I would gladly have fallen back to sleep in the shadow and comfort of that abyss. So this second phase was going to be different. I felt that immediately. It had to be.

I was going to put the FKT out of my mind. I needed to focus on just *being* here. I'd make it through the next few miles, few hours, few days by keeping my mind tethered to the ground. No more forecasting forward, no more lofty goals. I wouldn't be pursuing anything. I wouldn't be trying to prove anything. I would be a guy with two bad legs out for a long hike. The pain was still there, and it was still enough to rule out a record attempt, but I'd figured out a way to use my hiking poles as crutches and lighten the load on the leg that hurt the most. I wouldn't set any speed records, but I wouldn't cripple myself. JLu was right. I knew my body and how far I could push it. And maybe Horty's half-baked wisdom would turn out to be somewhat true.

After Unaka Mountain and seventeen miles of crutching myself up another vicious, rocky, hellish, sweaty, Rorschach-inkblot-looking stretch of land that most would hardly term a *trail*, I heard a familiar voice.

"Hey, peg leg," JLu shouted from just up ahead. She caught me midmaneuver; I was halfway over a huge tree trunk, straddling its girth with my bum legs.

I wasn't expecting to see her yet, miles away from Iron Mountain Gap, and my first thought was a funny one. When I'd left her that morning, I had been ready to give up, so I felt I needed to look suitably tortured now, but I was just too happy to see her. My plan from that morning—to keep things simple—had already begun to work its destressing magic. Jenny's presence made it even stronger. So what if I knew I wouldn't make the record? So what if she still thought I could? We were together, we were in the mountains, and we were alone. And at least I was making *some* progress. She hiked and I hobbled along to Cherry Gap Shelter so that we could sign the shelter logbook, another way to leave bread crumbs and proof of my progress. Transparency and documentation were high on my list.

JLu continued on the shorter outbound path that reconnected with the AT, and I crutched myself back up the way I'd come on the inbound shelter trail. Jenny asked what I was doing, and I told her that I was making sure I didn't miss any of the trail. If I was going to complete the AT, record-setting or relaxed, I was going to hike the entire AT. No shortcuts, even if it was only a hundred feet.

That kind of austerity was important to Horty and fundamental to the ultrarunning ethos. Honor and integrity were everything. Not that I'd needed reminding of it, but Horty called me anyway the week before we drove to Georgia. "Now, make sure that whenever you leave the AT, whether getting water or going to a shelter, you come back to the same point you exited. And at the end of each day, cross the road and touch a landmark, a tree, rock, or sign, where the trail continues. That way you'll know where to start the next day and you won't miss a speck of the trail. That's what I did."

I didn't do it because Horty told me to, nor was I some self-righteous stickler for rules; it's just that the mystique of the AT had always seemed to me to be its comprehensiveness. Not doing it *all* was the same as not doing it, period.

Not everyone pays as much attention to the unwritten code of conduct on the AT. The more obvious violators are easy to spot, if only by what they leave behind: Beer cans, toilet paper, empty bags of potato chips—the quality-of-life violations endemic to all public land in the nation. Then there are the more subtle transgressions: Cutting switchbacks, leaving fire rings, and making a lot of noise after dark, particularly in areas where there are likely to be other campers, like shelters. These are the misdemeanors of the AT, irritating and impolite but they often go unnoticed. Some people just don't know any better. And some hikers get accused of "yellow blazing"—that is, hitching a ride (*yellow* referring to the stripes on paved roads) to avoid a section of trail. Among the unwritten, wildly interpreted FKT ethics, there is only one inviolable rule: Cover every step of the trail under your own power.

Personally, I chose a strict FKT ethic because unfortunately, for whatever reason, people really do cheat. That was the primary reason I carried a seven-ounce GPS tracker, and why I'd decided to share the tracker online. There were plenty other smaller and lighter trackers available, but I heard this one was the best. Anyone could check on me at any time. I also made sure to take time-stamped photos, post updates on social media, and talk frequently to fellow hikers. I knew there would be doubters, as there always were when anyone was trying to break a record. As there should be.

Jenny and me starting our Pacific Crest Trail section hike, May 2013, Campo, California. *(Scott Jurek)*

Jenny climbing through the zigzags of Half Dome. *(Dean Potter)*

Jenny topping out on the Regular Northwest Face of Half Dome with Dean Potter, June 2011, Yosemite National Park. *(Dean Potter)*

Where it all began, Appalachian Trail southern terminus, Springer Mountain, Georgia.
(Luis Escobar)

Signing the logbook before setting off from Springer Mountain on May 27, 2015.
(Luis Escobar)

Wrapping up 53 miles on Day 1 at Unicoi Gap, Georgia. (Luis Escobar)

Morning of Day 4, crossing the Fontana Dam outside Great Smoky Mountains National Park. *(Luis Escobar)*

The start of my knee injury on Day 6, Lovers Leap Rock, North Carolina.
(*Luis Escobar*)

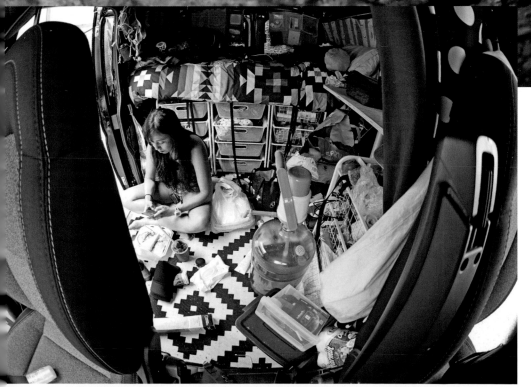

Taking it all in on Day 7, Cherokee National Forest, North Carolina. *(Luis Escobar)*

Jenny keeping it all together in Castle Black on Day 9. *(Luis Escobar)*

Cooling off with Jenny in Laurel Creek, Virginia, in the midday heat of Day 13. *(Luis Escobar)*

Trail magic from an athletic trainer on Day 15 near Trout Creek, Virginia. *(Luis Escobar)*

Signing the logbook at War Spur Shelter, Virginia, on Day 15. *(Jenny Jurek)*

Restocking at Castle Black, somewhere in central Virginia. *(Luis Escobar)*

Morning sunrise on McAfee Knob, Day 16. *(Luis Escobar)*

Speedgoat describing how tight the record is, Day 21, Shenandoah National Park. *(Jenny Jurek)*

I was well aware of the friendly rivalry between the trail-running and hiking tribes. I welcomed the scrutiny.

It was early afternoon by the time JLu headed back, and I was covering only two miles an hour. The terrain exacerbated my injuries and tested my newfound mindfulness.

I was a full-time hiker who was hobbling. I planted my poles on a mosaic of rocks that looked like a tile floor slapped down by a madman, swung my left leg, planted it again. Tapped the ground with my right. And again. And again.

It was a particularly tedious stretch of the trail, a section of slick rocks and shifting mud. These mountains were ancient here, which meant that I was hiking over a kind of graveyard of gigantic boulders. Over eons, the mountains had sunk into the earth and been worn down into low hills by unrelenting winds and rain. Now I clawed over their harsh, bleak remains, and I too felt ancient.

As I picked my way forward over the rocks, I heard some hikers approaching me. I felt a twinge of annoyance—I was feeling sorry for myself and wanted to walk it off in solitude.

It was two women, probably in their early fifties.

"Hey, you're *Scott!*" one of the women said. "We've been reading about you. How's it going?"

"Not very well right now," I said before I could censor myself.

Their faces fell; it was as if one of their own children were hurt. "I'm sorry," they both said, almost in unison.

I felt embarrassed that they'd caught me at a low point.

"Where are you ladies from?" I asked.

"Ohio."

I told them I was from Minnesota. They were section-hiking southbound for a week. I asked them to tell me more, to tell me all about their plans. They seemed surprised—they'd probably expected me to talk about my adventure, but I was much happier to hear about theirs. They had no rigid schedules, no timetable, no mission besides enjoying nature and their friendship. They had a confidence and cheerfulness that reminded me of my mother, and I found myself telling them about my injuries.

"That sounds bad," one of them said sadly, "but you can do this, Scott. I can tell that you've got what it takes."

"We're rooting for you," the other said softly. I guess I wasn't going to be the one providing inspiration this time. They left me and continued on south. Those women had given me something more than a nice story about their hike. They'd given me hope.

To be a trail angel, in the parlance of long-distance hikers, is to offer one or many acts of kindess. Some angels conjure their magic in quiet, subtle ways. Others are more practical and direct, bringing food and water and good cheer. I knew I could count on JLu for much of the latter. Without knowing it, the Ohioans had given me a bit of the former. (Later I would meet other angels: The stay-at-home runner moms who got me through a rough patch in Virginia. A seventy-year-old mother from Elizabethton, Tennessee, located me because her son, living across the country, said I would be coming through and she had to meet me. She told me he had taken up running after reading about me in *Born to Run* and *Eat and Run,* and it had changed his life. Then there were my tribe-based angels, the ones who brought vegan vittles to me or arranged rocks and leaves to spell out GO, SCOTT in the middle of the trail. I would encounter scores of them, and I would enjoy their smoothies, chocolate cakes, cold beer, fresh fruit, and notes of encouragement.)

Finally, there were the heavy hitters, the big-league angels who achieved trail-wide fame. One drove a van up and down the roads that the AT crisscrossed, looking for anyone who needed a lift. Another let hikers stay at her house for free. Some offered showers; others, laundry services. Some angels left coolers filled with cold water, soda, and even beer in the middle of the trail. However, in the hiking community, there was a growing concern that the activities of these angels led to littering and that they attracted hikers who weren't hardy enough to be on the trail.

Some angels set up grills at road crossings and cooked up burgers and dogs for hungry hikers. I even got a homemade tempeh burger from one of these barbecue angels. The veteran angels even had names: Baltimore Jack, Trail Angel Mary, Miss Janet. They, along with the quieter, more anonymous angels, all performed variations of trail magic, which was experienced by others as unexpected instances of serendipity or just moments of *Whoa, I needed that*. Some people outside the trail world might just call it performing random acts of kindness or being a Good Samaritan. Or maybe, at the core, helping someone reach a goal is what it means to be human. I would lose count of the angels I encountered as well as the doses of trail magic they bestowed on me.

As the long, slow day dragged into evening, I needed to heed nature's call. So I scanned the leafy ground cover for rattlesnakes and then walked into the brush. I was an ultrarunner and a lifelong outdoorsman; dropping a deuce in the woods was nothing new to me. But my right knee could barely flex forty-five degrees, and the quad muscle on my left leg couldn't support even half my body weight, so squatting became an acrobatic feat. I managed to get myself into a position that was more like an improvised yoga pose than a squat, but when I finished, I realized that if I tried to get up, I would either pitch face-first into the ground or fall backward, creating even bigger problems.

Then I heard the raven call. *"Kraaaaa!"*

JLu had apparently gotten concerned about my lateness and run in from the next crossing at Hughes Gap to meet me. Unfortunately, she arrived just in time to see me with my pants down in my absurd yoga pose. She asked, "What are you *doing?*" She tried to hold back her laughter but couldn't. I didn't bother to answer. Dodging the poison ivy, she found my hiking poles, put one in each of my hands, and magically pulled me upright. Trail magic in its most rudimentary form.

Before El Coyote left, he'd very solemnly looked me in the eyes and said, "I don't want to leave you, kid."

I faked some confidence and said, "Oh, don't worry—he'll be fine."

"I'm not worried about Venado," El Coyote replied. "I'm worried about *you.*"

I knew what he meant even though I tried not to think about it. Luis had been driving with me in Castle Black as I navigated (directions were not El Coyote's strong suit, as I found out) all these dirt roads and back ways, through mud and rocks at all hours of the day and night, often totally cut off from the reassuring resources of cell service and law enforcement.

And now Horty was leaving too. He didn't want to go—I could tell he was just getting started—but he had signed up to ride his mountain bike along the Continental Divide. I'm not sure how it happened, but Horty had grown on me, and his departure was bittersweet. He'd brought a ton of trail knowledge with him, he'd been in Jurker's shoes, and he'd given us confidence that we weren't doing it all wrong. Not only that, but he actually doled out a compliment on my navigation skills. I was shocked. "Oh, you mean not bad for a female Asian driver, right?" I joked, but I had to admit I was kinda killing it at the map-reading game.

After a week of chasing a moving target on the Appalachian

Trail, I was starting to be able to read the contours of the mountains and accurately guess where our next road crossing would likely be. Even through the thick trees, I could almost sniff out the trail. Though I wasn't following every step of the trail, I felt as though it was becoming a part of me.

I was also getting a handle on Castle Black. In our first week living out of the van, we'd fallen into an inefficient rhythm: make a mess, clean it up, make an even bigger mess, clean it up. We were drowning in too much stuff. Jurker was a classic just-in-case packer and he'd filled Castle Black with plastic bins and boxes of crap that were constantly getting in my way. I realized I had a golden opportunity in Horty's departure.

"Hey, Horty, do you mind if I give you some things to take home with you? We can pick them up on our way back to Colorado."

Before he could respond, I started loading boxes of nondairy milk and bags of rice into his trunk. I packed up all of Scott's casual clothes—jeans, shorts, button-down shirts, Birkenstocks— and loaded them into Horty's trunk. How naive we had been. I'd imagined us going out to dinner or grocery-shopping some evenings, but the sad reality was that Scott wasn't going to be wearing anything but running clothes for the next five weeks.

I also grabbed some pots and pans I hadn't used yet, as well as our only stove.

Horty said, "Hang on." He dug around in his trunk and came back with a tiny Jetboil camping stove. "Here, take this. This is all you need." It was perfect. Our camp stove was a bulky two-burner device with a two-gallon propane tank. Just as Horty and I were finishing our trade, I heard a voice in my head. It was Jurker saying, *You did* what *with our stove? Have you lost your mind?* So, on second thought, I brought our stove back inside the van. *Better keep this, just in case.*

I opened the back doors and glanced through Jurker's bins. I shouldn't go rifling through those; they held his essentials: trekking poles, hydration packs, headlamps, energy food, stuff like that. But then I saw boxes of unopened Clif Shots. They were the über-caffeinated ones, the double espresso and chocolate cherry shots. He hadn't had a single one; the last thing he wanted to do was stay up at night. At the end of each day, he just wanted to pass out. And the boxes were taking up room. I was tired of moving them to get to the other flavors.

"Hey, Horty, do you think you can use these on your bike ride?"

"Sure, I'll take those."

Little did I know this one decision would come back to haunt me.

Horty packed up and told me to call him with updates. I was sad to see him go, but I was more than ready for Jurker and me to blaze our own adventure.

Be careful what you wish for.

Just before leaving, Horty took me aside and gave me a final suggestion. He told me that I should make sure to drive up the side road to Roan High Knob when I got to Carvers Gap that night. The remains of the old Cloudland Hotel were up there, and on a clear night the views were incredible.

Cloudland, I found, was appropriately named—the road seemed to be cloaked in cotton. It was dusk and I could barely see five feet in front of me. I inched up the road, nosing the van through the heavy fog. It had an eerie feel and suddenly I was hyperaware of being alone.

Then headlights came up behind me out of nowhere and started tailgating me. Since I had no idea where I was and no desire to speed in these conditions, I pulled over to the far right and waved the car to pass. Instead, the driver pulled up behind me.

A man got out of the car. He started walking up to my door. I immediately rolled my window up. As he approached, he gave a friendly wave, and I cautiously rolled the window down halfway. I could still barely see through the fog, especially with his glaring headlights in the background.

A pause, and then his voice: "Oh, wow, we found you! I cannot believe it!"

I knew the voice. And when he shifted in the light, I recognized the face. It was the man from back in the Smokies who'd brought his son out to find Scott shivering in his towel. Team Father Son; what were they doing here? Hadn't they gotten their fill of Scott?

"Tomorrow is my birthday and I really want to run with Scott on my birthday!" the man explained, perhaps sensing that he was freaking me out. I thought that was sweet, and I relaxed and let my guard down. Just then, another set of headlights pulled up behind us. I waved at that other car to pass, but, again, this one pulled over to the side of the road.

"Oh, he's with us. I recruited a local to take us to all the trail crossings. We've been looking for you for days!" Suddenly, I felt myself stiffen up again.

It wasn't just that it was a little creepy. It was also deeply inconvenient to have to play tour manager to excited fans. I had a long list of tasks to do before Scott came in for the night. But it wasn't in me to turn them away. So we all took off and drove to the parking lot. By this time, the fog was lifting and the orange-purple light of sundown imbued the air around us.

Team Father Son started to suit up and get ready for a run and I told them if they started heading south, they'd run into Scott. It was a win-win situation: They would get some trail time with Jurker and I'd get some peace and quiet to clean and organize the van before he got here. Also, I wasn't sure if he had a headlamp with him, so it made me feel better knowing that TFS could offer him some light on the trail.

They asked their guide where the trail was and he said, "Oh, it runs right through here, goes along by this parking lot." He pointed them in one direction and they disappeared into the woods. It was a little strange because I didn't think the AT crossed here, but he was the local, so I shrugged and went on with my chores.

I parked Castle Black and filled my plastic washbasin with water from the bathroom. I was almost done washing all the dishes when I saw two headlamps bounding toward the parking lot. It was Team Father Son. They couldn't find the Appalachian Trail and they'd been looking for almost thirty minutes. I saw them huddling up with the local while I continued organizing. Had their guide sent them the wrong way by mistake?

After a few minutes, they took off again, this time in a new direction. Their guide stayed behind and seemed to be relaxing and taking in the sunset. I walked to the far end of the parking lot and searched the trees where he'd sent the father and son into the woods. No signs of white blazes anywhere. I jogged along the perimeter and didn't see any white blazes. "Hey, where did you say the trail comes out?"

He said, "The AT doesn't run through here; it avoids this parking lot."

I didn't even respond. This was too weird. I slammed the sliding door to Castle Black and peeled out of that lot as quickly as possible—and then I saw him hurry to his car and follow me out. *What the heck?* Why had he sent the runners on a wild-goose chase? More important, why was he following me? I sped up; he sped up. I took a hard left into a parking lot. He followed me into the lot. I backed out, and he backed out.

I thought about the one cast-iron skillet I still had in the van. It was within reach. I parked on the main road in front of the Carvers Gap sign. He pulled up next to me. I turned off the engine and locked the doors. He stayed in his car.

I started to panic: What if I'd missed Jurker while I was up there listening to this clown? I studied my atlas. I guess I wasn't killing the map game after all.

Suddenly, I saw a faint orb of illuminated fog. It got bigger and brighter, but it was moving too fast to be Jurker, especially on two bad legs. Was it Team Father Son? Why was there only one headlamp?

"Whoop-whoop!"

It was my Jurker! He'd come to save me!

Or maybe I was supposed to save him. When he got within a few steps, I unlocked the doors and yelled, "Get in! Get in!" He got in and I locked the doors again. I explained that I was being followed and he could tell I was freaked out. Then he did the Jurkiest thing possible. He got out of safe Castle Black, walked over to the creep's car, talked to him, and…posed for a picture with him. When he came back, he said he'd taken care of it.

I was so confused. I had no idea if that guy was a guide or a superfan or both. Maybe he meant well, maybe my loneliness was feeding into my paranoia. Whatever the case, everything was better when Jurker was with me. It meant he was safe and we had covered our respective distances correctly.

We drove down the road a few miles and tucked the car into a tiny, hidden pullout. I was glad he was done for the day. We caught up while I made him dinner. He was feeling better and walking well, which was a huge relief. We started cleaning up and getting ready to eat when suddenly headlights slowly rolled by.

"Turn off the lights!" I said. "Do you think he saw us?"

Before he could answer, the car made a U-turn and pulled in

right next to Castle Black. This time Jurker had had enough of the guy. He put his shoes back on to read him the riot act, but when he opened the door he saw it was Team Father Son. They'd never found the AT and had been looking for Scott in vain.

This was all too weird and too much for me to deal with. I just wanted everybody to give us some space so we could eat in peace. But Jurker had a solution. He told them they could sleep at the trailhead and he would meet them there at 6:00 in the morning, ready to run.

Happy birthday.

VIRGINIA

540 MILES

What matters most is how you walk through the fire.
—Charles Bukowski

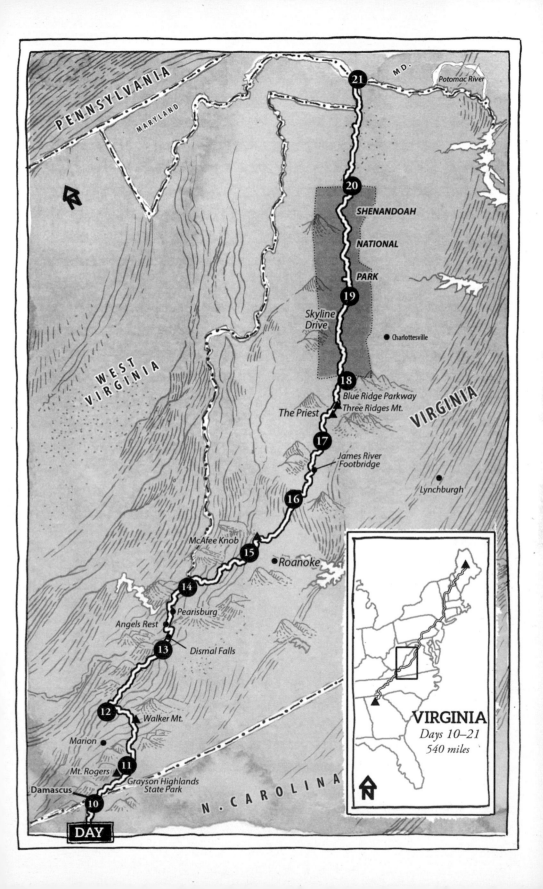

CHAPTER 6

IT NEVER ALWAYS GETS WORSE

Day Ten

THE MORNING SUN was beaming down over the bald expanse atop mile-high Hump Mountain, and I felt as free as the grassy fields rolling beneath me out to the Blue Ridge horizon. However, I wasn't free of pain, or of hobbling, or of doubts. I had spent the morning miles that day sorting things out. I had come face-to-face with the question that always, eventually, meets everyone on the trail (or on the highway, or in the office, or in class) as the initial thrill wears off and the rewards start coming less frequently.

What's the point?

The record seemed out of reach, so why was I still out here? Why keep tottering and anguishing along at two miles an hour?

There was a silver lining, though. JLu and I had wanted to get away and be together in the mountains, and now it looked like we'd have plenty of time for that. If it was going to take me two extra weeks to get to Katahdin, we'd have *lots* of time together. Maybe it was a sign that I should finally slow down and limp into retirement. Maybe a casual pace was my destiny now. Slow and steady, side by side with JLu—this could be the new normal. A couple on vacation in their camper van; JLu reading a book at a campground while she waits for her slow-ass husband to lumber in from another forty-mile trail day. No more of her stressing out trying to meet me at road crossings. I'd just become a happy AT slack-packer.

The only problem with that carefree vision was…JLu. There was no chance she would let me just walk it in.

We'd talked to our buddy and free-solo climber Alex Honnold before we left, and he'd said, "Well, if things don't go as planned, you can always call it a recon trip." And Speedgoat had made a similar comment when he'd called during our drive out and said, half jokingly, "Dude, if something happens, you can come back *next year* and we'll go head to head at the same time. You go NoBo and I'll go SoBo."

JLu just said three words: "One and done." No dry runs, no first drafts. There was no *next time* in her mind. And that had better be how I was thinking too. She hadn't sacrificed her summer to watch another "My heart wasn't into it" performance from me.

When I was with her, I fed off that energy. But on day ten, I was alone, high up on Hump Mountain. And the more I tried to screw my head on straight, the more it spun. *Maybe I just need to let go of the glory days and accept that the fire is gone.*

And yet…despite the swirling doubts, despite the stories I told myself of decline and retirement, somewhere deep inside, I still felt some of that drive, that old *ego*.

You *have to* have *some* ego.

I wish I could say that I was just channeling the vibrations and energy of the wilderness through my body, mind, and soul, that it was all beauty and joy. But at the end of the day, you have to *want it*. Plain and simple. The ego doesn't have to be destructive, and it doesn't have to make you lose sight of the real reasons you do what you do. It doesn't have to go to your head. But when push comes to shove, nothing motivates like winning does. I remembered that electricity. I still felt the young athlete inside me who thrived on winning. I'd gotten wiser over the years, and that wisdom had made me a more complete person, a better partner—but it also made me slower. There was no way around it. The more perspective I got, the more disconnected I became from the pure drive to win and dominate. Without that drive, the discomfort and pain that racing took didn't seem worth it.

I needed to find a bit of that old self if I was going to stick this thing. I had to tap into the fighter who came back from the dead to surge into first place, the young champ who won races with shredded ankle tendons and after vomiting in the desert. The long-haired hippie who explored the limits of his body for a mother who couldn't walk or even feed herself.

I needed a few drops of that elixir—or I needed to quickly find a new balance between running to win and running on wisdom.

JLu must have sensed this tug-of-war between me and my younger self because as we'd hiked together yesterday, she told me stories El Coyote had been telling her, stories about me that even *I* didn't remember. He had told her about a time back in 2005, at Badwater, when he was pacing his buddy Mike Sweeney, who was leading the race until halfway through. That's apparently when I showed up. Luis said that when I came up from behind, it was like I was in a different world. I remembered enough to acknowledge that I almost was; I'd bounced back from dehydration delirium, from puking my guts out, and I was keeping an eight-minute-mile pace again. I'd come back from damned near dead. Luis said that when I took the lead, I didn't pass Sweeney and his pacer on the right but ran straight between. Did I intentionally try to crush his spirit? Not sure. I can barely remember it.

That wasn't exactly the type of ego I was searching for in the woods of Appalachia, though. Perhaps I was asking for too much from my old body and mind, but what I really wanted was a kind of drive—a faith—that would carry me to push beyond what I thought was possible.

After Hump Mountain, the going got a lot harder. Long gone were the pine ridges and lofty, grassy balds of the Roan Highlands. Now it was the swampy, root-infested rhododendron lowlands of the South's interior. When the weather threw a thunderstorm my way, I was inspired to coin a nickname for my new biome: the Bayou. At least there were no water moccasins or alligators in this bayou.

My speed had taken a major hit from the injuries at the end of the first week. I'd gotten in thirty-six miles on day nine, and I hoped to get to forty today. It was still mostly walking, but I was optimistic that I could push forward and run for a few miles today. Last night's test-run mile down Roan Mountain had given me a sliver of hope. Maybe my body *was* remembering something. I couldn't believe that crazy Horty was right, once again.

The pain was still there; on day ten, I woke up, if anything, more beaten up than when I'd gone to sleep. But not all pain is the same. Pain can be high or low; it can be deep or shallow. Pain has more than one axis. As I wrestled through the Bayou, I checked in with my own pain load. It was increasing in intensity, no question, but decreasing in effect. My pain was getting less *painful*—which might sound ridiculous, but you'll know what I mean if you routinely push yourself in the gym or if you have the misfortune to live with a chronic illness or disability. Some of us are familiar with a whole bouquet of pains, each with its own special meaning and impact.

Pain is a biological fact, and there's nothing short of drugs that can wipe it away. But we do have some control over how much one fact or another will consume our thoughts and attention. Think about the first date you went on with your current partner, or the night you brought your dog home from the shelter. The love was all-consuming. The world felt like it revolved around your partner (or your dog). Do you love him any less than you did then? Of course not. It's just that when affection becomes predictable and routine, it loses its sharpness. And in the case of pain, perhaps the one we know hurts us less than the one we fear.

A few things were helping me manage my own pain. The first was the unexpected joy of Team Father Son. The second was sheer experience; I knew this pain wasn't the end of the world—or the end of my legs—because I'd been here before (or close enough to it). The third was based on a kind of faith: I knew I was healing. Well, I didn't *know it* know it; I couldn't get an X-ray out there or pull over next to a log and sit down for an MRI. I knew I was healing through the pain because I felt it at a molecular level. It's a kind of gut feeling, a distant but unmistakable sense from a part of your body you have only intermittent communication with. But I'd learned over the years to listen to my body. I could speak its language. Maybe it was pseudoscience; maybe it was a hopeless tautology (I was healing because I felt like I was healing?); maybe it was a placebo effect. It didn't matter to me. It was working.

My distance from the finish line also helped, surprisingly. Back in Boulder, I might have predicted the opposite—that the unimaginably long way to go would make the pain more acute by making the journey feel impossible—but that wasn't what happened at all. Instead, I was *freed* from thinking about the finish line altogether. It remained a faraway thing, an abstraction. My mind didn't have to whirl through calculations about whether or not I could withstand all this punishment for the next X or Y hours. I had to forget about how many hours or days I had left. Why bother calculating? So I thought about the step in front of me, and the step in front of that one. The scope was overwhelming. There was nothing to do but keep going.

It was at that moment that another prophecy from the Seer of Liberty University echoed in my mind. Before he left, Horty had told JLu, "Make sure you tell that boy: *It never always gets worse!*"

Horty was back home hundreds of miles away, but his deranged words of twisted wisdom were making guest appearances in my thoughts. *It never always gets worse.*

We'll see.

Even if it was going to take a miracle for me to get the record, JLu and I still needed to strategize, plan road-crossing meet-ups, set a daily schedule, and keep the battleship running as if we were going to war (and as if the record was still a possibility). I had to fuel my body each day, make sure I was consuming enough calories, grab water at creeks and springs, remember my headlamp for the last stretch of the day. As long as I stayed focused on the small goals—getting to the next road crossing, the next peak or even the next white blaze—I could continue moving forward. I could keep the FKT within sprinting distance, and I could keep the larger goal (just barely) alive.

I forgot about Katahdin being eighteen hundred miles away, about the FKT, about the loss of normalcy, about everything. I felt how sweet life could be when I wasn't looking at it through a prism of doing, but just being. That was enough for now. It was enough to start *running* again.

I took a few tentative steps, felt the same stabbing pains…and kept going. I was back running. Not elegantly, not with fierceness, not with anything near the speed I'd eventually need. But I was running. If I could just let life happen, everything could work. I didn't have to win, not yet. I just needed to *let* myself run.

Like all epiphanies, that one was great while it lasted.

When I wasn't connecting to a cosmic flow, I was stumbling forward and worrying about JLu. She had given me so much already. The astonishing capacity for suffering and perseverance she'd displayed through her miscarriages and subsequent health crises had played a big part in inspiring me to come out here and test myself. I hadn't thought that crewing for me would be such a test for her.

The guy from the night before—the bizarre stalker—had been odd. And I had to assume more weird scenarios were coming. It was no longer just strange; it was scary, especially when I thought about the fact that for the vast majority of time out here she'd be separated from me. How many more weirdoes were out there? How many were prowling around? How many might feel bold enough to mess around with a petite Asian-American woman roaming alone in the backwoods of the Deep South? We'd both noticed the flags down here, but Horty assured us it was a symbol of "Southern pride" (in other words, a "Leave us alone" attitude).

But it wasn't just *Deliverance*-inspired paranoia; I'd heard stories from people who'd been here. Former AT record holder Andrew "Trail Dawg" Thompson told me about an encounter his buddy Trav had had while thru-hiking the Appalachian Trail in North Carolina. Trav and his friends were hitchhiking on a remote dirt road and desperately needed to get to town for a resupply. After they'd walked toward town for a good bit, a beat-up pickup pulled up alongside them and a scraggly shirtless guy in bib overalls rolled down his window. In classic mountain-hillbilly fashion, he growled, "Git in!" Trav and his buddies all gave one another the same look, but hospitality is hard to turn down in the South. So they hopped into the truck, Trav and one of his buds in the cab, the other friend in the back. So far, so good. But then, as they were rolling down the road, their chauffeur grabbed a bottle from the floor, took a big swig, and passed the bottle to Trav. He declined—politely. "Thank you, sir, but we've got another ten miles to do before nightfall." The mountain man insisted: "Take a drink!" Trav declined again. The bearded driver then reached down below his seat, grabbed a .45, and pointed it at Trav. "Now, I said take a drink!" No hesitation this time; Trav took a big tug of the clear liquor, and the driver set down his gun and cackled. He dropped them off where he'd said he would and drove on to find some more drinking buddies or maybe other thru-hikers to scare shitless.

Who knew how many moonshined-up truck drivers were down here? Was he one in a million, or did most trail-adjacent Southerners enjoy pulling handguns on thru-hikers and making them drink from jugs of fiery liquor?

As I ran, my thoughts started to spin up and distract me.

Everywhere I looked seemed like a great place to stash a body. Sharp turns, dark roads, deserted hollows, forested hills, deep trenches, long gashes in the earth that no one had looked in for centuries, if ever. All these places were populated by my imagination with fresh corpses and their murderers.

But when the anxious spell passed, I realized that I could relate to the men and women down here. Peel away a few choice decals, furl up a flag or two, and they weren't that different from the folks I'd grown up around in rural Minnesota. Long, hard stares from dead-end-road inhabitants and a "Don't Tread on Me" mentality existed everywhere in this country. And most of them would probably have politely helped a damsel in distress with a flat tire. At least that's what I told myself.

I know now, with a little less on my mind and a little more distance from these events, that most of the people we ran into were almost certainly good, kind, hospitable people who were far more likely to lend a hand than bite one off. In fact, that part of the trail is particularly known among AT hikers for its Southern hospitality. Aside from the crazy local guide who seemed to be tracking Jenny and old Trav's chauffeur, the locals in the South were wonderful, especially at some of the cafés near the trail where JLu politely asked if they would cook my home fries in oil, not butter or lard.

Still. Night ten, we huddled up extra-close as we grabbed a few hours of sleep in Castle Black at Dennis Cove Road.

It was clear that we wouldn't be able to run together in the morning every day like we'd planned to. The big problem was Castle Black—who would drive it, who would be there with our belongings if the two of us ran. When it was just JLu and me out on the trail, she was often tethered to that fortress.

So we developed new traditions, one of which—making border crossings together—became a favorite. On day eleven, we were poised to leave Tennessee and enter Virginia. Right across the border was another milestone: the town of Damascus, a classic trail town that treated hikers well.

But fate intervened on the trail to Damascus. It arrived in the form of a text message, a shock in its own right, considering how rare cell service was on that section of the trail. As soon as I recognized the message's sender, I stopped dead in my tracks. I had no idea what it might contain, but I knew it would be worth a read.

If u get this and maybe u have thought of it but the northbound record is still easily in reach keep rolling great to follow progress u r doing great.

Karl "Speedgoat" Meltzer had made his first appearance on my journey north. And it was classic Speedgoat. Behind that veneer of support was the implication that I might—might—still be able to get the other record, the one for a northbounder (NoBo). The challenge, like a chiropractic manipulation, snapped my head back on straight. I disagreed. I could still get the overall FKT. Which I told him.

> Thanks dude! NoBo?!? I've still got the SoBo in sights. Putting in 50 today. Should be in Damascus by dark. Quad is coming around. I'll walk the record if I need to!:)

> Cool just keep ur head in it youll be fine when palmer went north he walked the first 1000 miles did not run a step

> Cool, thanks dude! Good beta. I'm able to run a bit today so we'll see. Jenny will touch base to see if you want to still come out. Can get you a ticket.

> im still game im working an aid st this wknd have jenny call me Monday keep movin

Here's the thing: if anyone had come across me hiking and hobbling toward Damascus and asked what I thought my chances were for the FKT, I would have been…more than cautious. I wouldn't have advised putting a single cent on me, despite El Coyote's advice "never bet against the Champ."

But Speedgoat challenging me from somewhere far away? Implying it was already game over? I knew the AT speed record was his baby and I'm sure he was concerned I might scoop it from him. Was he trying to mess with me, or was he just serving reality straight up like the emotionless old Goat always did?

His glib prediction set my jaw.

I would still get the FKT. Southbound, northbound, whatever- and however-bound. I would claw and crawl all day, every day, to Katahdin if I had to.

I had needed some ego fire starter, and I had desperately needed hope. The Speedgoat gave me both.

That evening as darkness consumed the woods, I backtracked half a mile with Jenny so that together we could touch the sign welcoming us to Virginia.

Jurker was still gimpy. He was moving slowly, but at least he was making progress north, and that was all I cared about. Friends back home were texting me things like *Hope he gets back to putting in fifty-mile days soon,* but I wasn't sure that would happen. His injuries weren't healing as quickly as he was used to, but such is the curse of aging. Or maybe it was the curse of the AT speed record and the insane daily mileage.

However, things were getting easier for me. I had finally gotten into a groove. I'd established some systems and routines for Castle Black and had a handle on crewing this juggernaut trail. The bugs and humidity didn't even faze me; I was adapting.

I hadn't grown up in an outdoorsy family, but I always felt safe in the mountains. In Seattle, I would drive up to the Cascades after work and run an eighteen-mile loop by myself. I'd often finish past dark. A lot of my runs back then were done in the evening rain, alone with my thoughts and my music. I figured that if I came across other people out there, they'd be my people: runners, hikers, and creatives just needing some fresh air or looking to clear their minds. Before Jurker, I'd never dated a runner; I was used to running alone.

But even so, with Horty and El Coyote gone and Jurker out on the trail almost all day, I had a lot more alone time than I needed. I missed my friends back home. My meet-ups with Jurker became my only social hour. We would sit on the floor of Castle Black for thirty minutes, eat lunch, and catch up on news headlines—he always wanted to hear about what was going on in the outside world. It was hard for him to leave the van and our sliver of normalcy, and it was hard for me to kick him out and send him back into the woods, leaving me with endless errands and my only friends, a Bluetooth speaker and an electric fan. They kept me company like Tom Hanks's Wilson in *Cast Away*.

All those hours on the trail allowed Jurker's mind to wander a little too much. One afternoon, after I'd spent the day chasing down frozen fruit for his smoothies, he appeared out of the woods, approached Castle Black, and said, "Hey, can you call Norm and ask him to mow our lawn? And then can you e-mail our electrician? I think he overcharged us for the solar-panel installation on the van."

Okay, in all my spare time I'll be sure to do those things. Right after I get gas, drain the water from the cooler, refill it with ice, wash the dishes, drive to the next spot, make dinner, and wait without cell service for your sorry ass.

Then, as he sipped his smoothie, he said, "This is good, thank you. But you know what sounds really good? Thai food." I laughed to keep myself from strangling him. I realized that he had no idea about my reality. His perception of what I did while he was inching his way up the trail was nothing like what actually happened.

On the morning we left Damascus, local trail runners J.J. and Beth offered to crew for Scott, which I was nervous about. I didn't really trust strangers to crew for him; our entire trip relied on the crew being where it was supposed to be when he got there. But

Jurker was so excited. "Enjoy your morning off!" he said to me as the three of them left. It was a nice idea, but I think he thought I was going to sleep in, eat breakfast in a restaurant, maybe even catch up with friends, check out the town some. Instead, I did two loads of laundry, cleaned and organized the van, called Norm about our lawn (we were ticketed for it being overgrown), and got groceries and gas. Then I made my way up to Grayson Highlands State Park. Horty had told me I had to go there and check out the wild ponies.

I waited a long time near the ponies, lying on the grass and watching them graze. Then I started to worry, so I hiked up the trail. I went two miles before I finally saw them. Jurker was moving so slowly that I felt bad for his gracious local companion Beth. I guess I could have slept in after all.

Even though I was most comfortable in the mountains, I wasn't actually *in* the mountains. It would be one thing if I was out on the trail; I knew I could outrun or out-karate-chop any assailant. I'd heard too many stories from friends whose cars had been broken into at trailhead parking lots. Trailheads are magnets for petty thieves. I felt safer in the trees. But I was stuck in a well-marked van on the side of a dirt road or in a tiny parking area. I had so much to get done at each meeting spot that when my chores were finished, all I wanted to do was take a nap, and I just had to hope that nobody would try to break in. Sketchy cars occasionally pulled up and strangers tried to talk to me, and I started to resent Jurker for being so slow, for leaving me stranded out there alone.

I had never spent any time in the South, so I had no sense of place, no connection to the community. I'd heard stories of murders on the AT not too far north from where we were, and while everybody knew where Scott was at all times, I didn't have a GPS tracker on me. I could end up in some ditch and nobody would find me for days or ever.

On day eleven, as Jurker was running, I was having a particularly hard time finding the road that would take me to our next meeting spot. When I finally found the little trailhead lot, I was surprised to see several cars already there—but that meant there'd be hikers around, which made things safer.

I parked Castle Black, got out, and opened the back doors to look for Jurker's headlamp. I knew he was going to come in late and he didn't have his headlamp, so I was planning on running back with the light to meet him. As I walked around the van, I felt the creepy sensation of eyes on me. I scanned the parking lot full of cars and saw a dirty white sedan with somebody sitting in the driver's seat. The door was partly open.

I tried not to look, but he was full-on *staring* at me. The dust on the windshield obscured my view of him, but from what I could tell, he didn't look like a hiker—he could have passed for Jerry Garcia's feral brother. I looked around and saw that all the other cars were unoccupied. It was just the two of us in that trailhead parking lot. I got back in the van and locked the doors.

Now I was in a pickle. If I ran down the trail to bring Jurker his headlamp, the Grateful Gawker might break into our home on wheels and find a lot of nice comforts. But if I stayed, who knew what might happen to *me?* I glanced over at my side mirror and, yup, there he was. Still staring.

I weighed my options. I decided that Jurker needed me and that this guy looked too fat to actually run after me. So I jumped out of the van, slammed the door, locked it, and ran as fast as I could up the trail. I kept looking behind to see if he was following me. Once I'd gone some distance, I stopped to see if I could hear him breaking a window or anything like that. Nothing. So far.

I was less than a mile down the trail when I saw Jurker—a huge relief. Big Thump was gonna thump down on Shakedown Strut.

"Jurker! There's a creepy guy in the parking lot sitting in his car, and he kept staring at me and casing Castle Black." I was out of breath and distracted, but I noticed that Jurker was moving well and at a good pace. "I felt like he might mess with me or the van."

Jurker bolted down the trail so fast I could barely keep up, but when we got to the parking lot, the guy was gone. At least for the moment.

CHAPTER 7

SOUTHERN HOSPITALITY

Day Eleven

I WAS FEELING good. Not based on my injuries, but based on the AT terrain and tread. I was actually *running* again. I was easing my way down the gentle slope of trail to the parking lot. Daylight was waning but I still had plenty of light—good thing, since I'd forgotten to grab my headlamp at the last meet-up with JLu. I was planning to run another eight miles, which meant I'd finish up around 10:00. A good day, all in all. Back on track. Back on schedule.

Then I saw someone running toward me. It was JLu and she was waving her arms wildly, like someone flagging down a cop car. When she got near enough, she immediately started telling me what was wrong. It was some creep again. I'd had it. I ran on ahead as fast as I could. When I got to the parking lot, he was gone, and Castle Black was intact. But it didn't matter—I was pissed and physically drained. I decided to call it a day and forget the next section; I could bang that out in the morning. We'd sleep here tonight. I didn't want JLu driving around alone that evening and waiting at yet another dirt-road crossing for two hours. She told me she was fine, that I should keep going, but I was done. I decided right then and there to stop sending her to remote and sketchy places alone, day or night. I would start doing longer stretches without support, twenty to twenty-five miles at a time, and we'd meet only at paved-road crossings. No more creepy encounters.

The next day, I woke up at 5:00 a.m. I had been feeling stiff and achy in the mornings, but that day I cranked out the eight-mile section in two hours. I was running, listening to music, carrying a running vest that held food and a hydration bladder with an inline mini–water filter. I felt in my element; I could have been on a long training run in the peaks back home. By the time I got to the next meet-up, at a gas station near an Interstate 81 overpass, I had finished thirty-two miles, and it wasn't even noon yet.

JLu seemed surprised to see me so early. She had taken a nap in a nearby restaurant parking lot and had just gotten to the gas station.

"Jurker!" She jumped out of the van to greet me. "Hey, you're early! You'll never guess what just happened. I was looking for a place to park when a red beat-up car pulls up to the van. This old dude asks, 'What time did Scott get in last night?' I was thinking to myself, *Who the hell is this and what is he talking about?* I thought maybe he was some superfan who wanted a live update, but he didn't look like a runner or even somebody who owned a computer. Then I took a closer look at his face. Same scraggly beard, same disheveled look. Different vehicle, but it could only be him. The guy from last night!"

"No way! Are you sure?" I looked around the parking lot to see if he was still there.

"Hundred percent. I'm positive. I figured out who he was! The

Grateful Gawker in broad daylight looked exactly like that guy who trolls your Facebook page!"

"Warren Doyle?"

"*Yes!*"

I laughed and sat down on the edge of the van. That guy had been talking trash about me while I was on the trail. The other day I'd caught up to two thru-hikers who were surprised to see me. They said, "We didn't know you were still out here! Warren Doyle said you were done, that your leg was injured. Said this wasn't gonna be your year."

Of course he told them that. Warren liked to position himself as the gatekeeper of the Appalachian Trail, and for some reason, he had a serious bone to pick with trail runners. He loved to try to pit the hikers against us. During Speedgoat's record attempts, he'd really laid into him online. It was like he had a personal vendetta against runners on the trail. He proclaimed on his website that "walking the entire Appalachian Trail is not recreation. It is an education and a job." Okay, Warren, but not everybody wants to *walk*. Let people choose their own speed.

Horty had said, "I've got my spies on the AT," and now I knew who he was referring to. But Warren seemed to take spying to another level. He probably was out here making sure that I wasn't cheating, that I wasn't faking it. After all, we were just visitors in Warren's world. He represented one special section of AT obsessives whose earnest love for the place had curdled over the years into a sense of possession. It was palpable online and on the trail. Forget checking to see if I was cheating—he probably had a laundry list of arbitrary trail rules, and he was keeping track of the ones I broke like a self-appointed AT hall monitor.

Some people loved him. JLu and I met part of his group and they were having a great time with him. To be fair, you couldn't ask for a better guide—Warren had hiked the AT more than anyone else (an astonishing eighteen times and counting). And Horty was friends with him, so who knew? But he rubbed a lot of people the wrong way. Just minutes after JLu's encounter with Warren, a thru-hiker asked her what the trail was like up ahead. She told him, "I'm not really sure, sorry. But Warren Doyle is right there—you could ask him!" And the hiker rolled his eyes and moved his hand like he was spanking the monkey.

I appreciated Warren's monitoring of record attempts and I welcomed the scrutiny, but the manner in which he carried out that monitoring crossed a line. He could have introduced himself to JLu; she would have been happy to answer any questions and show him whatever proof he was looking for.

It's one thing to post crap on social media, and it's another thing to spread rumors on the trail to fellow thru-hikers. But nobody spooks my wife.

On the climb up near Walker Mountain, as firehoses of water sprayed down from the black clouds and thunder boomed, I spotted a figure covered by an old-school poncho; the only thing visible was a long, grizzled beard with rain rivulets gushing through it. Some might take him for a character in *Murder on the Appalachian Trail*. There was no mistaking him.

"Are you Warren Doyle?" I shouted through the driving rain and thunder.

"Yes, I am," he said, a bit surprised.

I got up in his face. "You don't need to be spying on me. I'm covering every single inch of this trail and being completely transparent. If you question my integrity, you ask me directly! Don't just sit in your car and freak out my wife, next time I'll have State Troopers on your ass!"

He mumbled something in the pouring-down rain.

I raged on. "I thought you folks down here celebrated decency and etiquette! Whatever happened to Southern hospitality?"

By day twelve, I was only a fifth of the way to Katahdin, but I felt like I'd run the gauntlet already. I'd hit a towering wall, and a text message had catapulted me over it. I'd nearly given up in a motel in Erwin, but I'd gotten out and walked it off. My legs were feeling better—somehow—and I was beginning to remember what it felt like to be racing out ahead of the pack. I was outrunning my doubts for the first time, and I was back to doing fifty-mile days.

It wasn't all roses and runner's highs. I was also thinking about getting Jenny a handgun. It was a *ridiculous* thought; I knew she'd never touch a gun. But after twelve days, I was finding it impossible to ignore the darker side of the AT. The side that only slowly exposes itself to committed hikers and AT-history buffs.

When we arrived at the quintessential trail town of Damascus back on day ten, we drove through the little downtown. There were posters still up from the Trail Days festival, which is like the Woodstock of the AT community. We had just missed it and all the drama that surrounded it a few days prior. Apparently, the FBI had arrested James Hammes, a fifty-three-year-old man who had been a resident thru-hiker on this section for the past four years, a contributor to the *A.T. Guide,* and a regular guest at the Damascus boardinghouse where the FBI found him. Hammes, known to most by his trail name, Bismarck, sported an unruly beard and seemed to fit in well with the AT crowd. What none of us knew was that the FBI had interviewed him back in 2009, in Ohio, about the embezzlement of $8.7 million from the company he'd worked for. That was when he'd disappeared from Ohio.

He wasn't the first hiker to use the AT as a place to hide out. The trail has the same attraction to wanderers as railcars used to have in the old West—a kind of permanent itinerancy, a place to go where you could just keep going for as long as you liked. JLu and I both had experienced that pull and wanderlust. We just didn't pair it with evading authorities.

Certainly, there are some scoundrels among those who wander the trail, but there are redemption stories as well. For instance, David Lescoe. Back in 2005, David Lescoe started hiking south from Rhode Island. Along the way, he got into the habit of stealing other campers' food and gear. Then he came upon a trail angel in New Jersey. David didn't need to steal from the angel, because he freely offered him dinner, a warm bed, and a hot shower. Then he showed David a video featuring born-again Christian celebrity Kirk Cameron. Apparently, the video took, because the two men prayed together and David got religion and swore to make amends to those he'd harmed. The angel gave him some money and David kept heading south, mailing letters of apology, cash, and stolen equipment back to those he'd stolen from. He changed his trail name from Injun to Saved—the name he was known by when law enforcement caught him stealing food and gear from a cabin just south of Damascus. So in that case, the redemption was temporary.

Temporary also describes how things are on the AT and in towns like Damascus. The trail has something for everyone—peace, nature, and a chance to get away from it all. But this Eden has end points. And sometimes things get nasty. Sometimes it's the fault of the locals, like the fishhook booby traps Horty told us of. But hiker misbehavior was more typical, and we weren't immune to it. With my partner logos on Castle Black, the van was often mistaken for a company promotional vehicle. Some thru-hikers grabbed Clif Bars out of the back one day as JLu was unpacking and then, even worse, left the wrappers scattered all over the trail.

If petty theft and littering were the highest crimes on the AT, it'd be pretty much like any other parkland in the United States, but unfortunately, there have been far more serious offenses. Eleven people have been murdered along the AT since 1974. Randall Lee Smith brutally killed a thru-hiking couple in 1981. He was convicted of second-degree murder, sent to prison, and paroled fifteen years later—and he promptly tried to kill two *more* people on the trail. In 2007, a Georgia couple named John and Irene Bryant disappeared while they were on a hike not too far from Damascus, and the next year, a twenty-four-year-old hiker named Meredith Emerson also vanished. Later, their bodies were found. Some of the killings have never been solved. People disappear on the trail. Perhaps some of them intended to.

Hence my idea about a gun. The murders were rare, but by the time we crossed over into Virginia I'd heard enough disturbing stories from JLu that I'd had to recalibrate a bit. I knew a professional female climber who kept a Glock in her van's glovebox. JLu didn't even have a can of mace. The Appalachian Trail was a path toward higher consciousness and a test of character, but it was also a wild, lawless place. I called my buddy Rick, who lived out in the California desert and served as an EOD navy diver. We discussed the possibility of him accompanying JLu through Virginia. I wanted him to protect her and asked if he could pack some heat.

Luckily, I came to my senses, high up on a spine of the Blue Ridge Mountains. Well—my good judgment was helped by the fact that Rick wasn't able to come out. There'd be no gun and no backup from my friend. But still, I stuck to my decision to stop having JLu meet me at backwoods road crossings where she would have to hang out alone in the wilderness for long stretches. I would meet her at major roadways, with numbers and pavement. No more remote dirt roads. That was tough for both of us, and it meant fifteen-to twenty-five-mile stretches for me and fewer stops for food. After all the strange encounters, I was freaked out and kicking myself for thinking that JLu would be fine on her own. Why didn't I make sure we had at least one friend with JLu at all times? Man, I could be an idiot.

It was an anxious time for me, but it was also frankly… mind-numbing. The AT in Virginia is deceptively punishing. It's hot and sticky when you're heading up, rocky and root-filled when you're going down, and seemingly endless. Thru-hikers call it the Virginia Blues because the trail meanders 554 miles through the state. In fact, Virginia is home to nearly a quarter of the entire AT. And there are multiple rubble-laden mountains riddling those miles. The Smokies might officially end in Tennessee, but the Blue Ridge Mountains in Virginia are their formidable stepsiblings. Many of the four-thousand-foot peaks had foreboding monikers: Bruisers Knob, Dragon's Tooth, Buzzard's Rock, The Guillotine, and The Priest. Fittingly, this range was Horty's playground. As I climbed those mountains, I recalled many of their names from his training stories and tall tales.

The beginning of the Virginia Blues also marks the beginning of a surprisingly sadistic stretch of the trail itself. The AT becomes increasingly gnarly and demanding as it twists through the Virginia Appalachians, inspiring a witticism I'd heard plenty by the time I got through the state:

Q: Which is better, taking your chances with the rocks or taking your chances with the roots?
A: Which is better, being hanged or being shot?

My injuries were slowly healing up, as Horty had predicted they eventually would. Physically I was feeling strong, but the midday heat and the repetitious terrain lulled me to sleep. I started taking power naps on rocks, in leaves off the trail, anywhere I could lie down, and I got pretty good at it. One time I spooked a few hikers who were cautiously inspecting me, afraid I was dead.

I would have loved to sleep eight hours a night and not have to take naps that interrupted my progress. I would have loved to hang out at campfires, kicking back with all the colorful characters who had decided to spend a summer of their lives ambling through the wilderness. I would have loved to hear more stories about the weird history of the trail and its many eccentrics, from the dangerous maniacs to the gentle souls. There *were* opportunities to kick back. There were plenty of temptations.

A few days after we'd passed Damascus, JLu met a young group of thru-hikers who told her they were having a big "hicker" party next to Dismal Falls and really wanted me to join them. JLu immediately told them I would attend—she knew me well. I knew it would cut into my sleep, but I wanted to hang out and meet more of my clan.

It was pouring rain and near dark when I got there, but I had a beer while a dozen or so half-naked hickers danced in the river by the falls. One guy wearing only boxer briefs held a kid's pink umbrella and pranced on the rocks, unfazed by the rain. They were forest nymphs in their natural habitat.

As I made my way back to the trail, I thought about the differences between the AT and the long trails out west that I knew so much better. The Appalachian Trail is by far the most social of the three mega-trails in the United States, just by dint of being in a place where there are a whole lot of people. Population density is a lot higher in Virginia than in Colorado, and while the trail can feel like wilderness, it's almost always a short walk or hitch to a town. Some hikers even call it "the world's largest pub crawl." Others are no doubt disappointed by this; they arrive with a mental picture of isolated landscape but quickly learn that contact is the norm.

It would have been fun to hang out more and not think about mileage quotas or an itinerary, the way we'd traveled on the PCT. But we would get back to that later. This time it was about pursuing that edge.

I covered 51.6 miles on day fourteen, and made my way over Angels Rest and Senator Shumate Bridge in Pearisburg. I finished that night in a haze of déjà vu. I could have sworn I was walking in circles yet I found myself on Mountain Lake Road in the middle of nowhere at 11:00 p.m. Sketchy trucks had slowly driven past JLu as she waited for me to arrive; I was hours late. The next day I hiked over Lone Pine Peak, passed the three-hundred-year-old Keffer Oak (the largest oak tree on the AT in the South), went up Dragon's Tooth, and made it to just shy of McAfee Knob, all the while picking my way over softball-size rocks that were hidden among the roots and ground cover of the overgrown trail. I'd covered another forty-six miles by the time I closed out the fifteenth day. I survived the early Virginia Blues in the most tedious manner possible: by staying focused. No secret. No superpower. Miles became a moving meditation.

We were a quarter of the way through the Appalachian Trail. It was hard to believe we'd made it this far and even harder to imagine how much farther we had to go. We hadn't crossed a state line in a long time, which made the next sixteen hundred miles seem impossible to cover. It was easier to think of the trail in bite-size pieces represented by each state. Progress was just less tangible in Virginia; it felt like we were spinning our wheels and going nowhere.

Yet in twelve days, Jurker had covered so much ground that we were catching up to more and more company. Traditionally, north-bound AT thru-hikers depart from Springer Mountain at the end of March or the beginning of May. Most of the people we met were just out of college. We felt old, but at the same time, it was inspiring to be around these adventurous kids. I knew Jurker would get a boost from meeting more hikers out here.

When I drove through Marion, Virginia—the first big town I'd seen—I jumped at the chance to stop at a Walmart. Out here in rural southwestern Virginia, the store seemed like an oasis! I loaded up on plant-based protein sources, organic fruit, and a lot of Jurker's favorite vegan treats. He'd been going through them at an alarming rate. Normally a whole-grain, low-fat, healthy eater, out here he was all about oily, high-fat, sugary junk food. It was almost scary; he could drink an entire pint of melted vegan ice cream in one gulp. In the fabric department at Walmart, I bought a couple of yards of tulle to use as a makeshift screen for the van's sliding door to keep the bugs out. Hands down the best two dollars I ever spent.

When I returned to the van with my treasures, there was a fluorescent-green note stuck to the windshield. It read *Good luck Scott Jurek!! See you out on the trail! Best wishes, Cujo (Sam) and Sarah (no trail name yet).* It was simple but so sweet. Not only was he catching up to the thru-hikers, but some of them were rooting for him, and that meant a lot to me.

He had been spending more and more hours alone in the confining Green Tunnel, running through cobwebs and occasionally listening to music. Without others around to take turns driving the van, I could run only short out-and-back sections with him. I could tell he was missing the company. I certainly was getting lonely.

Our haphazard trip planning and our desire to be alone meant that most of our friends hadn't even known we were on the AT until we started. By the time we were in the belly of Virginia and realized we could both benefit from some friendly company, it was too late to ask anyone to join us. Nearly everyone had already made summer plans. A few friends offered to come out and pace Scott, but I couldn't tell them where we would be or even what airport to fly into on any particular day. Plus, they'd have to find a ride to meet me on the trail. Our friends were a resourceful bunch, but they were way too busy to seek a needle in a haystack on their days off.

Then, out of the blue, I got a text from Jenn Shelton. She was at a race in Arkansas that Luis happened to be photographing. Luis, Jenn, and Scott were part of the original ragtag group in *Born to Run*—they were family. El Coyote mentioned to Jenn that he was flying straight from Arkansas back to the AT. Jenn immediately asked if she could come with him. For some reason, he said no. Not being one to take no seriously, she texted me.

I wrote back.

What?!?! You want to come out to the AT? And Luis said no? Is he HIGH?

I was annoyed. I think Luis was trying to protect me; he knew I had my hands full out here. But I'd never say no to Jenn Shelton. I knew she was just what Jurker needed! Not quite a balm for his soul—more like rubbing alcohol in a wound. It stings, but you know that means it's working.

Last summer, Jurker and I flew out to support Jenn on her John Muir Trail FKT attempt. Jurker surprised her near Red's Meadow in the morning and ran with her through the night. Somehow, the two of them managed to forget some essentials. Jurker left behind all his warm clothes and Jenn neglected to bring any food, so the two of them came rolling into Tuolumne Meadows famished with Scott wearing a space blanket around his legs like a skirt. They were quite the pair, not exactly a dream team, but always laughing and pushing each other.

I told Jenn to get here however she could, even if it meant stowing away in El Coyote's monster backpack. We needed her. She changed her flights and I felt a huge wave of relief knowing that Jurker would have some colorful company in the hot, humid hills of Virginia, not far from where Jenn grew up.

This morning would be my last day alone, so I wanted to tidy up. I pulled into an empty gas station with a huge gravel parking lot and positioned Castle Black in the far end where I could clean and organize the van in peace. I wasn't doing it for Jenn but for Luis, Mr. Neat Freak. I was happily in my zone, listening to music and washing the dishes, so I didn't notice the truck approaching until it pulled in right next to the passenger side. Weird; this was a huge, empty parking area, and there was no one out here. Except for me. I turned off my music.

Knock-knock-knock.

Their truck was idling. I slid the van door open. There were three young guys, apparently locals. I assumed they had spotted the van and were fans of Scott. The one who seemed to be their ringleader piped up. "Hey, you're looking good this morning," the blond guy said. "Can I get my picture taken with you?"

I paused, then said, "Sure, I guess." I tried to laugh it off. Maybe they'd never seen an Asian lady before and I was about to be a joke shared with their friends. I didn't care; I just wanted them to leave. I posed with the blond guy while one friend took the photo and the other friend walked around Castle Black. He pointed at my license plate. "You're from Colorado, huh? Got any weed in there?"

I got it—they weren't running superfans; they thought I was transporting drugs in a black van with no windows. I laughed again. "No weed, just running shoes. My *husband* is running the Appalachian Trail and I'm supporting him. He should be here soon, so I better get ready."

The guys seemed to take the hint, and they got back in their truck. It was still idling. I quickly got back in the van and checked my phone. I had one bar of cell service. I didn't bother finishing the dishes. I cracked the sliding door open and poured the water onto the pavement. Just as I finished, a hand from outside slid the door wide open.

It was the blond guy again, and he was alone. His two friends were in the idling vehicle, and now I started to worry. Who the hell did he think he was to open my van door?

"Hey, that photo didn't turn out good. Can I get another photo?" he asked with a smile.

A thought creeped into my head, a line from the movie *The Girl with the Dragon Tattoo*. At one point the villain says, "It's hard to believe that the fear of offending can be stronger than the fear of pain, but you know what? It is." I didn't want to assume the worst about these guys and I didn't want to offend them.

I posed for an awkward selfie with the blond guy. He looked over the photo and approved. I got back in the van and slammed the sliding door shut as loud as possible. This time I wasn't afraid to offend. I saw another truck pull into the gas station. The blond guy walked up to the driver and pointed in my direction. Now the guys in the other truck were all staring. Who knows what they were saying, what they were plotting? I started the engine and peeled out of there as fast as I could. Thankfully, nobody followed me.

I made my way to the next trail crossing, where I was surprised to see the orange Honda Element, with Horty sitting on the tailgate. He was on his way to start his bike ride, but he'd made a side trip to drop off Luis and see Jurker again. But where was Jenn? Apparently, the airline had canceled her connecting flight. I was crushed. I needed some female energy, but I would settle for good old El Coyote.

Not long after I arrived, Jurker came running in with a few local runners in tow. He was moving great, the best I'd seen him do in days. It was early but already hot and humid, so we all jumped in the creek to cool off. Jurker thanked his local companions and then we headed off on the trail while Horty walked with us. Luis followed along snapping some photos but turned back quickly—he was going to drive the van so I could run the next stretch alone with Jurker.

Horty followed us up the switchbacks. I wasn't sure why he'd gone out of his way to pick up Luis and drop him off on the trail, adding to his already long drive out west. But I think he wanted to get his eyes on Jurker, to gauge for himself how he was holding up. Jurker was enjoying Horty's company but it was slowing him down. He went from running at a great pace to walking. Horty was rattling off a bunch of stats, telling Jurker what he could expect to see in the next few days and giving some trail-worn advice.

"Hey, you guys got the right attitude, you're really embracing the trail and the other hikers. Doyle always asks me, 'But how's his head?' I think he's hoping you'll crack like Karl." Horty looked Jurker in the eye. "I told him your head is right where it needs to be. I think you're gonna get that record."

We said our good-byes and wished Horty luck, and after a few minutes of running, Jurker and I were alone. I could tell Jurker was pleased with how well he was recovering from his injuries. He was almost giddy with his running progress. He was fired up by all the naysayers, the Warren Doyles commenting online and saying he was done. He told me, "JLu, I'm gonna show them. I'm going to crank this out in under forty days."

I followed his footsteps in silence. I was happy he was so confident. "All I care about is that we're back in time for my birthday."

He laughed. "Oh, don't worry, we are gonna finish this on the Fourth of July and be back by the eighth." My birthday was July 12, so at least he was giving himself somewhat of a cushion.

It seemed doable, but we would need to hustle. I got on his case. "Just try not to waste too much time talking to people!"

I could tell I'd touched a nerve. Very calmly and full of conviction, he said, "JLu, if it comes down to hours, then you can get mad at me."

Famous last words.

CHAPTER 8

NICKELS AND DIMES

Day Sixteen

I WOKE UP in a daze, rolled over, looked through the windshield, and saw a dozen runners milling about outside the walls of Castle Black. I slid open the door to go do my morning business. A running group from Roanoke would be joining me on the way to picturesque McAfee Knob. It was becoming my new routine: smile, greet, talk, run.

Jenny and I had come to the AT with visions of the two of us, mostly alone, out in the elements. But after seven hundred miles, the trip had become something else entirely. Our journey was taking on a life of its own. Perhaps I had let it happen. Perhaps I should have drawn stricter boundaries.

That's not to suggest that it was all bad, because it wasn't—not by a long shot. We were positively impacted by others and could tell they were inspired by the breadth of our jouyous struggle. Even as it became routine, I never stopped being amazed that people made such an effort to find us, support us, help us, run with us. That's what makes the AT one of the most magical trails on the planet. I loved the feeling of running in the world and with the world. I didn't want to be locked into the Green Tunnel all by myself, chasing some abstraction.

Still—we had a record to set. I knew I should've taken a couple of quick pics with the group and then headed out, but I ended up spending thirty minutes there taking photos and enjoying their company. It's a beautiful setting, and if you know people who've hiked that part of the AT, they'll almost certainly have pictures from there. It's one of the most photographed landmarks along the whole twenty-two hundred miles.

As I posed for photos and chatted, JLu started encouraging me to get going. I was spending too much time talking. She was right.

Last night had been another late finish. It was nearly midnight when I'd finally stopped. I was moving well again after my injuries, but the miles were taking longer than they had when I'd first started out. The late nights were tough on JLu too—she had to wait up for me, which meant she was getting the same five hours of sleep I was.

There was no question: I needed to be more efficient.

Before we left, JLu found a trio of Fleet Feet Sports Roanoke locals to accompany me for the next fifteen rough and remote miles. She seemed to be saying that if I was going to socialize, at least I could do it on the go. We shared vegan wraps and burritos they'd brought. Sharing a meal is one of my favorite things, even if I have to do it on my feet. It was a mobile smorgasbord of lunch, laughs, and musings on current events and the new season of *Game of Thrones* (which I was missing). The pop-culture conversations gave me a funny feeling; they brought me back to the real world while simultaneously reminding me of how very far away from it I had gotten. Perspective is always enlightening.

In the afternoon, my new running buddies disconnected from my northbound train and wished me well. I wanted to follow them—the humidity had just descended on the Virginia woods like a hot, wet blanket, and I was *wilting.* It was the kind of humidity that's wicked into your bones and drags you down from the inside out. While I was making my way through an exposed stretch of the trail that carved through a mowed and manicured field, I decided to take a walking break. I needed to get my mind off the elements, so I pulled my phone out and checked the comments on my most recent Facebook post. JLu had told me that there were a lot of remarks, and I needed a distraction.

I didn't get quite what I was looking for. One of the first messages I saw was from my mom's sister.

Your mother would be so proud of you was all it said.

I found my eyes welling up with tears. I was totally alone and exposed in the middle of a Virginia field, and a deep sadness gripped me in a matter of seconds. My emotional defenses must have melted down in the heat.

I had begun to notice that same phenomenon in other, less dramatic moments. In the course of two and a half weeks of running, I felt like my physical senses were increasingly finely tuned; I was becoming an intuitive animal. At the same time, my emotional equilibrium was tipping way out of whack, which had happened before. When you're pursuing hard challenges, emotions rise to the surface, and I was so much more fragile than I'd been back in Boulder. The two things seemed related; I was becoming stronger and weaker.

It was like the polarities of my mind and body were reversing. It wasn't a clean process—things were getting knocked loose in the flux. Memories, mostly. As I shuffled forward along the smooth winding trail, my mind went on a backward journey. Way back.

I'm sixteen years old, a sophomore in high school, and I run the household. I cook, I wash clothes, I split wood, I take care of my brother and sister. I've been looking after them since I was seven years old, when my mom first started showing symptoms of MS, back when I stood in left field in Little League and watched as she stumbled out of the car and made her way up into the bleachers with the help of my dad. After that, I was in charge at home. My dad tells me that every time he goes off to work.

But today is different. Today I get a break. Today I'm taking my siblings out in the car to pick up our great-grandmother, and then we're all going to the Miller Hill Mall in Duluth. It's beyond exciting to just get to be a teenager for a bit.

Dad's at work, so my mom will be alone at home. She knows how excited I am. She probably feels guilty for keeping us around all the time. She tells us to have fun and not to worry about her. She's on the couch; she'll be fine.

We set off in our Dodge Grand Caravan, and I drive with the special kind of joy only a sixteen-year-old with a newly minted driver's license knows. When we pick up our great-grandmother, she's as excited as we are. She relishes any opportunity to leave her apartment, and a trip to the mall is a big deal for her. We're happy she's there with us, not least of all because we know she'll give a twenty-dollar bill to each of us and tell us to go buy something nice. She'll pass the time in her own special heaven: JCPenney.

At the mall, we scatter. I'm off to look at clothes. New jeans! Twenty dollars goes a long way at Miller Hill Mall, and pretty soon I've got a couple of sale items picked out. I'm a teenager and options are everywhere.

It's getting kind of late, but I'm not too worried about my mom. She can get around with a walker when she needs to. She's a little shaky these days, but she's able to transfer herself from couch, bed, and toilet.

I can't help feeling great. I'm free. I'm not in charge of anyone. No one depends on me. I'm just another teenager at the mall.

On the way home, I gas up the car because my dad is a stickler for things like that. Everything has to be just so or he'll let me have it. When we get back, we rush in, still saturated with excitement from our shopping trip, and I yell out to my mom. She doesn't respond. She's not on the couch or in her room.

I hear a low moaning from the bathroom. I try to push open the door but it hits something and gets stuck. I push harder. It's my mom.

We're at the hospital. I don't know if my dad came home and packed us all up or if an ambulance came. I don't remember anything—except one image. I remember my dad looking at me like he hated me and saying, "If you'd been around...if you'd been around like you were supposed to be..."

She never walks again after that. Not even with her walker. The broken hip sets off a negative chain reaction. I know whose fault it is.

Her muscles atrophy. She's confined to her wheelchair. I change too. I'm no longer careless, not even for a second. I become a state-ranked Nordic skier and valedictorian. I privately dream of Dartmouth College after requesting an application, but I stay in Minnesota to help take care of my mom. I study physical therapy. I live at home. My mom is in terrible pain, but I'm never far away.

I resolve to make things better.

I kept trudging over the rolling terrain and sprinting through a lifetime of memories. I'd screwed up that day, and the guilt was heavy. What's more, compared to my mom, I'd had it easy—I could walk. I would have taken her place in that wheelchair if I could, taken the disease on myself so that my mom could have her life back.

I felt like that teenager and that angst-ridden young adult.

When I grew out of the guilt, I found myself seething instead. I wasn't angry at the disease alone—although, God knows, I could rage and rage and rage at it—but at my mom too.

After I moved out west, started to make a life for myself, it became harder and harder to get back to Minnesota to spend time with her. So every time I did, I wanted to make the most of it. I wanted to get her outside, make her happy, break her out of the institutional sameness of the nursing home.

I took her to movies and restaurants. Her legs would spasm as I moved her from the wheelchair to the rental car. Even though it was ten degrees below freezing outside, even though the nurses were increasingly reluctant to sign her out, I still took her. I just wanted her to get some pleasure somewhere. To taste something again. And I could tell she liked it. Her eyes would light up in the movie theater before closing as she inevitably fell asleep. And the joy she got from restaurant food—anything, even the junkiest stuff—was incredible. I'd mash up some French fries and she'd be over the moon.

Then I'd ask her how she was doing, if she was having any pain. She'd invariably reply: "I'm tough, I'm tough."

I'd nod. I'd apologize for not getting back home more often. It was hard to get from Seattle to Minnesota. She would cut me off.

"You have to live your life. Don't worry." And: "I'm tough, I'm tough."

She was repeating herself a lot by this point. The MS was ravaging her central nervous system, and she was losing more and more of her short-term memory. I knew that. But still, it grated on me. It sounded like she was covering up how she was really feeling. I would respond, "I know you're tough! But you need to tell me how you're doing. You need to tell me what's going on."

She wouldn't. It wasn't just me. She never complained about pain to anyone—doctors, nurses, PTs. She never, ever complained. Even when her muscles twisted and cramped and her face contorted from discomfort and pain. Even when she couldn't operate the buttons on her remote control, and even when swallowing became so painful that her food had to be pureed down to the consistency of baby food. Cooking had been her passion and profession, and now her doctors wanted to put in a feeding tube. Still no complaints.

"I'm tough, I'm tough." It felt like a cop-out. I imagined her raging with me against the disease, or at least acknowledging what was going on. Instead, she used those words like a kind of magic spell. She wouldn't admit what I wanted her to: that she was suffering, that her life sucked. Why wasn't she mad? Why was she rolling over and letting this disease win?

Why wasn't she struggling like I was?

Maybe I was still an adolescent, raging at lack of control.

It was only years later, well after her passing, that I began to understand what she had been doing. Certainly as I limped in pain and doubt along the Appalachian Trail, I was giving myself a crash course in the power of a mantra, in the power of single-mindedness, of stubbornness, of codes, of real toughness. When I was a younger man, I was angry, and I'd wanted my mother to be angry too. But she wasn't. She was reminding herself that despite the hideous disease that was stealing everything else from her, she still had her toughness. Because she said so, and because she could say so. And did. Often. Her physical strength was gone. But her toughness only got tougher; it became her essential feature. If she hadn't been a tough old lady, she would have had to just be a bitter teenager like me.

She was still teaching me things, still reminding me what toughness looked like.

My pain was voluntary; I'd brought it on myself. But if I wanted to do it justice, I would have to be tough. I would have to get tougher.

As I struggled through these memories—an unexpected side effect of the dreaded Virginia Blues—I drew resilience from memories of my mother. I also drew strength from JLu, who embodies that same "I'm tough" attitude. Knowing all that she had been through—the surgeries, the invasive medical tests, and almost bleeding to death—I could surely handle the pain and fatigue out here on the Appalachian Trail.

Those days in Virginia passed in an almost surreal rainbow of miles and memories. I was crossing some kind of mental/physical threshold, one I'd never crossed before, and I felt like I had passed a nondescript yet profound test of my resolve.

On day eighteen in the woody hollows of Virginia, JLu and I reached the Tye River Suspension Bridge. We hadn't planned on stopping, but there were a bunch of people swimming and lying on the rocks, and we had no choice but to jump in and cool off. As we walked across the bridge, we overheard a thru-hiker say to her friend, "Is that Scott Jurek?" Her friend looked up and nodded. "Shouldn't he be *running?*" I probably should have been, but an opportunity to cool down and escape from the stifling muggy air was too good to pass up. For fifteen minutes, life wasn't heavy and our minds weren't occupied with the past or our current struggles.

Then, on day nineteen, I was shocked out of my cogitating and lazing about by the arrival of a mythical creature.

Jenny had been trading calls with the Speedgoat over the past few days, and somehow, using that special goat magic, he found me deep in Shenandoah National Park.

The smile on his face couldn't have been bigger. On the AT, he was like a kid in a candy store. He lived in Sandy, Utah, but out here he was home. He was unquestionably already plotting his own FKT, but I didn't mind. It was great to have him there. Like Horty, he was an old hand at this, and he could relate to my experiences in ways that almost no one else could.

He was usually a man of few words, but when it came to the AT, he gushed multiple sentences. "Yep, just get on the AT treadmill and go three and a half miles an hour. That's how you get the record, dude."

Right after he joined me on the trail, he pointed out a nondescript spot that we passed. "Dude! Right here, yeah, this was where I almost fuckin' called it quits! First time I took a crack at the old AT speed record. Damn, feels like yesterday."

After we'd run for a mile together, I pulled off the trail for a pit stop. After a few minutes, I returned to the trail, where Speedgoat was waiting. He snapped at me: "You gotta button that shit up, be quicker! How many dumps you taking a day? Is it all that vegan shit you eat or what?"

I wasn't at all surprised. I knew the Speedgoat was in rare form when he was in his element.

The Speedgoat was built like his ungulate namesake: a compact, wiry 130 pounds. But when his deep, foghorn voice boomed, you'd swear he was a giant. Like Horty, Karl Meltzer loomed large in the ultrarunning community. So did his *nom de trail,* Speedgoat, and everything that the name connoted. In 1993, while he was driving home from Pikes Peak, a jackrabbit crossed the road. Karl randomly said, "Hey, it's a speedgoat." And the name stuck. Tough, crazy, ornery, unique. A nimble climber, like a goat, but speedy. Not only had the Speedgoat won the "Wild and Tough" Hardrock Hundred five times, he had also won more hundred-mile races (thirty-eight) than "anyone else on earth." (That's a direct quote from his website.) And he'd set the 2,064-mile Pony Express Trail (Sacramento to St. Joseph, Missouri) speed record in 2010, completing the run in forty days. Of the hundred-plus ultras he'd entered, Speedgoat had won sixty. For sixteen years he'd won a hundred-miler annually.

But despite all those accomplishments, Meltzer was *obsessed* with the AT, particularly the speed record. He had chased the AT FKT twice—in 2008 and 2014. On his second assault, he'd pulled the plug in Virginia with nine hundred miles left to go. The day before he quit, he had logged sixty miles, and on the day he quit, he said, "Yesterday I was on fire, felt like I could do a hundred, but today I can't go a step more than nine miles. I'm done. What the hell, dude?"

He had physically and mentally cracked. I was beginning to know what that felt like.

He wasn't unusual only in the running world; he was eclectic everywhere and in the things he did. I never saw him wear anything but a T-shirt, hiking shorts, and running shoes or wool house slippers. He always raced with a hydration waist belt; no newfangled high-tech hydration vest or torso pack for the old-school Goat. He wore bicycle-racing gloves while he ran, because, well, you know: "Dude, you think I want my hands messed up when I eat shit?" For years he raced with a bulky, low-tech MP3 player and big-ass headphones with a wire headband. He did it way before most runners ran with music and then way *after* more compact and convenient devices came out. In some ways, he was both a trendsetter *and* a throwback. And it worked for him. Monotony and boredom were absent from Speedgoat's mentality. In hundred-milers he could eat gel after gel, consuming sixty of them in twenty hours. Everyone was shocked he didn't get sick of gels. Speedgoat's response? "Dude, I just suck them down, doesn't matter." Evidently, palate fatigue was not a part of his mind-set either.

He was also a fanatic golfer. And no surprise, given his nickname, the Speedgoat played world-class *speed* golf, setting a record for 230 holes in twelve hours. He had a secret life goal of playing on the Masters tour.

He was simple and stubborn to the core. He still ate like it was the 1950s. The nutrition revolution had reached nearly every corner of the running world—even nonvegans were at least eating *consciously*—but not Speedgoat. Burgers, steak, pizza, whatever was around, Speedgoat was game. Well, except mayonnaise—or anything white, for that matter. Oh yeah, and most vegetables. But he loved his brewskis. And, of course, Red Bull. The beverage giant was one of his sponsors and it was a match made in heaven. Karl was always well stocked with Red Bull in every flavor, including prototypes no one had ever heard of. "Dude, I got the keys to the warehouse," he would joke as he thrust a kiwi-flavored Red Bull into the hands of someone nearby.

But he wasn't even consistent in his craziness. As careless as he was in his eating habits, Speedgoat was exceptionally fussy in other aspects of his life. His necessities of "Speedgoat livin' " were always ready in his van, and it was a meticulously curated collection of stuff. I rarely saw any item switched out or replaced or upgraded. Speedgoat had his *stuff*, and his stuff was a symbol of his simple yet calculated existence.

Now he was out here with me. At least I'd have some entertainment for the last stretch of the Virginia Blues. But I wasn't sure JLu was ready for two weeks with the Goat.

By the time we got to the Shenandoahs, we were different people than we'd been when we left Boulder. Horty wasn't with us, but his words pervaded the air; this was who we were, and this was what we did. Our systems were dialed. We were making up for lost time and we were in a groove. So I was less than excited about another person joining our team, even if it was the legendary Speedgoat.

It's not that I didn't like him; I barely knew him. I knew he and Scott had developed a happy rivalry over the years, and he'd come to our wedding, but he and I had never established any kind of relationship. Some of my friends had crewed for him and I'd heard he could be a real grump, so I didn't want that energy here because we were having fun.

But I've been told that you should be careful of being too happy—it makes you soft. Speedgoat was here to remind us of that.

Jurker had schooled me on the history of Speedgoat and the AT FKT. I knew the AT was his obsession, I knew he had gone for the speed record twice before and had come close both times, which only fueled his mania. I wondered if he would be upset if Jurker scooped his project on the first try. Maybe he was coming out here to sabotage us or spy on us? He'd jumped at the opportunity to help out, so I was a little suspicious of his intentions.

But Jurker really wanted him here, and he could use the company. He wasn't the least bit worried; he assured me that Speedgoat was a true champion and would welcome the competition. Karl knew the AT like the back of his hand; he had rehearsed sections and driven to literally almost every single road crossing. That all sounded like it would be helpful, but I really didn't need another know-it-all out here. We were unlocking the AT FKT puzzle on our own terms. Far from precise, we had no idea if one bad decision or disappointment would be our demise or the very thing that bolstered us up over the next mountain. That's what made it exciting; the uncertainty kept us sharp.

Speedgoat texted me a few days before he met us to make sure I had reserved a campground in Shenandoah. I hadn't figured that out yet and I wasn't able to reply right away. When he showed up, he had already reserved a campsite for us. Okay, maybe he was going to be a helpful addition to this team of two. He found us out on the trail and all my anxieties went away when I saw how relaxed he was out here; he had the same youthful expression I'd seen on Jurker on day one. I could see that Speedgoat was genuinely excited to help Jurker succeed.

Karl referred to his vehicle as "the Inconspicuous White Van," which was equal parts creepy and funny and exactly on-brand. When we pulled into a trailhead parking lot, I was curious to see his rig. This was the vehicle he'd used in his last attempt on the AT, so I wanted to see how ours compared. It was bigger than ours, for sure, with lots of windows, but it was more rustic inside. He had a raised platform for a big bed, two inflatable Therm-a-Rest mattresses and some sleeping bags, plastic bins under the bed for storage, a nicer cooler than ours, a two-burner propane stove, and a blue plastic cube-shaped water jug. He didn't have installed solar panels, just portable ones, so he always parked his van in the sunniest spot possible and then unrolled the panels and lay them on top of his van.

Castle Black was no palace, but I'd tried my best to make it cozy. I hung curtains to cover up the patchwork of steel walls and duct-taped insulation. I threw a rug on the plywood floor. We had a twin-bed-size foam mattress and a comforter with a cute duvet cover (it was the little things that kept me sane). Speedgoat's van was for survival; it reminded me of a college dorm on wheels, minus the tie-dye tapestries.

I was getting ready to meet Jurker here in the parking lot, grabbing his food and setting his supplies out. Speedgoat pulled out his lawn chair from the back of his van and walked over to me. "Ready?" he asked.

"For what?" I was confused.

"To hike down. The trail doesn't run through the parking lot." Blunt, always blunt. I liked that about Karl.

"I know, but I think it's pretty close."

"Always meet him on the trail; never make him walk extra steps. Doesn't matter how short it is—it all adds up. A tenth of a mile here, a half a mile there, and next thing you know, you're looking at an extra mile per day over forty-six days. That's forty-six miles, which equals a full day on the AT. So, do you have a chair? If not, I have one."

The man had a point. I grabbed my camping chair out of Castle Black. It still had the price tags on, since it had been a last-minute purchase before we left Boulder. I loaded his energy food and water into a backpack and locked up.

"Do you have any hot food for him?" He read the answer in my face. "Always have something hot to offer him. He's so sick of eating energy food. Have a couple different options of real food every time you see him. And whatever you make, be sure it has a ton of calories."

Right. Normally I do not like taking orders from people, but I had to hand it to him—he knew what he was talking about. I got back in the van and fired up the stove. It was the first time I'd used it during the day. I slathered two pieces of bread with coconut oil and made a grilled vegan cheese sandwich with avocado slices. That was about the fattiest thing I could make, and I was proud of myself for not burning it!

We hiked down to the trail, which was longer and steeper than

I'd expected; good thing I hadn't made Jurker hike up that. Karl plopped down in his big lawn chair on the trail, put on his reading glasses, and started paging through his guidebook, occasionally jotting down notes. I set my chair next to his and began looking for signs of Jurker. Like a beater truck with high mileage and bad suspension, Jurker rolled our way, much to my relief.

I offered him my seat and he took a bite of the sandwich. I told him about my morning, about the Speedgoat rig, and caught him up on the daily news. He took off his pack and sifted through his food supply, assessing what he would need for the next section.

"You guys are taking too long," said an authoritative Speedgoat. "No sitting down; you can eat that sandwich while you walk out of here. Jenny, you need to grab his pack as soon as he gets here and do the resupply. No chitchat."

I was starting to really like Karl. He was a no-nonsense kind of guy and he approached the AT speed record like a NASA scientist. He had all these detailed maps of the trail that I hadn't known existed. He'd taken one look at us and could tell we didn't have our act together. I'd thought we were moving like a well-oiled machine, but apparently we were leaking at every seal. Guess we wouldn't be stopping for swims and backtracking for border crossings anymore. Without sounding righteous or bossy, he initiated an overhaul of our go-with-the-flow, easy-breezy attitude.

After Jurker left, Speedgoat and I hiked back up to the vans. "Listen, this record is legit; there is no room for error. Every second matters. How often are you meeting him?"

"I don't know…we try to meet up at least every four hours. Sometimes every six, or even eight." That was the rhythm we'd gotten into down south.

"From now on, we meet him at every road crossing; that way he can carry less. Plus it's a huge mental boost for him to see you more often." The advantage Speedgoat brought to this one-woman-crew operation was that he could put himself in Scott's position better than I could, since he'd made the run himself. Sometimes he seemed to know what Jurker needed even before Jurker knew.

I followed him to the Big Meadows Campground, where Speedgoat had made reservations for us. We found our campsite and he parked his van. Then he backed into a different spot, came out, backed in again, then did it once more at a different angle. He spent about ten minutes positioning his van in just the right spot. It seemed like a lot of work to make sure his van was level. But then he told me about how he took care of his lawn at home. He had a croquet court in his backyard that he manicured daily and meticulously mowed every three days. And not with a power mower—with a push one, and a battery trimmer. He didn't trust anyone else to maintain it, not even his wife, Cheryl.

I found the Speedgoat's quirks endearing. He was like an old man set in his ways. I think when you race ultramarathons or attempt something like the AT, there are so many things out of your control that the few things in your life you can control, you want to master. For Jurker, it was his diet. That was the one thing he liked to have complete control over. And out here, he handed the reins to me, which was no small task.

I dropped Speedgoat off at Pinefield Gap so he could run with Jurker that evening. He pulled on his waist belt and slid two beer cans into the water-bottle holders. Legendary. I saw three black bears in the direction they were running and I'd seen three more by the time I drove to the final meeting spot of the day. I had asked Speedgoat if he was worried about bears in this notoriously bear-filled section and he said, "Nope, I just put on my headphones and turn the music up louder." Jurker was in good hands.

MID-ATLANTIC

450 MILES

Train yourself to let go of everything you fear to lose.
—Yoda, *Star Wars*

An afternoon nap in the Blue Ridge Mountains of central Virginia on Day 17. *(Luis Escobar)*

Midpoint sign on Day 23, Pine Grove Furnace State Park, Pennsylvania, 1,095 miles. *(Scott Jurek)*

oother stretch in
sylvania, Day 23.
'Alexis Berg)

Guiding my blind buddy Thomas in Bear Mountain State Park, New York, Day 29. *(Scott Jurek collection)*

Running across the Hudson River, New York, on Day 29. *(Jenny Jurek)*

Jenny says good-bye to Speedgoat and the "Inconspicuous White Van" in Dalton, Massachusetts, on Day 32. *(Walter Edwards)*

50 m.p.h. blowing rain on Mount Greylock, Massachusetts, on Day 33. *(Jenny Jurek)*

Horty all smiles in Vermont on Day 33. *(Jenny Jurek)*

A dark night about to get darker on Smarts Mountain, New Hampshire, Day 36. *(Mark Godale)*

Taking a nap on a rock just before Galehead Hut in the predawn of Day 38. (Timmy O'Neill)

Zealand Falls Hut potato chip binge, White Mountains, New Hampshire, on Day 38. (Timmy O'Neill)

Mount Washington on the Fourth of July, Day 39. (Luis Escobar)

Lunch break at Mad
Spring Hut, White Mounta
New Hampshire, on Da
(Luis Esco

Climbing Mount Jefferson, White Mountains, New Hamsphire, on Day 39. *(Luis Escobar)*

The slabs and slots of the Mahoosuc Mountains with my Jedi guide Ryan Welts. *(Timmy O'Neill)*

Celebrating our final state border crossing, into Maine, Day 40. *(Timmy O'Neill)*

Mahoosuc Notch, AKA "the hardest mile on the AT," Day 41. *(Luis Escobar)*

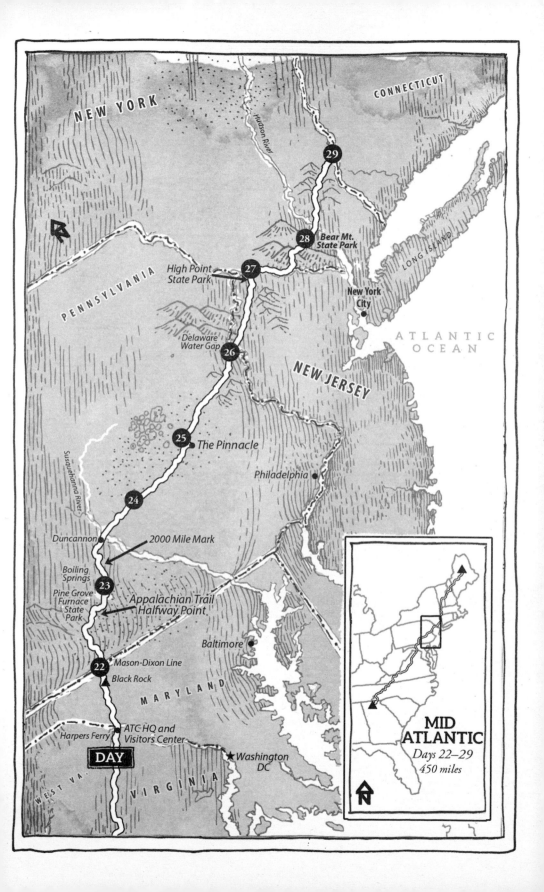

CONNECTICUT

NEW YORK

Hudson River

29

28 Bear Mt. State Park

High Point State Park **27**

LONG ISLAND

New York City

PENNSYLVANIA

ATLANTIC OCEAN

Delaware Water Gap **26**

NEW JERSEY

25 The Pinnacle

Susquehanna River

Philadelphia

24

Duncannon

2000 Mile Mark

Boiling Springs

23

Pine Grove Furnace State Park

Appalachian Trail Halfway Point

Baltimore

22 Mason-Dixon Line

Black Rock

MARYLAND

ATC HQ and Visitors Center

Harpers Ferry

DAY

★ Washington DC

WEST VA.

VIRGINIA

MID ATLANTIC
Days 22–29
450 miles

CHAPTER 9

ROCKSYLVANIA

Day Twenty

"YOU HEAR THAT?" I asked.

"What?"

JLu and I were headed to Hogwallow Gap, running the evening light away on one of the last stretches of Shenandoah National Park. Speedgoat had offered to shuttle Castle Black there, so we took the now-rare opportunity to run together. It had been days since we'd had trail time alone, and we were catching up and chatting so it wasn't surprising she didn't hear it. But I did. By day twenty, I'd already become attuned to the circle of wilderness that had evolved into my entire world. My Spidey sense was on alert.

"That growl," I said. "Listen."

JLu and I paused, listening closely this time. Nothing. Maybe I was wrong. We took a few strides ahead. And then the growl again echoed through the thick woods, louder, reverberating into our bones. I scanned the surroundings and quickly located our visitor on the left.

A huge black bear materialized from the forest's natural camouflage. She had reared up on her hind legs and was about twenty feet away—a distance the bear could cover in only a few seconds if she chose to charge.

My first thought was *cubs*. I knew that if we were positioned between the bear and her cubs, we could be screwed. We might already be. Keeping my body mostly static, I swiveled my head around and searched for cubs in all directions—nothing. After that, JLu and I remained still. If we moved toward any cubs, we'd almost certainly provoke an attack.

But something eventually had to give. I took a breath, raised my arms, made my body look as big as I could, and hollered back at the standing bear. She looked to be about three hundred pounds and six feet tall, and she stayed up on her hind legs, glared at us, shook her head, and growled again, totally unfazed by me. A standoff.

I couldn't help thinking of old Horty in that moment, even with the threat of death in the air. Horty loved talking to bears; he spoke to them as if they were humans. He'd holler at them as they were running off scared: "Hey, bear, get back here. Yeah, you! I said come back here!" Unfortunately, one time we were running together and came across a bear that seemed to understand English. Horty unloaded his typical threats and taunts and actually provoked the bear to turn back around and full-on chase after Horty and me. Sometimes I couldn't believe he was still alive.

On the trail, I spoke to the bear again. Louder but calmer this time. I even took a step forward. Then I spotted two cubs. They were about fifty feet up a tree, just above their mama, only a few paces off the trail.

Now Mama went *ballistic,* roaring like mad and slamming her giant paw on the tree. It sounded like somebody was pounding the trunk with a baseball bat, and it seemed to be a clear warning for us to get the hell out of there. The only problem was that we were heading north. She wasn't letting us past her even though they were off to the side of the trail. But I wasn't about to head back to Georgia on account of one bear.

"She's not gonna let us by," I said to JLu. "We've gotta give them space."

"Space? What space? We can't step off the trail, what if we walk into a rattlesnake den or tick colony?" JLu had a point. The trail was a thin ribbon through dense brush that hid hazards of its own.

Mama Bear tracked us with her eyes and stood her ground between us and her cubs. She stopped smacking the tree but remained on her hind legs. We inched forward on the farthest tangent of the trail possible. After we got far enough past the bear and saw no indication that she was following us, we resumed running with intensity.

Speedgoat loved hearing about our mama-bear showdown when we closed out the day. He shared a story of his own about being charged by a moose while racing the Bighorn hundred-miler. "Dude, that was a close one. Almost my last hundo." Every trail runner knows that an aggressive moose is about as terrifying an experience as there is out there. Speedgoat had escaped multiple lethal assaults by ducking behind aspen trees. He was lucky he was no wider than those aspens and that moose have terrible vision right in front of their bodies.

When I woke up on day twenty-one, I already felt the pull of a new section of the adventure. The Appalachian Trail linked disparate places and feelings together in a way that was unlike any other trail I'd ever run. As Speedgoat, JLu, and I approached the northern border of Virginia and the sliver of Maryland just beyond it, we became increasingly aware that we were leaving the South behind. Or, rather, that the trail and the world around it seemed to be slowly transitioning. It hadn't been easy to make it this far. But there we were, and we were still moving. That thought, at least, gave me comfort. Perhaps I was weathered now. Perhaps the oldest mountains in the world and their endless peaks were shaping me into something stronger.

Not that I didn't have doubts. There were plenty of things that made me question myself, but they could also fuel my fire.

I'd met an older runner who was checking on me. He asked how many zeros I had taken. *Zeros*, in trail speak, are days when no miles are hiked. A lot of hikers take zeros occasionally, to rest, to socialize, to clean up and refuel. When I told him none, that I couldn't even consider setting a speed record if I took any zeros, he laughed and said, "Record? There's no way you're going to set the record. I've been following you—you're way too far behind."

He wasn't even close to getting in my head; I had been shutting down the critics my entire racing career. Nobody expected a twenty-five-year-old from Minnesota to show up and win the Western States 100, first try. Nobody expected a sea-level Seattleite to win the Hardrock Hundred, and certainly nobody expected a stagnant forty-something to run the Appalachian Trail in record time. Nobody—except the man in the ring. I thought about that Roosevelt quote printed on my 1999 Western States race guide: "It is not the critic who counts; not the man who points out how the strong man stumbles…. The credit belongs to the man who is actually in the arena, whose face is marred by dust and sweat and blood; who strives valiantly…who at the best knows in the end the triumph of high achievement, and who at the worst, if he fails, at least fails while daring greatly, so that his place shall never be with those cold and timid souls who neither know victory nor defeat."

I think most people we ran into meant well. But there were outliers. A few days back, JLu stopped at a popular brewery to get me some french fries. She felt too grimy to wait inside with the well-groomed customers, so she stayed in the foyer near some thru-hikers. One of them asked how many days I'd been on the trail so far.

After a quick calculation, she replied, "Eighteen."

He looked surprised. "I've taken more zeros than days he's hiked," the young thru-hiker said. "That insults me."

Before JLu could respond, another hiker stood up and said, "Hey, man, hike your own hike. I think it's cool what he's doing," and asked to take a picture with her.

There it was again, that age-old rub. I could hear the man yelling at me in the Smokies "What's your hurry?"; the people online posting that I was missing the point; the guy who said I was too slow to get the record—and now this hiker felt insulted by my pace.

Hike your own hike and I'll blaze my own trail. These comments only motivated me more.

The South was where we had gotten our bearings and lost our minds. I'd bumped up against my mental and physical limits and thought it was over. But I'd bounced back. JLu, for her part, had been harassed and overworked, but she'd held her own. And now she was running a tighter ship than ever. Castle Black had gotten more professional. She'd turned it into an efficient food, comfort, and lodging machine for one very ragged runner.

We crossed the Mason-Dixon Line on day twenty-two, leaving the South behind and approaching the halfway point. Mile markers were one thing, but it felt more significant that we had crossed into the geographical midsection of the trail. We were done with the Blue Ridge Mountains and heading into the mid-Atlantic bluffs and forests. My body had healed up from the first major blows, and my head was back in the game. Up next would be Pennsylvania, then quick dips into New Jersey and New York before I officially entered New England—the last section of the trail.

That was what progress felt like.

The differences, day to day and region to region, were incredible to experience. Especially since I was carried between them by nothing more than my own muscle and willpower. There was none of the strange disorientation that comes from flying across time zones—it was just me and my legs, pulling the world toward me.

Or running away, depending on the situation. The mama bear was still fresh in my mind as we left Virginia behind. But threats would always be a part of nature and the trail. When they weren't imminent, they deepened my respect for the place. I welcomed the wild; that was part of the experience. There was darkness and danger on the Appalachian Trail, both known and unknown to me.

Just a few days after I passed through Great Smoky Mountains National Park, a hiker was attacked by a bear. It happened near Hazel Creek and involved a bear that hadn't even been provoked. Prowling for food at about 10:30 at night, the bear had pulled a sixteen-year-old hiker out of his hammock and mauled his leg and head, even though the boy, camping with his father, had done everything right and taken excellent bear precautions. He'd hoisted his food, pack, and equipment far above the ground. The boy's dad, who'd also been in a hammock, beat the bear back and then helped his son limp to the shore of a nearby lake. Campers there who had a boat took them across the lake to a dock where paramedics were waiting. He was airlifted to a hospital in Asheville, where he was treated for his injuries.

In all, there were an average of nine bear attacks on the AT every year, most of them during the late spring and early summer, before the summer fruit had ripened.

In addition to big mammals, there were other dangers hidden in those mid-Atlantic woods—less dramatic, but ultimately more vexing.

First of all, there were the rocks. Jagged and uneven stones covered the trail, inspiring thru-hikers to name the middle stretch Rocksylvania. It seemed like every step was its own little adventure: uneven, slippery, and often bordered by boulders that raised the stakes of tripping and falling by promising you a cracked skull or mangled knee. The earth itself was a danger here. The rocks had been compressed into sharp layers and then pushed upright like spears about two hundred million years ago, when the landmass that would become Africa rammed into North America, shoving this part of the continent westward. That primeval push still echoes through the contours of the Pennsylvania landscape, most obviously in the westward-curving ridges of the Appalachians.

AT legend has it that Pennsylvania hiking clubs and trail crews are proud of their state's nickname of Rocksylvania and don't remove rocks from the trail. In fact, some people claim they actually dump wheelbarrows full of rocks onto the trail. Speedgoat kept saying, "Dude, why'd they route the trail over the rocks? That makes a lot of sense." Often there were no rocks to the left and right of the trail but the trail itself ran directly over boulder fields and rock beds.

Pennsylvania's rocks were notorious on the AT for causing disabling injuries and ending trips. The mountains' diamond-hard, multicolored quartz rocks—used as arrowheads by the Iroquois and as building material by the early European settlers—were so plentiful and so inhospitable to plant life that many of the blazes here were painted on rocks instead of trees. Even in relatively—and

I use the word *relatively* with caution—flat stretches of Rocksylvania, it was impossible to develop any kind of rhythm or pace. Some of the especially treacherous sections, popularly known as the Knife Edges, required a hybrid of scrambling and hiking.

Pennsylvania's rocks were perilous in their own right, but they also provided shelter for two of the AT's three types of poisonous snakes, northern copperheads and timber rattlesnakes. (The third type, the aggressive water moccasin, lives in the South and ranges only up to southern Virginia.) Karl spoke of the Pennsylvania rattlers as "big fuckers." He said their bodies were the diameter of a coffee can and claimed he could hear them rattle even through his headphones blasting Strangefolk. Speedgoat hated all snakes; fortunately he'd grown up in New Hampshire, where they have only one species of poisonous snake.

The copperheads were more likely to bite than the rattlers, though. Like other pit vipers, they have muscular, thick bodies that range up to three feet in length. Their brown and rust-colored patches help them blend into the rocks to the point of near-invisibility, and they compound their camouflage by freezing when people approach instead of fleeing or offering a warning as rattlers usually do. They're especially troublesome in the narrow straits of the trail that are bordered by rock shelves on one side and cliffs on the other. But the copperheads weren't nearly as dangerous as the timber rattler, the most feared AT snake of all. The timber rattler can grow up to six feet long and has the girth of a man's arm; its hollow fangs—large and sharp enough to puncture clothes and most boots—inject a notably powerful venom.

About a month after I was scrambling up the Knife Edges in Pennsylvania, a timber rattler bit a thirty-nine-year-old camper on that stretch of trail. He received antivenin on-site and got airlifted to a hospital, and he still died.

But bears and snakes didn't even come close to the most fearsome creatures out there. The blacklegged tick and the common deer tick, no bigger than the tip of a pencil, were the menaces that loomed largest in my mind. The woods of the Northeast are responsible for the country's highest incidence of Lyme disease, and even a mild bout of it could wreck my chances for the FKT and extend well beyond that. Even after treatment, Lyme disease can manifest as a mysterious, disabling condition that can last for years.

The poisonous spiders were the least of my worries, even though black widows and brown recluses inhabited the trail. I was usually the first person on the trail in the morning and the last to leave it at night, so I inadvertently cleared the trail of webs, earning myself the trail name of Web Walker, a moniker bestowed on me by my fellow thru-hikers. I'd started at Springer Mountain with a trail name I'd been called for years, but I especially loved this one. It made me feel a part of the Appalachian Trail Class of 2015.

In spite of the rocks, I'd been pushing myself so hard that I was making up for some of the time I'd lost during my thirty-mile days after the injuries. I was laying down fifty-four to fifty-eight miles a day, thanks in part to the Speedgoat, who reminded me every time I was ready to pack it in that I had to "chip away at some extra miles *every* day. Nickel-and-dime and even *penny* your way to Maine, dude!" At some point, I guess Speedgoat had come around and decided I did have a shot at the record after all.

After years of knowing Karl, I had grown comfortable with his idiosyncrasies and philosophies. The passions of running and hiking bring together an eclectic stew of individuals who are all trying to get to a finish line or reach a destination. And beyond that? Almost nothing. Often these are people who would never interact with each other at all in everyday life, let alone spend hours or days together. Horty and I are a good example. His friends always asked why he went on long running adventures out west with "that Jurek guy." I guess crew-cut, buttoned-up Liberty University professors aren't supposed to hang with long-haired vegan hippies. I love it. We respect each other's differences and appreciate each other's strengths. Our sport shows there's hope for different kinds of humans to get along and not hate each other—at least, if they all have a similar goal to concentrate on.

Karl was different from me in about a million ways, but he was a venerable champion. He had a thirst for domination but he also genuinely wanted to help me get the record. Something in his makeup made him both ruthless and selfless, often at different times during the same day. But there is always plenty of that contradiction throughout the ultrarunning community. When we're out on the racecourse, we duke it out, but after the race we're all buddies, sipping some post-race brews and enjoying the afterglow of a good clean fight. That strange camaraderie was what drew me to the sport and has kept me in it for decades.

Perhaps the emphasis should be on *strange*. Ultrarunning seems to be a harbor for outsiders of all kinds, Horty and Karl most certainly among them. I'll never forget when Speedgoat and I roomed together in Hong Kong for the 2002 Oxfam Trailwalker 100K. As far as I know, it was the first time he'd ever traveled outside of the United States. The day after our team won the four-person team race, most of us went on an excursion to a famous Buddhist temple, and I encouraged Speedgoat to join us even though I could tell he was over the Asian experience. "Dude, I'm kinda tired of all the Chinese food and this crazy city," he said. "I'm gonna get whatever American food I can find, some beer, and watch golf on TV all afternoon." The Speedgoat was way out of his comfort zone and far from his curated routines, and he was not about to break the routine that had gotten him there.

When I got back to the hotel, there were empty beer cans and minibottles of liquor on the desk and nightstand; chip bags and candy wrappers were strewn on the floor, and the minibar had been cleared out. Karl, lounging in bed watching golf, was lit up and pumped as shit.

"Dude, they left all this free shit in the fridge for us! Want a drink?"

He didn't realize that he'd just demolished two hundred dollars' worth of minibar refreshments. Like I said, the ol' Goat didn't usually roam far from home. And the type of lodging we generally inhabited most definitely didn't include stocked minibars.

Around 8:00 p.m. on day twenty-four, Jenny and I arrived at PA-325 near Clarks Creek and checked the maps. I'd gotten forty-five miles already—not bad, but not finished yet. Most days around that time, I'd have only a few more miles, maybe an hour or two to go. I even thought I might finish up the day before having to break out the headlamps, which would have been a true milestone considering how late into the night the past week's runs had gone. But the Speedgoat had been scheming, and he had a different plan at the trailhead.

"Dude, sweet! You've been rolling, right on! Now I told you we'd give you a lighter day today, but I really think you should bank some more miles. There's talk about a huge front moving in and it's bringing inches of rain with it. Some kind of tropical storm. Better lay them down tonight; tomorrow night could be brutal. Here's the deal—it's fourteen miles to the next road crossing through Pennsylvania State Game Lands and I know it's already getting dark, but I think you gotta crank this shit out. I'll run in from the other side and meet you halfway."

At this point I was doing whatever Speedgoat told me to do. I let out a sigh and stretched my headlamp onto my sweaty skull. It was going to be a long night; fifty-nine total miles for the day. I knew it would be great to catch some extra miles when my body was working well, but I was dreading it to a certain degree. The dark, lonely nights were quickly becoming my least favorite part of the experience. The heavy lifting happens in the darkest times—but the glimmer of the record was starting to come back into view.

As JLu was reloading my pack for the night, we were interrupted by a stranger, a gray-haired farmer who was at the trailhead. He handed JLu a fresh-baked blueberry oatmeal cobbler and a bottle of something home-brewed. The old-timer called it "switchel." While it seemed wildly reckless to take food or drink—especially the fermented type—from strangers, I just couldn't say no. Besides, I had hardly been rigorous about not accepting food from strangers so far, and I hadn't yet gotten a trip-derailing stomach bug or food poisoning. On the contrary, the random food and drink from followers had been a godsend.

The switchel was crazy-good, gingery and vinegary, and it really hit the spot after a long hot day. Ginger can work wonders on the stomach and it was a common tool in my nutritional tool kit, on and off the trail. Surprisingly, Speedgoat took to it quickly too and downed half the bottle.

I set off while Speedgoat and JLu drove on to the next trailhead, the final destination for day twenty-four.

For thirteen miles, I cut through the sodden Pennsylvania darkness, following my narrow little cone of light and pumping my legs to the old familiar rhythms of techno that I'd been listening to for years. It was lonely, but it was loneliness with a purpose.

Long after midnight and hours after giving up on Karl, I spotted a headlamp in front of me, slicing through the mist and fog, and I heard the boom of the Goat's voice before his face came into focus.

"Nice, dude! Way to bang that shit out." He had run out to meet me from the destination trailhead. He was also, somehow, sipping a cold beer as he ran.

"How much farther is the van?" I asked.

"Little over a mile. I dropped my other beer can on the trail exactly a mile from the parking lot."

We found it in a few minutes.

The final two days in Virginia were fun, hanging with the Speedgoat. It was a relief to have somebody around who knew where we were going so I could relax and take a break from the navigation, the most stressful part about crewing on the AT. More than that, I had a quirky companion who was quickly becoming my best and only friend. He was not one to volunteer personal information, but I loved asking him about how he'd met Cheryl, how they'd decided to get married, if he ever wanted to have kids. "No. Runners with kids always say, 'You can keep racing, you just have to rearrange your life a little.'" He paused, crinkled his forehead in a puzzled look, and said, "Why would I want to do that?"

On the morning of day twenty-one, Speedgoat left to pick up our buddy Rickey Gates from the airport. Rickey was coming to the East Coast to race a classic race, the Mount Washington Road Race, and he'd decided to drop in on us for a few days. I loved Rickey; he was an elite trail runner renowned for utilizing multiple modes of travel. Whether by foot, thumb, cycle, or train, he'd arrive, and for the constant voyager, the conveyance is as important as the destination. He was thrift-store chic in a western shirt and moccasins at our wedding, where my designer friends voted him best-dressed. Rickey could eat with kings and sleep by dumpsters. I always enjoyed his company and I knew Jurker did too.

Rickey ran with Jurker while Speedgoat and I drove to Ashby Gap. We had some time before they'd arrive, so Speedgoat wanted to strategize. Jurker was optimistic that we were back on record pace, but I was a little concerned because we had fallen far behind our itinerary. Karl asked to see our spreadsheet, and after some rummaging around, I found it buried under the maps. He studied it and then, very matter-of-fact, very Speedgoat, he said, "It's not humanly possible to stay on this schedule. His mileage up in New Hampshire and Maine is not possible; nobody has ever covered that distance that quickly."

I let that sink in. *So he's saying that we've been out here busting our asses for three weeks and Jurker doesn't stand a chance at the record?* I was so disheartened and angry at Scott. How could he have squandered so much time talking to people, posing for pictures, swimming in creeks, hanging out in the van? Then I started kicking myself for not being more involved in the planning. Why had I left him in charge of the itinerary? I was fuming. I knew it! I'd tried to tell him he was wasting too much time but he was too busy wasting time to notice. He was going to get a rude awakening when the AT analyst told him it was out of his reach. I cleaned the van to calm down before he and Rickey arrived.

As a family rule, we try not to argue in front of friends, so when they got there, I bit my tongue and restocked his pack and then sent him on his way. He took off running with Karl while Rickey and I ate lunch. As starving as I was for the company of an old friend, I was distracted. I vented to him about the cruel reality Speedgoat had spelled out for me, that it wasn't possible for Jurker to get the record now.

Rickey just leaned in like he was telling me a secret and said, "But Karl's never done it either."

Point taken. Speedgoat knew everything about the AT, but he still hadn't nailed it. Rickey continued educating me. "We just need to be positive. Jurker needs positive energy. He'll do it."

Rickey was right and I decided then and there to put my cynicism aside and be nothing but positive to the best of my ability. Later that evening, Speedgoat, Rickey, and I drove to the Blackburn AT center. Speedgoat was taking notes since he'd never been up that road. We hiked up to the trail and sat on a log in the dusk. I was dressed and ready to run the next six miles with Jurker. It was gonna be a late night and those guys were laughing, sharing a oney bat, relieved that it was me and not them who had the last night shift.

When Jurker came running toward us, he had a train of about a half a dozen headlamps behind him, and their energy cut through the air like a lightning bolt. One of the runners had filled a backpack with dry ice and brought Popsicles for Jurker. It seemed like a fun group, which prompted Rickey to say, "Man, I wish I was running the next stretch." The excitement was contagious even for me. I could see why people drove for hours to meet up with Scott. I think they wanted to experience the energy, to be a part of the record attempt. I don't know what it was exactly, but I was suddenly so grateful to run into the night with him. And as it turned out, all the other runners peeled off, so we were alone.

It was a particularly dark and eerie section. I was leading and the trail markers were hard to see at night. The grass and trees were all dewy, so everything seemed to reflect in the beam of my headlamp. We could hear the road crossing well before we reached it. There was an all-night crew doing construction right next to the parking lot. We fell asleep to the bright lights, deafening generators, and jackhammers and slept like babies.

I woke up the next morning elated. Rickey and Scott took off running and I knew that in four miles, they would cross the West Virginia state line. We'd be officially out of Virginia, and as luck would have it, Jurker was set up to do the Four State Challenge! It's a classic challenge that trail-hardened thru-hikers like to do; they travel the forty-three miles from Virginia through West Virginia and Maryland to Pennsylvania, hitting all four states in one day.

Speedgoat and I met them in Harpers Ferry, the home of the Appalachian Trail Conservancy. I'd been in touch with the ATC, and Jurker wanted to stop in, but unfortunately when we got there it was 7:00 a.m. and nobody was in the office. I was surprised anybody was even awake in this sleepy town, but there were some local runners who brought Scott some rocks on which they'd painted *The time is now.* It was the kind of positive energy Rickey had been talking about and I appreciated it.

We were close to Washington, DC, now and there were a surprising amount of runners waiting to meet him at each trailhead. As the day went on, the weather turned dark and it was pouring rain again. Speedgoat ran the last section in the rain while Rickey and I found a laundromat. He said Jurker's clothes smelled like apple cider vinegar, a fact I had been ignoring for the past week or so. Not uncommon for ultra-endurance athletes, I knew it meant he was breaking down acids in his body, that he was tapping into his reserves or something worse.

He completed the Four State Challenge plus six extra miles and was soaked through. Since Rickey was leaving the next day, instead of drying off and jumping in bed like he should have, Scott wanted to spend the evening drinking a beer with his friends. I wanted him to sleep, but even more than that, I wanted him to enjoy this little slice of normalcy. Karl eventually went to bed but the three of us stayed up late, sitting in our van, talking about everything but running.

At some point late in the night, a car pulled up. It was two ul-trarunning French photographers, Alexis and Roan. I have no idea how they found us out there but we laughed at the randomness. They were going to try to find a hotel and then meet us tomorrow morning.

The rain didn't let up and Jurker was grateful for the clean dry clothes to start day twenty-three with the Frenchies. Karl left to take Rickey to the airport; Roan was running with Jurker; and Alexis followed me to the crew stops, sleeping in his car whenever possible. I knew he must have been hungry, so I offered to drive into town with him to get food and gas.

I looked up a grocery store and led the way. A few miles from the trail, the terrain got more urban, and, weirdly, I recognized the strip malls. Why did they look familiar? Had I been here before? Suddenly it hit me. I was in Chambersburg, Pennsylvania, and this was the road Jurker and I drove to find the AT a few years ago.

It was surreal. It's hard to explain, but back when we first stepped on the AT, it seemed pretty basic. I didn't understand Jurker's reverence for it. But now, knowing what I knew and after everything I'd seen, felt, smelled, and experienced since stepping foot on it in Georgia, it blew my mind. Just a few miles beyond the strip malls and neighborhoods lay this unassuming trailhead, a portal to a whole other world, like Alice's rabbit hole. We'd been living a different life in a parallel universe, so close to the rest of the world, yet so removed. I thought about the AT's proximity to major cities up and down the Eastern Seaboard. Half of the U.S. population lives within a day's drive of at least one of these rabbit holes.

We got food and drove to the next meeting spot. Alexis fell asleep in his rental car. I walked to the trailhead and found a fluorescent sticky note that read "You got this, Scott! HALFWAY!!!" When Scott arrived with Roan, we said *au revoir* to the Frenchies and I ran the next stretch with Jurker. We were alone and anticipated what was coming, so we ran fast and with purpose. After about a mile, there it was: the official 2015 Appalachian Trail midway-point sign. Holy shitballs.

There were a lot of runners waiting for Jurker at the AT Museum in Pine Grove Furnace State Park. The rain was torrential but when Scott got there, the excitement of crossing the midway point gave him extra energy and he was running with ease. He left with a handful of runners and I was alone again. I wandered around the state park and drove to a lake somebody had told me about. It was completely empty because of the rain, but luckily, just then the storm started to break. I jumped in, and, as clichéd as it sounds, I felt all my cares slip away as I floated on my back and stared at the rapidly clearing sky. We made it halfway! We had a crazy 1,095 miles behind us and another 1,095 to go. We had everything we needed—each other—and that was enough. I closed my eyes, held my breath, and felt the water get colder as I sank below the surface.

CHAPTER 10

RUNNING THROUGH THE STICKS WITH MY WOES

Day Twenty-Five

"DUDE, IT'S THE friggin' Forrest Gump show out here," Speed-goat grumbled. "Virginia and Maryland were nuts. Don't know how you're doing it, man. All these people would drive me insane. Well, they *are* driving me insane and I'm not the one doing fifty-mile days! We gotta ditch that GPS tracker, delay the live feed by a day or two."

I just kept running on the AT treadmill, acting like I was working too hard to give an answer.

Speedgoat wasn't wrong; it often was a bit like the Forrest Gump show. With the weekend in full swing in Pennsylvania, there were lots of people in addition to countless rock piles. On the one hand, it was hard to be "on" and working my butt off while also answering questions and letting people join me. I often wondered how much energy and time I was expending by opening my record attempt to whoever wanted to join in; most professional athletes wouldn't even consider letting strangers play alongside them in a championship game or match. On the other hand, I wanted to be myself, the approachable guy who hung out after races for the last finisher, the guy who stayed at events well after the venue had closed to answer questions and pose for photos. It was by no means easy, but that was me. And all of these people were part of my tribe. The hip-hop artist Drake describes his tribe as his Woe. "Woe is my crew. It stands for 'working on excellence.' It's just my whole brand and my whole movement and my way of life for everyone. I want everyone to work on excellence. So all my friends are my Woes and I feel anybody working on excellence in life is a Woe in life as well."

To me, anyone who runs or mindfully moves their body is working on excellence. Could JLu and I get the record while still sharing our experience with my Woes? For the time being, I was managing to do both. I'm sure I wasn't perfect, and people coming out didn't know what mental or physical state I would be in. They had to take what they got.

My tribe wasn't coming out only to catch a ride on our train; they were also providing material support. One family brought us six grocery bags filled with plant-based rarities: cheese and meat substitutes, nondairy ice cream, and other items that were hard to come by. The outpouring of support and generosity was humbling. Locals wanted to help in any way they could. As we got farther north, the trail came closer to larger cities and population centers. We appreciated all the donations, but JLu had a hard time finding room in Castle Black's limited storage. Managing the company of strangers was physically and mentally draining on JLu more than on me. She was the one who was bombarded at trailheads; she was the one who had to answer questions while she was trying to prep things for me; she was the one who was interrupted when she was taking a nap. I felt bad for her additional woes.

While it was hard to measure the costs and returns, I knew that even though I was giving life energy to complete strangers, I was also receiving a form of energy. It was another give-and-take relationship with a cycle of working on excellence. What I gave was returned to me in the form of inspiration, motivation, and perspective.

As I ran down a ridge at sunset, my thoughts wandered away from the rocks below my feet to the amazing people I'd encountered on the trail the past couple of days. The crowds at trailheads, twenty or thirty at a time, a lot of them bearing inspiring signs, some with quotes from my book: PAIN ONLY HURTS! and BE SOMEBODY! They were giving me a dose of my own medicine. A local cross-country team met me in the late-evening darkness of rolling farmland in the Cumberland Valley, and during the day parents brought their little explorers to run a mile or a few yards with me.

Then there were the big hits of unexpected inspiration that made me realize my struggles on the trail were nothing in the big picture of life. One local runner came out and told me he was there to run thirty miles with me. My initial reaction was an internal cringe. Thirty miles is a long way to go with a stranger. And then he told me about the hellish year he'd just been through. He'd been diagnosed with leukemia and had almost lost his life. He was my age, had a wife and kids. It was easy to put myself in his shoes. The thirty-mile run with me was a gift he was giving himself, a kind of celebration for getting through it. And here I was, feeling bad about my torn muscles and rocks and roots on the trail. My day was transformed. Perspective can be both humbling and inspiring. Those thirty miles wound up being the easiest of that whole stretch.

It was becoming increasingly clear to me that I wouldn't even come close to the record without the fans, friends, and supporters who were showing up to run with me. The trail was torturing my body every day. Finishing—let alone owning the record—was coming in and out of focus daily, even hourly. But the presence of other bodies, other minds, and other stories made my pain feel like a part of something bigger. And something I couldn't complain about. There were a lot worse things I could be dealing with besides boulder fields and tropical storms.

As we crossed the Delaware River and left Rocksylvania behind for a brief trip through New Jersey, I made sure that JLu and I ran together. We loved hearing the accents change along with the geography, and we laughed as we did our best to replicate lines we had heard from locals. We needed that time together—time she didn't have to spend cooking for me, feeding me, scouring my body for ticks, bandaging me, or otherwise tending to my basic needs. Time to simply be a couple. Not a couple fixed on the big goal. That was hard to balance, and occasionally I wondered if we were drifting apart rather than coming together. I got the sense that her spirits were flagging, even though she and Speedgoat had become buddies to the point of mutual admiration (how that had happened was a mystery, yet it also seemed meant to be). She was sacrificing so much to be out here supporting my FKT attempt. On the outside, it appeared to be all about me, but we were a team working toward something we both needed. Something beyond a record.

That is, if we actually got the record. I had made up ground by adhering to the Speedgoat principles of averaging three and a half miles per hour on the AT treadmill and nickel-and-diming my way to Katahdin if I had to, but I was still just barely clawing back to a record-setting pace. The ground I'd lost in the South over just two days was taking me weeks to regain, but I was doing it. I was starting to transform into someone or something else. A sort of AT castaway, a trail animal; I was haggard, bony, and somehow permanently dirty, but I would need to dig even deeper into that bony body if I was going to get to Maine.

New Jersey. It was hard to believe we had made it this far. The runners and hikers came out in force, giving us an enthusiastic welcome, Jersey accent and all. Signs saying NJ LOVES EL VENADO were taped around trees. I was more than halfway done, and the distances between states got smaller and the trail supposedly easier (according to Horty). The mid-Atlantic states brought with them the almost instant gratification of daily border crossings: New Jersey, New York, then Connecticut, which signaled our arrival in New England. Connecticut and Massachusetts would each take a day. It was Vermont, New Hampshire, and then Maine that had humbled many a thru-hiker. They were the undisputed crux of the entire AT.

It was heartening to look at a full AT map and see how much ground we'd covered. I loved feeling the progress and knowing how far I had traveled by human locomotion. The squiggly red line that went from where I was to the end of the Appalachian Trail was getting shorter and shorter.

It was a good thing, too, because by the time JLu and I ran across the Delaware River, I was starting to feel an obstruction that was hard to describe. Not the early wall I'd hit a few days in, and not a mental wall or a sense of doubt or the physical barriers of injury and crippling soreness. It was a heaviness, an imaginary fifty-pound pack that felt all too real.

It was in the Kittatinny Mountains in New Jersey that I struggled with the daily despair of *How can I keep doing this for another two weeks?* It was a strange form of depression. I would be happy throughout the day, with some ups and downs. Running and hiking tens of miles a day isn't always a joyful experience. I would finish the day flying high on the satisfaction of completing another fifty-plus-mile day. That moment of glory would last a few minutes, and then I'd feel a sinking sensation as I remembered that in less than six hours, I would be waking up to do the same thing again. I was caught up in a cycle of emotions every damn day.

The runner who patiently waited outside Castle Black at 6:00 that morning was bubbling with excitement, but I told him I might not say much as we ran. I couldn't confide in him. I couldn't even confide in JLu because she had her own emotional roller coaster to deal with. And I sure as hell didn't know how to describe it to the data-driven Goat, even though he probably knew exactly how I felt. He had been there, and he'd cracked. Maybe this was how depressed people felt. I could put on the happy face, soak up motivation from those who came out to run with me and cheer for me, feel the power of my legs propelling me, but deep down inside, I was faltering, sinking.

There was one other person I needed in my corner. He had seen me at the height of my career and at the darkest times during my divorce. He'd helped me climb up and out of that, and now he might be able to lift me up and push me forward, regardless of the heaviness I felt.

Don Makai was like an adopted father to me. I valued his expertise—he was a runner too—but what I really needed was his comforting paternal presence. He was the opposite of Horty and Karl; he was a genteel, agreeable, buttoned-up attorney from Seattle. But he was also as strong as steel. He'd trained extensively in the martial arts. His own teacher had been trained by the karate legend An'ichi Miyagi, the inspiration for Mr. Miyagi in *The Karate Kid*, and that legacy seemed to live on in Don. He carried himself with that same Zen-like dignity, but he could quickly switch to Mortal Kombat mode.

Don practiced a form of Okinawan karate called *goju-ryu*, a discipline whose adherents could do things like catch arrows and break concrete blocks with their bare hands. I'd thought that was the stuff of movies from my youth, but then he showed me pictures of himself breaking through stacks of wood boards.

Years ago, he had introduced me to the Japanese philosophy of Bushido, or the "way of the warrior," which stressed honor, simplicity, and courage. There are echoes of its lessons in the stoicism of Marcus Aurelius, especially in the tenet that has most influenced me: The mind of a warrior (or anyone performing a difficult task) should be so attuned to the *moment* that thoughts and emotions do not impede proper action. A mind in this condition is thought to function so optimally that the right decisions come naturally and pain and fear disappear. I often saw similarities between this mind-set and what elite athletes refer to as being "in the zone." When I successfully adopted the mind of the warrior, I felt a great sense of must-ness replace my confusion and anxiety. I must keep going—no question. Was I going to release my heaviness or carry it the rest of the way north? Was I even going to make it to Maine, much less break the record for doing it? I had no idea. Literally. I had no idea in my head beyond the overwhelming *must*. Keep going; it's as easy as that. A single focal point. Keep going. Stay in the *now*. Every moment contains only one thing: the potential to keep going.

JLu intuitively understood what I was going through on some level, even more than Horty and Speedgoat did, and she e-mailed Don and included a list of provisions he should try to bring. When he arrived at the trail, she was so happy to see him that she almost cried. Having an old friend she could trust to look out for us, she finally let her guard down. I wasn't so much happy to see him as relieved. Just knowing he was coming had already started to lighten me.

Once he settled into our crew, he displayed the goods he'd graciously brought from Seattle—everything JLu had requested, and about five times the amount she'd asked for. It was generous—and overwhelming. He'd packed a giant box of delicate Japanese pastries that had already begun to spoil. He also brought the special type of vegan cinnamon roll she'd wanted for me, a two-thousand-calorie loaf that was shaped like a baguette. In fact, he had six of them. Because of the summer heat and the size of our compact cooler, many of his gifts had to be smashed, folded, and crammed into the cooler. It was a tragedy, but Castle Black was a war room, not a pantry. It's funny in retrospect, but the situation challenged us at the time. Don—wonderful Don—had brought exactly what I needed most in that moment: stability, authority, grace, and groundedness. He almost instantaneously shook me out of my depression, and I was grateful once again for his ability to intervene in my life and make me focus on the here and now.

And then…the reality of the AT overtook us all, Don especially. Within a day, it became clear that Bushido Don was not ready for the gnarly old AT—and we were not ready for Don's unreadiness.

To add more senseis to the mix, Horty had returned to the trail after biking the Tour Divide race for only a few days ("Stomach problems," he'd said, and he ended the discussion). Now we had two AT veterans on deck, each with his own expertise and dogma. It was fun to watch them jockey for the title of chief officer. Although they probably didn't want to admit it, we all knew JLu was the ship's master. Prior to this, the two had spent little time side by side, although Horty was there when the Speedgoat pulled the plug on his own AT attempt in 2014. And of course, old Horty had his own opinion on that scene.

If Horty wasn't sliding open Castle Black's door at 5:00 a.m. with a "Let's go to Maine, boy" wake-up call, Speedgoat was simply knocking on the van wall ten minutes before he'd be back with a cup of hot coffee as he pointed me directions to his camping toilet seat somewhere deep in the woods, often engulfed in knee-high poison ivy. (Speedgoat was immune to its itchy oils.) He had started digging a hole despite grumbling to us later, "Dude, you think bears dig holes?" Speedgoat kept showing us his graphs and charts, explaining that I needed to cover more miles, to make it to this or that landmark or road crossing, if I wanted to own the FKT. Each chief officer brought something different to the table. One brought grit and irrepressibility; the other, obsessive calculation and strategizing. And they were both crazy as hell.

On the afternoon of day twenty-eight, we left the Garden State and entered New York, which some hikers on the AT call "Little Maine" for its networks of ladders over mossy boulders, rock scrambles, and root infestations. The foothills of New York felt as remote as anyplace on the trail. I don't know what special magic lived there, but the darkness was darker and the night was more solemn and more thorough than anywhere else. I couldn't believe that New York City was just thirty-some miles away. Perhaps the trail's proximity to the busiest place on earth made it that much darker. If the weather cooperated, the next day I'd be able to see the city's vast skyline. I felt like I was on another planet, but in reality I was a short train ride from Times Square.

To add to our problems, a fierce windstorm had recently plowed through the area and uprooted thick, towering trees that were now scattered throughout the woods—and across the trail. We had to climb over them, crawl under them, or wade into the dense forest to go around them. Just as in Maine, blazes on the trail were infrequent and tricky to spot, and the downed trees added another dimension to trail travel. If this was a little taste of Maine, I was in for a real treat in five hundred miles.

As we crossed a slab of granite, Horty and I had roused a couple of very large, gorgeous emerald-tinted rattlesnakes. Even Horty marveled at their beauty. He had stopped crushing them with rocks years ago. I joked that he was turning into a peace-loving hippie. For someone so stubborn, old Horty surprised me with his potential for change.

Like with Horty, this wasn't Bushido Don's first rodeo. He had supported me on numerous hundred-mile races and was a fully qualified and valued crew ninja. However, the crewing of an AT speed record is a whole different mission. Sometimes a team member's qualities may have worked seamlessly on previous projects, but if you change the project scope, that trusted team member may struggle and affect the team's dynamics. I needed Don's presence, but he was adding another stressor. Not to me, but to the rest of our tight crew. He was constantly getting lost and couldn't follow Castle Black even though it was the only large black van for miles and miles. At one trailhead, gracious Don offered to take trash from thru-hikers and asked Horty where the trash went. Horty said, "It goes nowhere." Instead of nurturing us, Bushido Don needed his sword held. He was in over his head and was stressing JLu out. She confided in me that it was too much for them, that they didn't have the bandwidth to take care of me and my sensei. With mutiny on the horizon, I had to tell him one morning that he needed to "bushido focus" on following Jenny; she couldn't wait for him or give him directions to remote trailheads narrowly found. I felt bad. I probably didn't have the best delivery and Don was the last person I wanted to hurt.

Bushido Don meant well and he did well most of the time. I felt responsible; I hadn't given him a warning of what he might walk into on the Green Tunnel. It was like jumping into the middle of a work project. I couldn't give him a training manual ahead of time like he once did for me with copies of *The Book of Five Rings* by Musashi. And there was no time for JLu, Speedgoat, or Horty to do on-the-job training. Sometimes you keep a team member on because you know they are needed. Don was needed by me. So being the master team leaders they were, JLu and Speedgoat figured out a way to work with Don for the next few days before he left, giving him clear and direct instructions. Most often these were the Mr. Miyagi–style tasks of wax-on, wax-off, like peeling a case of mangos that we had been given—JLu knew plenty about single-minded focus. And I had plenty of experience with that too.

That storm Speedgoat had warned us about arrived and it had a name—Tropical Storm Bill. It rolled into York County, Pennsylvania, around the same time we did on day twenty-five. It was a Saturday, so there was a crowd of runners with Scott all morning. But as Bill started dumping almost two inches of rain, the locals rapidly thinned out, and I needed to come up with a plan. I knew Jurker would be finishing a fifty-two-mile day soaking wet, and he'd be lucky to be done before midnight.

I looked in the guidebook and saw that down the road from our ending location was an organic farm called Common Ground Farm and Retreat. It sounded like our kind of place! Speedgoat had never heard of it—a rarity—so he couldn't vouch for it. I knew Jurker would appreciate a hot shower and a real bed after this giant effort.

Not only that, a vegan bakery in Bethlehem, Pennsylvania, had reached out about delivering Scott some treats. The owner dropped off two giant boxes filled with the kind of desserts you see at weddings and fancy hotels. I knew this organic sanctuary coupled with the vegan treats was going to soften the blow of this long and soggy nighttime push.

We checked into the retreat that evening. I expected Jurker to arrive around 11:00 p.m., so around 10:15, I walked out of the room and looked for Speedgoat. He had parked (and leveled) his van in front of the main lodge, and I thought he was going to come with me so he could run back on the trail to meet Scott. But as I got closer to his van, I saw he was not in running clothes but freshly showered and curled up in his sleeping bag, reading his guidebooks and jotting down notes, so I decided not to bother him. I drove alone to the trailhead, but before I got there, my phone rang.

I looked at the caller ID. It was Jurker.

Panic. *If he has time to call me, it means he's not moving. He never calls me.* The rain was coming down in sheets that the headlights were reflecting off, so it was difficult to see where I was going. I couldn't answer the phone, and he left a voice mail. I kept driving toward the trail and a few minutes later, I saw headlamps and people waving me down. It was Jurker and three other runners. They had been waiting for me for only five minutes, but I felt terrible. In this kind of weather after that kind of day, I knew how disheartening it must have been for them to reach the road and not see anybody there. I would have been so mad if the tables were turned. But not Jurker; he waved at me enthusiastically and thanked his local companions, and they left to run back to their cars five miles down the trail. He wasn't mad at all; he'd just been worried about me.

I drove us back to the farm. Our friend had driven down from New York, and he'd brought Thai food. After Scott took a hot shower, we ate pad thai noodles and curry together, and then Jurker finally lay down in a proper-size bed and dug into the pastries.

Jurker was in paradise. While he was holding a Boston cream doughnut in one hand and a chocolate chip cannoli in the other, I put on my headlamp and started doing our nightly tick check.

If I'd been in the van where it was a lot darker, I would have missed it. There on his left biceps was the tiniest tick I had ever seen, smaller than a pinhead. At first, I thought it was a speck of dirt, slightly raised, so I tried to flick it away. It didn't move; the head was already buried in Scott's skin.

I let out a whispered scream. "Jurker! A *tick!*"

"What? Are you *serious?*"

"*Yes!*" I ran outside in the rain to Castle Black and dug around for our first aid kit. I found the tick-removal tool and followed the instructions, but the tick was so small, the tool was useless. I grabbed tweezers from my toiletry bag and carefully pulled it out.

"Holy cow, let me see that thing. It's so tiny; how did you even see it? I wonder if I got it when I took a nap in a pile of leaves off the trail."

"You did *what?*" I was stunned. That was the most idiotic thing he'd ever done. I threw the covers off him and doubled my efforts to find ticks on his hairy legs. I found two more that had burrowed into his shins. "How could you be so stupid? Have you lost your mind? What is wrong with you? Don't you know that our lives go on after this trail? Hello! Remember me? I *need* you when this over. Lyme disease can mess you up and I need you; our future family needs you. I don't care if you're so tired you can't walk, don't you *ever* lie down in the leaves again."

The storm passed and it was hot and humid in our final days of Pennsylvania. Yes, it was rocky, but getting through Pennsylvania was a huge transition for us. We started to feel the population density close in around us. More people, more houses, more road crossings. And better food. It was in Pennsylvania that the vegetarian community really showed up. One lady brought us a dozen black-bean burgers, another guy made us raw vegan cookies, somebody else brought a bag of homemade granola, all comforts that we appreciated.

But apparently, not everybody was up on the latest evolutions of plant-based foods. I heard from people about some chatter on Facebook that Scott wasn't following a vegan diet anymore. I can only guess that some visitors saw things in the van that didn't look vegan, like the cream puffs and burger patties. But I couldn't worry about that. At every trailhead, whenever the van door was open, enthusiasts would stick their heads in, take photos and videos, and post whatever they wanted on the internet. I knew people were curious, but it basically sucked. Castle Black was our crew vehicle but it was also my home, with my underwear, sports bra, and running clothes hanging to dry, dirty dishes everywhere, our unmade bed, and so on.

Keeping our tradition alive, on day twenty-seven, Jurker and I crossed the Pennsylvania–New Jersey state line together at the Delaware Water Gap. It was a bluebird morning and even though the trail paralleled a major highway, it was serene. After that, the border crossings came fast and furious. The next day, we were in New York.

Good old Horty came back and found us in New York. Apparently, he'd ended his bike ride early; he didn't say why and I didn't ask. I had my own theories. You know when you spark up a new relationship and you make any excuse to see that person? That was Horty with the AT. Any chance he had to stop by and check on Scott's progress, he jumped at the opportunity.

On the morning of day twenty-nine, Horty and I met Jurker outside Harriman State Park. He was running with some locals, and Horty razzed them as they crossed the road and started climbing up a hill. Horty and I were discussing the game plan for the day when we heard voices, and this loud *"Damn it!"* Then we saw Jurker running down toward us with the group of locals trailing behind him. Apparently Jurker had been following the locals when he stopped and said, "Hey, I haven't seen any blazes in a while. Are we still on the AT?" Before they could answer, he had already turned around. It wasn't far, but they had climbed uphill for about a quarter of a mile on the wrong trail. We saw him retrace his steps back to the AT and cringed. Everybody means well, but you still can't let your guard down. In the end, he was responsible for covering every step of the trail on his own.

I drove to Bear Mountain State Park to meet Jurker. I hadn't realized it was a steep two and a half miles to the summit where we planned to meet, and I thought for sure I was going to miss him. When I reached the top, there were news vans and a lot of runners hanging around. I found Scott sitting on a rock wearing a fluorescent yellow mesh vest that said GUIDE next to a guy wearing a similar vest that said BLIND RUNNER. They were doing an interview for a local TV crew. Jurker introduced me to his friend Thomas, whom he had guided at the Boston Marathon just a few months ago.

From the summit of Bear Mountain, we could see the Manhattan skyline, such a strange juxtaposition. We'd been to New York City countless times and I'd never realized how close it was to the AT and its rugged trails. A doctor friend of ours who has a house close to the AT met us on the trail. She was a well-known ob-gyn in SoHo. We'd gotten to know her on a trip we'd taken to Tanzania earlier that year with an organization called Every Mother Counts, a nonprofit that aimed to make pregnancy and childbirth safe for every mother, everywhere. Its mission became very close to us after my first miscarriage, when the nearness of the hospital (just a mile away) was critical to saving my life.

I was relieved to see the ob-gyn, Dr. Flagg, because I'd started to worry about my own health. Two months had passed since I'd had my D and C surgery after the miscarriage, and I still hadn't gotten my period. When I asked her what she thought about that, she said the average time for the uterus to heal could vary, but eight weeks was a bit on the long side. In other words: *Don't worry, but keep me posted.*

NEW ENGLAND

452 MILES

I love the fight and when things are easy I hate it.
—Ernest Shackleton

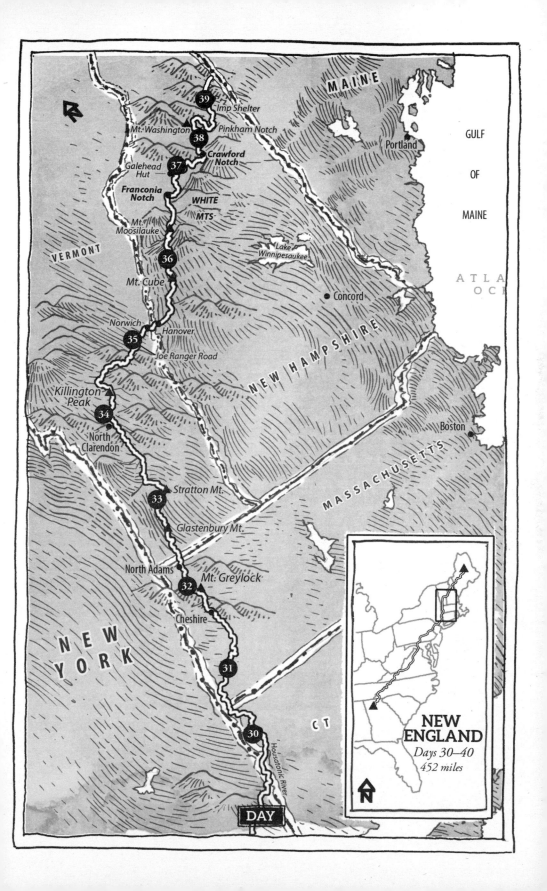

CHAPTER 11

NASTY

Day Twenty-Nine

"BET YOU DIDN'T think you'd see a black dude out here in these woods!"

He was up above me, sitting on a large rock that overhung the trail. I could make out his spiked dreadlocks and a green running singlet that had BLACK ROSES NYC printed across the front. We were about thirty miles north of New York City, in Bear Mountain State Park. I just laughed.

"Remember me, brotha? We ran thirty-one miles around Manhattan when you were here for your book a few years back," he said, climbing down.

"*Knox?* No way! That's crazy." I was surprised to see him, but now I knew exactly who he was. Knox was one of those guys you just do not forget. I immediately thought back to the run we did together. He'd told me he had to meet me because I'd quoted Tupac in *Eat and Run*. I remembered how cool the Black Roses running group sounded. Knox was the leader, and he seemed to have a curator's touch in bringing together interesting, disparate groups of people; it was part book club, part elite track team, part motorcycle gang. I wanted to be a member but I didn't know if I was boss enough.

We reminisced about that run we'd done in NYC years ago and discussed my state of the union and the FKT. The miles clicked by, barely noticed. We talked about the history of our sport, and we talked about someone we both deeply admired: Ted Corbitt, the legendary African-American ultrarunner and Olympic marathoner.

Running with Knox gave a boost to my spirits. I set aside my way-of-the-warrior worldview and slipped into what might have been an even more powerful mind-set: having fun. Shooting the shit. We didn't even stop when Knox bonked hard (he wouldn't eat any of my gels), and we were only somewhat fazed when a thru-hiker named Karaoke joined us for eighteen miles, twenty-pound pack and all. Karaoke earned his nickname. He wasn't exactly an opera singer, but we enjoyed his company nonetheless. There must have been something in the water up there in the Hudson Valley, because the trail was full of colorful characters. On the way to a little shelter near Fishkill on the east side of the Hudson, we passed one totally naked thru-hiker holding a strategically placed sign that read, HEY, SCOTT JUREK, THIS SAUSAGE IS VEGAN.

The next day in Connecticut, I knew what Speedgoat was probably thinking, but I didn't stress. I was having fun for the first time in a long time. I even guided my blind buddy Thomas for two miles to the summit of Bear Mountain, which inspired me.

Besides all the new runners, there was something else changing around me; I could feel it in my bones. The rivers sounded different—stronger, louder, meaner. Evergreens were becoming more prevalent. Even the rocks were different. I don't know how to describe them, although you'd think I would have been a geologist by this point, given all the billions of rocks I'd seen the past thirty days. The AT was shape-shifting, and I could feel it.

I tried to share this observation with Speedgoat as we cut through the beautiful Housatonic Valley that runs through New York, Connecticut, and Massachusetts. He was predictably unmoved. I was out here for adventure, but Speedgoat was out here with one thing on his mind. There was no time during an FKT for musing about the *trees* and *rocks*. To him, everything was another benchmark, another box to check. I wondered if there was time for him to wax poetic. On day thirty we'd crossed into New England, his homeland, but for him, Connecticut was just another state on the AT, one that we'd be through in a day. Just another chance to get a few more miles completed on mellower terrain before, as he ominously put it, "Shit gets real."

Old Horty understood what I meant. But to him it wasn't a mystery. He met me at one of the many crossings of River Road in Connecticut and I hollered out to him, "You can feel the rivers changing. It's different up here. Almost like we've crossed into another realm."

"You bet, boy. I was wondering if you could tell. You're heading to the big mountains, and you're going to love it!"

Day thirty-two dawned in Massachusetts, and I could sense Speedgoat silently bursting with the pent-up energy of "I told you so." I hadn't finished until midnight yesterday, and I wasn't going to finish much earlier tonight. Speedgoat had stopped staying up for me days before, back in New York.

I finally started imposing some discipline on myself when it came to other runners. Speedgoat probably would have counseled me to "turn off that fucking tracker," but I needed to stay true to myself, so instead of adopting any kind of fake coldness or rudeness, I just got efficient. Rather than stopping for photo ops, I asked that people take their pictures on the go. Selfies were fine, but they had to keep up as they snapped them. I wasn't going to break stride anymore. It felt good. I didn't turn anyone away, but I managed to put my (and my team's) priorities first. I felt like it was the kind of middle way that should have pleased everyone. Of course it didn't. Speedgoat still rolled his eyes when I signed a book or took a pic, even on the run.

But his hardline approach wouldn't matter soon, because he was about to take off. It was time for him to get to the Hardrock Hundred. I could tell he was antsy about leaving, and he spent the last several days poring over maps and crunching numbers like he was cramming for a final exam.

Right before he left, he asked if he could have a private powwow with me. I had been dealing with extreme nausea and fever while running all morning, and I was worried a virus or stomach bug was settling in, but I needed to get every last piece of trail wisdom Speedgoat had to offer. I asked the half dozen or so runners with me if they could give Speedgoat and me some space for the next mile.

"Horty and I have a master plan; we got you scheduled all the way to Katahdin. Gonna have to plow through fifty-mile days in Vermont, but things let up into manageable high thirties in the Whites and Mahoosucs. Just keep doing what you're doing."

He filled me in on the numbers and mileage goals. As he outlined the plan, I realized he really, truly did not want to leave us. I knew he would anyway—he couldn't skip Hardrock—but I could feel his regret and anxiety. I understood. Even though my name would be on the FKT (if I actually made it), this was his adventure too. He was invested. To walk away? Especially now, when I was gaining momentum but also (in his view) taking big risks? It was eating him up. I had noticed a similar dynamic in play with people who'd never even been out here on the trail. Social media had connected thousands and thousands of people to our FKT, and it was shocking to me how deeply many of them were invested in the run. JLu and I were constantly getting requests for more photos, more updates, more, more, more. Followers online would observe my progress throughout the whole day. They woke up with me, they went to work with me, and they went to sleep wondering how far I would push through the night.

It was another reminder that I was running with the collective ambitions and hopes of a lot more people than I'd ever anticipated.

With Speedgoat and Bushido Don gone, Jenny and I were briefly down to a skeleton crew. I'd been averaging a little over fifty miles a day for the past week despite the rough terrain, which was good. Not good enough, but good. I was holding steady but not making up additional ground. The idea that I was going to build up any more of a cushion on the record was beginning to seem more and more impossible. The days were ticking by.

But first we had to get into those big mountains that Horty had talked about back at the Housatonic River.

Just as the team got low on personnel, my longtime buddy Walter came in, fresh from the corporate world, ready to escape his high-stress work life by getting muddy and destroyed in Massachusetts and Vermont. We started day thirty-two running through the Sages Ravine in Massachusetts. It was a magical section of trail—pristine, verdant, and prehistoric. The trail lies deep in a quiet gully shaded by an old forest, and it's lined with glaciated boulders that have been sanded smooth by millions of years of ice, wind, and water. It felt like someone could have run this same route a few thousand years before us; it had a mystifying ancient feel to it.

We made good time, and by late in the day we were making our way to Mount Greylock, the highest point in Massachusetts at thirty-five hundred feet.

We ran fifty-one miles that day, and much of it was dark, cold, and wet. A storm blowing in from the Midwest announced its impending arrival. Meteorologists were calling it an "atmospheric river," and it had been kicking up hundred-and-twenty-mile-an-hour winds and bringing tornadoes, drenching rains, floods, hail, and mud slides to much of the country. The forecast for Boston was for winds of fifty miles an hour and possibly a tornado. I thought of the mile-long mud holes of Vermont that I'd heard so much about. And those were supposedly on a *good* day. They were probably turning into ponds of morass now.

Walter and I ran past Pittsfield in the beautiful Berkshires, the town where Herman Melville had written *Moby-Dick,* and a group of locals fell in line with us. One was a talker. He wanted to know what we had seen, how we were feeling, how many miles we were planning for the day, what we thought about Massachusetts. Then he wanted to talk about start-ups and the problems with a lot of technology and the beauty of data. Were we running for a charity, and if so, could he donate? And had I heard about the weather coming in? I don't think he took a breath. Finally, Walter spoke up.

"Dude," he said, "you sure can talk."

"Oh yeah," the guy answered. "My friends call me Word Count."

It turned out that one of those friends was four-time Boston Marathon champion Bill Rodgers, and as we ran through the town of Cheshire, he got him on the phone. It was surreal. The legendary Boston Billy was giving me words of encouragement as I ran along the AT!

After that, we felt more comfortable asking for some quiet time (we figured he was used to people requesting that), and when Word

Count peeled off in Cheshire, Walter and I got to catch up in earnest. Walter was the opposite of Speedgoat; he didn't care about numbers or hard facts. If Speedgoat were a TV show, he would be something on CSPAN, whereas Walter would be a reality show on E!. He was mindless entertainment for me and knew me on a different level. He wasn't a fellow competitor and he finished hours after me in races. He had once weighed close to three hundred pounds and lived a real all-or-nothing life. He'd had a lot of fun (which JLu and I vicariously enjoyed after we had settled down). He transformed his life in an incredible way and got sober and stable, so he could then be my wingman and designated driver when I needed to go out in Seattle after my divorce. I'd party and he'd throw back soda water, having just as much fun as me, until we closed down the bars. He was a great friend, one who I could confide in.

I've always loved hanging out with people who'd manifested their own destinies, people who have made things happen despite the odds. There are no better runners, no better human beings. At least—they're the people I like to roll with. And often, they weren't the fastest runners or the most successful. They endured and they were real to the core.

On the trail, I let Walter's Tinder updates and his stories of the latest dating scene entertain me. He filled me in on the Boulder gossip and told me what our friends were up to. It was a world I felt so far removed from, yet I remembered it well. We ran and hiked as if we were on a training run, catching up with each other with no worries and no places to be.

It was just Walter and me for the night shift of day thirty-two, a three-thousand-foot climb up Greylock. As we neared the summit, the wind screamed and pushed huge clouds of fog through the evergreens. It was summer and hours before sunset, but the trail went dark as midnight. Walter and I felt like we were back in the Seattle foothills of Tiger Mountain, where we'd both spent many wet, dark miles. We laughed at how running those tough miles were some of our fondest memories, the ones full of Type 2 fun that you appreciated after they were over.

By the time we dragged ourselves to the summit of Mount Greylock, the winds were gusting to sixty miles an hour, the temperature had dropped to forty degrees, and we were soaked with icy water, exhausted, and starving. JLu cooked us some pasta with marinara sauce and kalamata olives, and the van trembled and shook in the gale. I told Walter to forget about the tent he had intended to set up and to find some floor space in Castle Black, El Coyote–style.

For nearly an hour, we had the coziest little dinner party in all of Massachusetts. It was one of those perfect nights where the screeching bleak weather outside only made the warmth inside more pervasive. We ate to our hearts' content, tried to remember some of the crazier things Word Count had said, and pressed Walter for more stories from his wild dating life. Three old friends, laughing and eating and talking about failed dates and awkward hookups, all on the top of a mountain in the middle of a storm, crammed into a dirty van whose wheels were just barely holding on to the earth.

Three old friends and...Horty.

An icy gust of rain blew into the van as the sliding door opened and Horty's voice, ferocious as the gales outside, rattled the van. "Hey, boy, better try and get some sleep, Vermont is gonna be *real* nasty."

Horty said the word *nasty* with a pirate's breathy gusto; he loved to launch into his new and wild adventures when seas were at their highest. Horty relished the gnar. To him, true adventure should be steeped with elements of failure, risk, and even death, preferably all

Squeezing through the
Mahoosuc Notch.
(Luis Escobar)

One of many bogs and ponds
in the Mahoosuc Mountains,
Day 41.
(Luis Escobar)

Day 42. Going over the numbers with Jenny and Timmy and realizing time is running out. (*Luis Escobar*)

Descending the gnar of Saddleback Mountain, Maine, Day 42. (*Luis Escobar*)

On Day 46, I finally got my first glimpse of Katahdin. *(Aron Ralston)*

Topher giving me the game plan for the final 10-mile push to the base of Katahdin. *(Luis Escobar)*

Down to the wire, running toward Katahdin with Walter and Special Forces. *(Luis Escobar)*

Going for a birthday hike.
(Luis Escobar)

Scrambling on The
Greatest Mountain.
(Luis Escobar)

Pushing through the false summit on Katahdin. *(Luis Escobar)*

I'd been dreaming of touching this sign for years. *(Luis Escobar)*

The A Team. I couldn't have done it without them. *(Hunter Nolan)*

Raven Jurek (one year old) in her first race, Pearl Street Kid's Half Mile, Boulder, Colorado, August 2017. *(Glenn Delman)*

three. He was especially fond of the Shackleton quote "I love the fight and when things are easy I hate it."

He was right about Vermont, I knew it. I was exhausted, but as I drifted off I saw the fields and forests of Vermud, as Vermont was known, turning wetter and muddier and wetter and muddier. Horty the soothsayer. Horty the piratical harbinger of doom.

Things were going to get *real* nasty. It was nice to have a night to forget about it.

Crewing for a hundred-mile race has its challenges, but it's usually over in a day. I'd been crewing for Jurker on the Appalachian Trail for an entire month straight. Every time Luis or Horty came back, he would remark, "I can't believe you're still out here." To be honest, I couldn't either. I know that Horty's wife, Nancy, didn't crew for him on the AT, and Speedgoat's wife, Cheryl, crewed a couple sections. I understood why.

Since I was Scott's only constant crew, and neither of us had an opportunity to take any real breaks, it meant that both members of our typically happy household were reaching their limit at exactly the same time. We were both stressed; we were both sleeping poorly; we were both sacrificing so much. It was hard for us to support each other in any meaningful way.

Some stressors were avoidable. Some *people* weren't. I loved everybody on our team and appreciated all the people who came out, but every once in a while, I wanted some alone time with my husband. It felt like we never had a single moment of privacy anymore and I was actually starting to get a little jealous of the friends and fans who got to run long stretches with him all day. He had promised me we could run the next section together alone but when

Jurker arrived, a few local runners were already with him and more were waiting to join.

I gave him a look that said, *I need to talk to you—alone.* And he gave me that *Not now, I'm busy* look right back, without hesitation. Then he invited the next group of runners to join him. I gave him another look, one that said, *Oh no, you didn't.* After a month of waiting on him hand and foot, I felt completely disrespected.

I gave the van keys to Walter and took off running down the trail. There was a side trail and I knew he thought I'd taken that because I heard him calling my name: "JLu! JLu!" Good; I hoped he went down that trail looking for me. I was in full sabotage mode now. I kept running as fast as I could just to make the point that he didn't deserve my company. I descended a series of bluffs, and after a few switchbacks, I no longer heard his voice in the distance. He must have gotten the hint and told the runners he needed some privacy. I heard him calling after me some more: "JLu! JLu!"

Once I hit the base of the bluffs, it was relatively flat and I tore through the trees even faster. I muttered between breaths, "I will break you," and ran for my life. I was pushing myself, and the surprising/annoying thing was, he was gaining on me. I knew he'd been feeling good, but not that good. How was that possible?

He inevitably caught me and I stopped. I was silent yet poised to bound off again as I waited to see what his first move would be. It felt like we were back on the PCT, having a blow-out fight about everything and nothing at once.

"JLu, I'm sorry. I know I should have told them they couldn't run with me, but what was I supposed to say? 'No, I'm sorry you can't run with me today, I need to talk to my wife in private'?"

"Yes! That would have been a perfect thing to say. People have to understand they can't always run with you whenever they want to. I'm so sick of you not standing up for me, not giving our relationship space. This is my trip too, remember?"

Without giving him a chance to respond, I grabbed the tracker out of his vest pocket and held it in the air, scanning for the nearest cliff. Unfortunately, we were on a flat and wide section of trail. Undaunted, I cocked my arm back and prepared to chuck it as far into the trees as I could. At the top of my lungs I shouted, "It's *me* or the tracker!"

His eyes widened. *"No! JLu! Don't!"*

Another big storm blew in along with a high-wind advisory for eastern Massachusetts. Jurker and Walter were slogging their way up Mount Greylock, battling rain, mud, and gusts reaching forty-five miles an hour in town and closer to sixty miles an hour near the summit. Par for the course; this was our storm du jour.

Speedgoat flew home but was following our progress and always available for remote consultations. I didn't throw the tracker into the woods. I made my point and Jurker understood. We were a team and there was no time for holding grudges. We had other things to worry about.

On day thirty-three, the torment raged on while we ran over and under storm-downed trees and right into the town of North Adams, tucked up in the northwestern corner of Massachusetts. In a wonderful coincidence, there was a music festival going on there that weekend that our friend Timmy O'Neill was emceeing. He was planning on joining our team so we met up in the parking lot of a Big J grocery store. I'd never been so happy to see him. We were old climbing buddies from my college days in Boulder, and over the years he'd become a best friend and mentor. He'd actually presided over our marriage on a hillside in Sunshine Canyon.

Seeing Timmy on that blustery afternoon after a month of that grind was a huge morale boost for me and I knew he would provide the same for Scott. Even better, his emcee gig was almost up, and he was free to join our team the very next day.

Jurker had been referring to Timmy as his secret weapon for weeks now. Everybody warned us about the White Mountains and their granite slabs and peaks. We had heard stories of exposed cliffs, and while Scott admitted he had a slight fear of heights, he always downplayed it. Unfortunately, I had seen with my own eyes how bad it truly was.

When I worked for Patagonia in Ventura, California, I would routinely make the six-hour drive out to our friend Dean Potter's shabin (that was his term, a cross between a shack and a cabin) in Yosemite for the weekend. Ever since those days, climbing the Regular Northwest Face of Yosemite's famous Half Dome had been a dream of mine.

Dean had promised me that if I trained for it, he would guide me up the route. Jurker knew this was an opportunity I couldn't pass up, and he was psyched to help make it happen in June of 2011. We left the shabin at 3:30 in the morning and started hiking in the dark toward the Death Slabs.

The name alone should have tipped us off, but we were riding on Dean's confidence in our skills, so we didn't even think twice. In the darkness, our headlamps cast just enough beam to illuminate our immediate area, which helped quiet Jurker's fears of falling over the edge. If you can't see it, it can't hurt you. We scrambled up easy yet serious third- and fourth-class terrain, connecting steep sections rigged with fixed lines, often old, sunbaked ropes tied off to trees or predrilled bolts.

We negotiated massive jumbled boulders that eventually led to a particularly steep and long section of vertical, water-polished rock.

There were a couple of knotted lines dangling down from the inky-black rock faces. A skeptical and sketched Jurker looked up at the ropes, then to Dean, and finally to me and told us that he was "beginning to understand why this approach is called the Death Slabs."

Dean assumed that since Jurker was a world-class athlete, this would be no problem. But he's not a technical rock climber, and here he was, scrambling up steep, wet, fifth-class slabs. He was also wearing worn-out running shoes that probably had five hundred miles on them.

It had been a long winter, and there were more than a few spots where the snow still accumulated on narrow stone ledges. Ice-cold water was running down the face and seeping underfoot.

Jurker didn't complain but we could tell he was struggling. He had been carrying all of my gear so that I could save my energy for the climb, always the knight. But I insisted I take my pack for this stretch and he reluctantly handed it over. He muscled his way up the first fifty feet of terrain, hanging on to the wet, tattered ropes with white knuckles. If you're not comfortable slab climbing, you'll tend to not trust your feet and overgrip with your hands. This means your arms rapidly fatigue.

Before the final lip, Jurker's arms were completely pumped. About fifteen feet off the narrow ledge, his feet slipped out from under him and his body went slack. He was dangling like a rag doll by his arms. Freezing-cold water was streaming underneath him.

Dean sprang into action and hand-over-handed the same rope as Scott, and when he was just below him he yelled, "Whatever you do, do not let go!" Then he gave a do-or-die command: "Put your feet on my shoulders now!"

Jurker couldn't even look down; he was gripped with fear. Dean reached up with one arm and grabbed Scott's feet and placed one on each of his shoulders. Then Dean pulled his body up on the rope, raising Jurker up a few feet. But Dean saw that Scott was losing his grip. Dean moved higher up the rope and put his head right under Jurker's bottom and hoisted him up with his head. Scott reached for the ledge and managed to slide his whole body onto it, like a beached whale.

He was completely soaked through and shaking. Dean and I quickly scampered up and helped Jurker move away from the cliffs. We tried to downplay it, but later Dean told me it was about as close as he'd ever seen someone get to dying. For the Dark Wizard to say that freaked me out.

Dean and I climbed the face of Half Dome in just over ten hours. That was fast for somebody of my moderate ability, but Jurker was carrying our hiking shoes and extra clothes, so we were able to go superlight. Scott hiked up to the Half Dome Trail and then took the John Muir Trail eight miles down to the valley floor, staying safe on terra firma. He bought us sweet drinks and salty snacks and then quickly turned around and hiked back up to meet us at the summit. I was spoiled, I know. But that's the kind of guy Jurker is. We all hiked down together, laughing and reliving the Death Slabs. All told, Scott hiked thirty-five miles that day.

Four years later, the image of the late great Dean Potter's head almost literally up Jurker's ass was still engraved in my mind. So I was grateful Timmy, an experienced climber, was going to be with Jurker through the White Mountains.

CHAPTER 12

VERMUD

Day Thirty-Three

HORTY'S MOUNTAINTOP PROPHECIES about the challenges of Vermont began to manifest themselves immediately after I crossed over from Massachusetts on day thirty-three. "Vermont can be *real* nasty," he'd warned me. It was even nastier than that.

The storm that had rocked us to sleep on top of Mount Greylock must have roared its way north in the night, because as soon as I descended and crossed the border, I ran into mud pits unlike anything I had ever seen. Pools of muck pitted the trail so frequently and expanded so quickly, it was often hard to tell where the trail was. A lot of it was underwater, submerged beneath a soup of rocks, leaves, and wind debris. It seemed more like a streambed than a trail.

It would end up being Vermont's wettest June in three hundred years. Horty in his many trips to Vermont had never seen it this bad. "Vermont is usually bad, but this is *unreal*!" he said. "Usually it's runnable section, runnable section, muddy section. Right now, it's muddy section, muddy section, runnable section."

Thru-hikers call the state Vermud and it's a joke among locals up there that there are four seasons in Vermont: mud, mud, mud, and mud. I think that's probably unfair to winter, when the mud freezes solid under a layer of snow, but it was otherwise accurate in my experience there.

The mud wasn't just messy; it became a real obstacle. Forward progress slowed to a crawl. Each mile took longer to cover, and the mud sucked more and more energy out of me. Everyone knows the feeling of accidentally stepping into muck and not knowing where the bottom lies. Just imagine that, but for miles and miles and miles. Every step ended in a cold splash, and then the next required me to pull my back foot up and out of the sticky grip of the trail. My shoes filled with sludge and suctioned to the bottom. It was awful. It was like running with weighted boots and in high gravity. Horty told us that the bedrock was so close to the surface of the trail that the mire had nowhere to go and just floated on top. Trail maintenance was impossible. I could do nothing but wallow along and laugh at how ridiculous the conditions were.

Perhaps to keep my mind off the here and now, Horty went over the Vermont game plan once again as we slogged through the endless muck. The next hundred miles of the AT would track the gnarled spine of the Green Mountains, and the following fifty miles would veer eastward, crossing against the grain of those same mountains and resulting in many sharp climbs, descents, and a lot of likely falls. It was a real pick-your-poison stretch of the trail, and I looked forward to putting Vermud in my rearview mirror when we got to higher ground in New Hampshire.

One reason this part of the country was so weather-worn was that it was by far the oldest stretch of the whole AT. For 105 miles, it runs with the Long Trail, which was created well before the AT, back in 1910, by men with handsaws, axes, and shovels. It took twenty years to finish the 272-mile footpath, which stretches from Vermont's southern border all the way to Canada, and it was the first major recreational trail in America. So it had vintage charm and storied mystique. It was also kind of like one long, sludge-filled wheel rut.

Horty knew whereof he spoke. He'd established a Long Trail FKT of four days and two hours back in 1999. It was also up here that he'd overtaken his rival Scott "Maineak" Grierson during their mano a mano duel along the AT. After 1,606 miles of chasing each other north, Maineak tried to throw Horty off in this stretch by listing the wrong time when he signed in at the registers at the start of the day, an attempt to make it look like he was far ahead. It worked at first, and Horty was devastated—until he got to a register where Maineak had mistakenly signed in on *the following day*. Later, he saw someone coming out of the Congdon Shelter and he knew it had to be Maineak. He told me that he'd been fantasizing about that moment since he'd found out about the deception, and he had planned to say, "Guess who I am? Your worst nightmare!" But in reality, he just said hello, and he and Maineak walked six miles together. They played leapfrog for the next three days, trading the lead back and forth, until Horty left him for good. I think Horty liked toying with his prey.

Around midday, with almost comically bad timing, a local runner found me and proceeded to extol the virtues of wearing huarache sandals while running the Vermont trails of mud. As someone who had huaraches handmade for him by a Tarahumaran in the Copper Canyon, I laughed. *What is this guy talking about?* You could have worn snow boots or socks out there, and it wouldn't have mattered; the mud would suction your feet down just the same. Nothing was gonna help me get through this muck except one shoe-sucking step at a time.

I'd been feeling great in the last stretch of Massachusetts and had entertained the thought that maybe I'd turned the last corner and was going to bolt into Maine just like old times, old races. The muck ended my optimism, quickly. More disruptive than the mud, I was beginning to feel the first real effects of sleep deprivation. There were moments when I was all but hallucinating. I'd been running for thirty-three days, and for most of those days, my eyes had been on the trail and the passing ground, scanning for obstacles. I'd spent hundreds of hours and hundreds of miles like that, my eyes fixed downward, watching half focused, taking in the endless procession of rocks and roots and ruts that streamed past. Every once in a while, I'd look up at Walter or JLu or just toward a white blaze. Instead of the solid, real world, I'd see a strange waterfall world—everything streaming toward me, everything falling down. I wondered if I would see anything but the passing trail for the rest of my life.

Walter snapped me back to reality. He was steady, strong, and cheerful. On the trail, he talked about how beautiful everything was and how great it was being outside, hanging out. He talked about how nice it would feel to have dinner later, to stretch out. Walter never once complained to me. He was a stoic on the trail. I didn't know how miserable he was. Later he told me, "I kept having to bite my tongue because it was *so* heinous, but I couldn't complain to you, because I'd only been out there three days!"

As the gray-dark sky faded to the black of night on day thirty-three, Walter and I ran past some thru-hikers at the Goddard Shelter, below the rainy summit of Glastenbury Mountain in Vermont, and I felt desperately envious of the warm sleeping bags they were curled up in. But we still had thirteen more mountainous miles to go before our day was over. Chilled to our bones in the steady downpour and silent from our muddy efforts, Walter and I finally reached Castle Black at 11:00 p.m. in the shadow of Stratton Mountain.

The alarm went off on the morning of day thirty-four, but I was sure I was dreaming. It felt like I was swimming, or diving, or drowning. As I shook myself awake, I realized I wasn't any of those things—but I was definitely *wet*. Had I accidentally lost control of my bladder in the middle of the night? Then I saw JLu. She was looking at me with an odd expression. I was in bed, in Castle Black, but there was no doubt about it: I was soaked.

After a quick inspection, we surmised I had just been sweating in my sleep—a lot. Neither of us knew why but it felt like a lingering virus from a couple of days back. Or was it the beginnings of Lyme disease? It was a new development, and an unwelcome one. JLu insisted on giving me a thorough examination, and she got more and more worried as she looked me over; my ribs were visible, my eyes were bulging, and I was covered with a mysterious red bumpy rash. Not to mention I still reeked of vinegar, but that was no mystery.

The vinegar scent was a byproduct of metabolizing amino acids and the protein in my muscles; I was literally cannibalizing myself. Even though I was eating upwards of seven thousand calories a day and plenty of carbohydrates, I was dangerously tapping into my essential reserves. Being on my feet for sometimes twenty hours a day meant I was always at the edge of gnawing away at my own muscle, muscle I was going to need for the larger mountains ahead.

As I stumbled up out of Castle Black, the weight of sleep deprivation hit me like a humid day. It was dense. My legs were dense. I needed to be like an alchemist and turn my lead feet into golden wings. But I was moving and thinking too slowly for any magic, and my morning routine seemed to pass me in a series of stills. I lost track of things and only had time to eat a banana and grab some Clif Bars to go.

There was one piece of excellent news that day, something I'd been looking forward to for weeks. Timmy O'Neill, our good friend from Boulder, was scheduled to arrive that day. With Walter already with us, it meant that I was going to push through Vermud with close friends on my wing.

Timmy was definitely unlike the other friends and fellow ultra-runners who had joined me so far. For starters, he wasn't even a runner. He'd never done anything like fifty miles a day before. I'm sure the only times he ran was from the police as a kid and from commitment as an adult. He'd been assuring both Jenny and me for months of his excitement, claiming that he'd even been training with extended solo climbs in the Flatirons above Boulder. He loved trying new things, declaring that once he found what he was really good at, he did it as little as possible in order to continually develop his discomfort zone.

He was also hilarious, a stand-up comic, and had made a career expressing the droll side of adventure sports. He had outdoor chops—he was a Patagonia- and Clif Bar–sponsored climber—but I was most looking forward to his spirit and sense of humor. He lived with virtually no material possessions, deciding instead to purchase them for others: a house for his mom and a car for his brother. He read a book a week and said he would rather help a friend through a divorce than go to the wedding "because everyone will help you party but few will help you grieve." He and Jenny were friends from way back, and I knew that she had turned to him whenever she went through a difficult breakup (there had been a few).

On the trail, he was all smiles when he greeted us, and he told me that he felt great even though he'd been roofed backstage at a concert the night before. I didn't ask for more details; there were plenty of miles ahead for that story. I just shook my head and said it was awesome to have him out here with us.

As we headed north, the Green Mountains seesawed up and down endlessly along an eternal ridge.

The mud was bad, but it would have been hard running even after a long dry spell. This was some of the most jumbled-up country I'd been on yet, thick with rocks that seemed glued together by mud and grass. Making our way forward meant constantly having to seek out stable places, lunging, torquing, twisting. Every surface of my body came into contact with the trail. The storm hadn't helped; many of the downed trees still had fresh white wood where they'd been broken by the wind, which was still whipping around in gusts of fifty-five miles an hour.

The Stratton area was beautiful and one of the more inspiring points of the whole trail. It's renowned for its great skiing, but I was most enraptured by the quiet loveliness of its fire tower. These towers used to dot the national forests everywhere, especially out west, where they'd rise up several stories in the air and terminate in a small covered platform. There, a diligent and self-possessed fire watcher would spend a few months of the year looking for the telltale signs of wildfires. If any were spotted, he or she would leap into action and send coordinates of the inchoate blaze to administrators, who would send out firefighters. Most of these towers have been decommissioned and deconstructed, but a few remain. The tower on Stratton had been renovated and its caretakers were an old French-Canadian couple who seemed so happy, so at peace with their little perch in the sky that I immediately hoped that JLu and I could be like them one day. They reminded me that atop this tower, Benton MacKaye first conceived of the idea for the Appalachian Trail. I wished I could have stayed and tapped into their wisdom and cheer more, but after signing my book for them, I was back in the white-blazed track of muck.

I was mentally foggy all that day and happy to listen to Timmy and Walter tell stories that had nothing to do with running, records, or mud. I started to slip into a comfortable mode in which I deferred decision-making mostly to them or to the crew more generally. It was easier than weighing options and making judgment calls. The weeks of little sleep had accumulated, and I was finally starting to notice the difficulties that it brought.

And yet, there were still moments every day when I felt a sense of certainty that I was in exactly the right place, doing the right thing at the right time. I wanted it to end, but I already knew I'd miss it when it did.

That night, bruised and beaten, we stayed in a hotel in North Clarendon, a little town just past the Green Mountains. Horty had booked the rooms and thought we should all get a night indoors. It had been a wet nine days since the last real roof I'd slept under.

I woke up on the morning of day thirty-five and realized that I had a little over ten days to go if I wanted to break the record. Close enough to begin to seem urgent. Close enough to seem possible.

For the first few weeks on the trail, I'd wake up craving more sleep, but I'd also feel like I'd rebounded from the night before. My body was still finding ways to reknit its tears and heal all the damage I'd loaded onto it. That started to change in Vermont. Whether it was a physical tipping point and whether sleep was a factor, I didn't know. But the feeling was undeniable—I was losing a piece of myself every day now. I wasn't recuperating overnight.

Horty had a theory about motivation. He told me that a lot of motivation could be boiled down to this: How bad do you want it? He would ask people, "What's the furthest you can run without stopping?" After they replied whatever distance, he followed up with "Could you run a mile further if I gave you a million dollars? What if I was running behind you holding a gun to your head, could you run even further?"

He said, "It's easy to say you want it real bad when you're sitting at home on the couch. But when the going gets tough, do you want it enough?"

We often think we can't go any farther and feel like we have nothing left to give, yet there is a hidden potential and strength in all of us, begging us to find it. We arrive at it via different means— sometimes reward, sometimes fear. There was something to Horty's motivational theory, and finding that desire was the most vexing problem. How bad did *I* want it?

The question became less and less theoretical in Vermont, where I started to come up against my own limits. I've heard it said that ultramarathons are 90 percent mental. And the other 10 percent? That's mental too. I was in the thick of that other 10 percent.

About two-thirds of the way through day thirty-five, I began to worry that Timmy might break before I did. He kept stopping to stretch his legs, especially his calves and ankles. The marathon distance yesterday coupled with the forty miles he'd done today ruined him. It seemed likely to me that he had a condition common among distance runners called Achilles tendinosis, compounded with gross effusion—which he prosaically called his "cankles." He was done for the night, and maybe for his entire tour. At the first meeting point in the mountains, JLu and I huddled up. Timmy's overuse injury didn't only complicate *his* life, but we had been counting on him to help us get through the White Mountains coming up next, in New Hampshire. He wasn't a runner, but he covered challenging terrain like a mountain goat and could have helped me navigate the most technical sections.

It was raining again. In fact, it had been raining ever since that storm overtook us at Greylock and it seemed like we'd been caught in one continuous torment ever since we'd left Springer Mountain on day one. I could probably count on the fingers of one hand the number of days it hadn't rained in the past month. Timmy had had to bow out, and the skies had opened up even wider, and I was starting to have those visions again, the ones where the world rushed by even when I was standing still.

At one point, the trail began to plummet almost vertically, serving as a kind of funnel for all the millions of gallons of water falling on Vermont that day. The deluge turned the trail into a stream and then into a ditch. My body was so used to bending over and seeking out safe spots for my feet, I was constantly pitching forward and sliding and bruising the same areas over and over.

With Timmy sidelined, Mark "Fat Boy" Godale surprised us for the night shift, driving nine hours straight from Cleveland in a car that appeared to contain all of his possessions: children's car seats and items from his four daughters, running gear and shoes, a potpourri of trash, and select items for this trip, including a folding lawn chair he planned to set up for sleeping inside his car. The car and its contents were like his current life situation: everything was within arm's reach, but nothing was useful. A recent divorce had left Godale hobbling mentally as much as he was physically, due to numerous injuries and surgeries. He needed this quick trip to the AT as much as I needed him for the night shift. Over his twenty-five years of running ultras and setting records, he had seen a lot, but I don't think he knew what he was getting into. He didn't care. Fat Boy always had the right attitude.

By nightfall, I was holding on by a thread mentally. I asked Fat Boy why there was a house lit up on the top of a mountain in the middle of nowhere. He laughed and told me that it was the moon rising behind the ridgeline of trees, not a house. I didn't have the energy to care what was reality. And yet I was still moving forward. My decades of running had trained my brain in ways I hadn't even anticipated. It was triaging itself, shutting off certain systems to allow others to keep going. Above all—my legs, my lungs.

Fat Boy and I staggered on into the night. It seemed like we passed one perfectly fine stopping point after another, and somehow Horty was there at each one, waving us on, telling us to keep going, to stay on schedule and get fifty miles in today, keeping track of some master plan known only to him. I was too tired to stop. The path of least resistance was in front of me, and that path kept going until 2:30 a.m.

JLu had to keep driving miles out of her way to accommodate Horty's extended stopping points. The final stop that night was at single-car-wide Joe Ranger Road. She found the best parking place available for Castle Black. It felt like it was on about a twenty-degree slope, and I spent much of the night at the edge of the bed, clinging to JLu so I didn't roll off. It didn't matter; we could sleep like babies anywhere by this point. I felt bad for Fat Boy, who was trying to sleep reclined in the driver's seat of his car while pitched downhill.

In the morning, Horty slid open the van door with his usual greeting, but I thought I could hear some doubt and sadness in his customary "Let's go to Maine, boy." We ignored him and tried to go back to sleep since we'd gotten only a few hours of sleep the previous night. It was pouring outside. I told him I wasn't getting out this early, even if he was leaving today. I was *completely annihilated*. Horty came back ten minutes later. "I know this is really hard, and you've barely been getting any sleep, but you better get on the trail. Come on, boy, I'll join you to the next road crossing." Like a father trying to coax his teenage son out of bed, Horty got my pack ready.

I asked him if he could wash out my shoes, which would give me some bit of comfort.

He did. He went out to a muddy creek along the roadside. I saw him briefly swirl my shoes in the water and call it good. I was touched that he did it, though I don't think he actually got any mud out of them. It was day thirty-six, July 1, and it was going to rain every day until the end of the world. It was really testing my faith in Horty's favorite aphorism: *It never always gets worse.* We still had the White Mountains to go. Things would surely keep getting worse. They always found a way. The homemade sign I'd seen late last night while stumbling and sliding in the mud was probably a more suitable adage: "WHEN IN DOUBT, THE 'AT' ALWAYS GOES UP!"

I stumbled along with Horty, somewhere between wakefulness and sleep. Horty talked about the latest sleep-deprivation research and how most people could function pretty well on three and a half hours of sleep night after night. What mattered most was the quality of sleep. He told me that I could get through this, that I would have to go deeper than I'd ever gone before.

"I've seen you give it everything you had, way back in Erwin, Tennessee, then in Virginia, and now you're gonna work harder than you've ever worked in your life. The greater the price we pay, the greater the reward. You can do this, boy!"

JLu and I were set to run the next section across the state line into New Hampshire, two distressed peas in a pod. As we slogged through the mud, she told me how hard the previous night had been for her. She told me that she hadn't slept and that, even before that, she'd almost lost it while driving the van up muddy unmarked logging roads in the fog. She reminded me that I had once promised her she would be the crew chief no matter what, but that last night, she'd suggested stopping for the night and Horty had suggested continuing, and I hadn't listened to her. I was on autopilot, just following the controls that Horty manipulated. I had become occluded to the person who was my lifeblood. I couldn't believe how I had forgotten her.

I told her I was sorry, and I was. I choked up and then began to full-on sob. It was all too much. I couldn't protect JLu out here; I couldn't even help her. *I* was the danger to her. Me and the AT record.

"I'm sorry. This is crazy. It isn't worth it. Look what I'm doing to you. Look what I'm doing to us," I said between sobs. And in a pleading voice, I muttered, "Let's just go home."

We were exactly four hundred and fifty miles from Katahdin, only four hundred and fifty miles from finishing what we had set out to do seventeen hundred miles back, in Georgia. We had come so far and had gotten through so much, yet we had so much more to go. And now, after all we had been through, I was ready to hang it up.

She shook her head, and we kept going. Without her, I would have stopped in Vermont, stuck in the mud.

It was the second time I'd ever seen him cry. He almost never cried.

Not when his mother died.

Not when his friend committed suicide.

Not when we got married.

Not when I nearly died.

The first time was in April, just two months before we wept in each other's arms in the middle of Vermont.

We went in for an ultrasound when I was eight weeks pregnant. It was hard to know what we were looking at on the screen, but we could see the tiny grain of *something* that we were told was the baby.

We were so excited. It had been almost a year since my first miscarriage and ER visit. We were in the middle of final preparations for the Appalachian Trail, where we hoped that our baby would spend its first trimester on its first big adventure. Then the ultrasound tech measured the speck and typed two words: *No heartbeat.*

She didn't say anything; she just went to get the doctor who would review the images with us and deliver the news with more ceremony. But we already knew our dreams were over.

At the doctor's office, we were stoic and composed for each other. I tried to be positive, and I said all the things that people always said to me: "It wasn't meant to be. It will happen when it's right." Jurker tried to console me, but it wasn't necessary. I was numb to the disappointments by now.

When we got home, I lay down on our couch and put my hand over the place where the baby should have been thriving. I felt sick, like I was carrying around an empty promise. Jurker scooted me over and lay down next to me. And then he started crying. Not just crying, but shaking and sobbing. It broke me, and we were suddenly sobbing together over the loss, over our misfortune, over our dwindling hopes of ever having a family.

Sometimes it felt like Jurker wanted a baby more than I did. When we first met, I'd thought he was the quintessential hippie. He certainly exhibited some of the traits. He wore his long curly hair pulled back in a ponytail and always rocked Birkenstock sandals. I'd see him riding his mountain bike all over the hills of Seattle. He didn't own a car. He would take the bus out to Issaquah to train in the mountains. I used to see him shopping at my co-op, Madison Market on Capitol Hill, with his reusable canvas bags, filling up on bulk items on Member Appreciation Day when everything was 10 percent off. He would fill these heavy five-gallon glass water jugs with reverse-osmosis water and haul them back to his studio apartment in a bike trailer. In the early 2000s, he was definitely that quirky vegan guy who seemed so extreme. He was an environmentalist and an idealist.

When we started dating, he didn't want to have kids. It's not that he didn't like them; he just didn't need to have his own. His grandparents were foster parents who took care of infants with high needs until they were well enough to be adopted. He grew up changing diapers and swaddling and bottle-feeding babies. He had been groomed to be a great father; he just didn't have a desire to be one. At the time it didn't bother me—I never thought we would get that far anyway.

I wasn't even looking for a relationship. In 2007, I had just run my first hundred-mile race, and I'd broken up with a long-term boyfriend. The following year, I left my beloved city of Seattle to start the next chapter of my life in Southern California. I was living my dream of designing running clothes for Patagonia and I wasn't in a state of mind to slow down for anybody.

The truth was, even when we became good friends, I felt bad for him. When he was newly single, I set him up with one of my hot climber friends in Seattle who was also recovering from a breakup. When that fizzled, I suggested that he visit me so I could introduce him to my single lady friends in Ventura, but he ended up spending all of his time with me.

But we were both transitioning and neither of us was willing to break stride the way you need to in order to nurture a relationship. And yet we did. Without even trying, we fell in love. By the time we decided to move to Boulder together, in 2010, he'd had a change of heart about kids. The angst he felt about the world was a little softer, and his outlook was a little brighter. The idea of raising a child sounded almost *fun*. I don't know what it was exactly, and I didn't pressure him (I wasn't sure I even wanted to get *married*). I think that, in me, he found somebody who appreciated life the way he did, and he wanted to share that same joy with the next generation.

But it turns out it's not always that easy. First he had to have his vasectomy reversed. As an idealistic thirty-year-old, he'd been staunchly anti–population growth. Seven years later, he told all his running friends that he'd had a hernia fixed, so he couldn't run for a month, but our close friends knew why he was walking around like he'd just gotten off a horse. One joker opined, "Holy shit, you had your balls cut *twice* for *no* reason!" Love makes you do crazy things. Or *un*do them.

For instance, this. Here we were on day thirty-six, holding each other in the pouring rain in the middle of the woods and sobbing uncontrollably together for the second time in less than two months.

And like we always do, we put our heads down, leaned into the rain, and kept moving forward. We were physically and emotionally drained, at the end of the line. Scott had one last bright idea. "Should I call Toph and Kim?"

It sounded useless; there was no way Topher could break away from his hectic job as the CEO of an outdoor company to help a friend on the East Coast. But we had nothing to lose, so when he found himself hiking alone in the rain, he made a desperate SOS call. Of course, he got Toph's voice mail.

"Hey, Toph, I hate to do this to you, but I need you guys to come out here. I know you're busy but we really need you for the Hundred-Mile Wilderness in Maine. Call Jenny and figure out where to meet. The trail is gnarly out here but you could use the extra mileage; I heard you came up short at Western." Trying to make light of the desperate situation, Jurker jabbed at him for having had to drop out at the Western States 100 a week earlier.

We ran into Hanover and crossed our second-to-last state border, going from Vermont into New Hampshire. I went to the Hanover Co-Op and loaded up on vegan groceries at this little oasis.

The dramatic day didn't end without an absurd final act. That afternoon, somebody took a picture of Jurker sitting by the side of the van. His soaking-wet clothes were sagging off his body, his eyes were bulging from the sleepless night, and the photographer applied a filter that made him look even more gaunt than he really was. Then, as the machinery of social media whirred on, someone *else* snagged *that* picture and pasted it next to another photo of Scott from day three. The difference was stark. Of course it was—he'd been running fifty miles a day for weeks. But then another poster, a respected member of the running community, used the cheap photo trick to claim that Scott was wasting away *due to his vegan diet.*

It was amazing how many people had advice for someone they didn't know who was doing something they could never do. I bit my tongue; I had other issues to tend to on Facebook. Somebody had created a fake account using Scott's profile photo, soliciting unsuspecting female fans for money. Strangers were constantly sending me messages and when I didn't respond, they'd get offended. In what was perhaps divine intervention, I accidentally spilled the contents of my water bottle onto my phone and completely fried it for the remainder of the trip.

CHAPTER 13

SPECIAL FORCES

Day Thirty-Six

IT WASN'T A hallucination.

There really was a chocolate cake on top of the mountain.

"Do you think it's for you?" Fat Boy sounded appropriately suspicious. He'd been out on the trail for only a couple of days, so he still had standards of hygiene.

I just grabbed it and peeled back the foil. It was still warm.

"Of course it's for me!" I dug in and devoured it. I told myself it was vegan, and it tasted sufficiently vegan for me not to think too much about it. Godale and I ate the whole thing. He didn't earn the name "Fat Boy" for being overweight. It was given to him by Horty, of course, after Godale recounted a story from Western States. A runner passed and asked, "Are you Mark Godale?" When he replied yes, the guy seemed puzzled and remarked, "You don't look as fat as you do in *Ultrarunning* magazine."

"Aren't we getting close to the road? This is the longest three miles I've done in my life," he said as we descended from the summit of Mount Cube. He was stating the obvious. The story of my life, every night on the AT.

Godale once again had the graveyard shift with me on day thirty-six, in the foothills of the Whites. I knew he had a lot on his mind but I knew he needed this. He was a real OG from my era, a seven-time 100K World Championship competitor, and he'd held the twenty-four-hour American record before I set a new one in 2010, but he'd been plagued by a series of chronic injuries. Despite his wounds, every April for the past twenty-four consecutive years he had willed himself to complete the Boston Marathon.

Years ago, he'd messed himself up running in a slot canyon in Se-dona and broken a bunch of bones. He'd undergone many surgeries and was lucky to be alive, but even now, he still half hobbled on the trail, and his gait almost twisted him sideways. He was in constant pain, which he was candid about. During easy stretches, I'd ask if he was feeling any better, and he'd inevitably reply, "No, it hurts like hell every step." I sort of appreciated having someone next to me who was as beaten up as I was, if not more.

And yet, even with how broken he was, he still took pity on me. As we descended Mount Cube, he remarked that I seemed to be starring in three movies at once: *Forrest Gump, Groundhog Day,* and *The Truman Show*. The comparisons were painfully spot on.

Godale was an excellent partner during a rough couple of nights. He knew when to indulge me and when to push me on. That night, at a particularly narrow corridor of switchbacks with sharp drop-offs on one side, I hit a wall and I told him, "I gotta lie down. Like, now." He said it was a bad place for that—and he was right—but instead of vetoing the idea, he let me lie down, and he stretched his leg out to put something between my body and the cliff in case I rolled over in my sleep. "Ten minutes," he said as I closed my eyes.

I woke up with a start, panicked. I felt like I'd been out for hours. "Already? Scott, it's been two minutes."

It didn't matter. We got up and got going. My body had its own clock and I was at its mercy.

It was 2:00 in the morning when we finally got to the road crossing that I decided would mark the end of the day. Everyone was already asleep, so I crawled into Castle Black and Mark crammed himself into his car for a few hours of partially reclined rest. Nothing came easy in the Live Free or Die state.

Even though we had pushed deep into the night, I hadn't met the mileage goal on the plan Horty had laid out for me. I should have gone another five, to Lake Tarleton Road near a town called Warren, but I was finished, and Horty wasn't there to yell at me. I'd nickel-and-dimed my way back into contention for the FKT and now I was at risk of nickel-and-diming my way out again.

Day thirty-seven dawned brightly, along with the hope of rebounding before officially entering the Whites.

I was greeted in the morning by an old hand, at least at the Appalachian Trail. He had the bravado of a drunken cowboy, loved to mess with my mind, and went by the name of Trail Dawg.

"Think about it! You're forty-seven miles from Galehead, and lately you've been going two miles an hour. That's a twenty-four-hour day, my friend! You won't be done with today until tomorrow. Bet that fucks with your brain a bit."

He shot me a cocksure glance and a wink for good measure and didn't wait for me to respond.

"No fancy calculus needed out here. Yep, the ol' AT speed record is just simple arithmetic, a harsh math teacher that will bust your balls every time. Man, I fuckin' love this shit!" he said.

Trail Dawg (aka Andrew Thompson) was an acolyte of Horty, once a cocky puppy at Liberty University whom Horty had brought into his rabid pack of Horton disciples. They did the twisted stuff, like running Horty's fifty-mile racecourse out and back for a "fun" hundred-mile training run. The Masochistic Professor had taught Thompson well in the arts of extracting pleasure from endless struggle and reveling in the gnar.

But most important for me: Trail Dawg had set the AT record back in 2005 after a bunch of wild attempts. So he knew what I was going through and what I needed, even if that included a few jabs at me to see how I was holding up.

I pressed him for wisdom as we began a day that would involve a four-thousand-foot climb to Mount Moosilauke, the traditional gateway to the White Mountains. The wisdom he shared wasn't exactly the wisdom I wanted to hear, since he noted that I was already behind Horty and Speedgoat's battle plan and that this day was definitely going to bleed into tomorrow, as my last few nights had. Another graveyard-shift finish. Another lonely broken night.

Timmy decided to try to take my mind off the bad news. He made several calls to local contacts; he quipped that it wasn't what you knew but who you knew that opened doors. He mentioned that he recruited a running brother of a climbing friend who was willing and able to help us out. I imagined a lanky climber, like Timmy, so when Andrew Drummond showed up, I was taken aback. He was at least six foot two and had the build of an Paul Bunyan. He was formidable and his presence alone boosted my confidence. He seemed capable of dealing with a multitude of difficult scenarios, from grim weather to the gnarliest sections of trail; we could send him in and expect results. Timmy called him Special Forces, which was perfect. As soon as he showed up, he said he was game for an all-nighter in the Whites.

About fifteen miles into the day, Special Forces and I finished our forty-eight-hundred-foot ascent to the granite plateau atop Mount

Moosilauke, a name that came from the Algonquin word for "bald place." For the first time in eighteen hundred miles, I was above the tree line. The summit was energizing. The sun was shining, and chains of mountains stretched far into the distance. Franconia Ridge was out there, and beyond that, our destination of Galehead Hut. It looked so near. I felt a surge of short-lived optimism. Everything lay at my feet—the whole trail, the whole world.

It was the first of many dispiriting illusions of the Whites.

It's a strange thing, but even though I remember feeling triumphant and optimistic when Special Forces and I summited and then began our descent, I would later hear that this was the point in the journey when I really started to frighten people. Strangers stared at me when I picked up my food with my dirty fingers and shoved it into my mouth. They said I looked like a shadow of myself, a weaker, sicker version. My skin was stretched taut over my cheekbones, and I had grown scraggily facial hair. More than a Heisenberg but not quite a beard.

My high spirits were partly due to the company of my two newest crewmen and several locals. Special Forces radiated intense adventure, and Trail Dawg—well, he was a trip. As we ran, he regaled us with stories about Maineak's winter AT SoBo hike aided by a bottle of whiskey and a rickety aluminum-frame pack. He told us how last summer he'd climbed all forty-eight of New Hampshire's four-thousand-foot peaks in three days and fourteen hours, beating an eleven-year-old record by an hour. He shared tales from the Barkley Marathons, the gleefully perverse Tennessee nightmare that pulls entrants a hundred miles through bramble, across raging rivers, and over almost impassable Appalachian terrain via unmarked paths with nicknames like Rat Jaw, Hell, and Nun-Da-Ut-Sun'Y (Cherokee for "the trail where they cried"). The race began in 1995, and since then, only fifteen people have even *finished* it.

Horty was one. Old Trail Dawg was another. If a challenge was especially burly, he wanted his name on it.

He had attempted FKTs numerous times on the AT and finally
cracked the code going SoBo in 2005. His most impressive accom-
plishment on the trail, to me, came on his last attempt. That's when,
after he ran the first two hundred miles SoBo, fighting his way
through Maine, he found that the rivers and creeks he needed to
cross were too high to continue. Instead of heading home, he drove
straight back to Katahdin, waited a couple days for the rivers to recede, and started over. That sounded utterly mental to me.

The Whites were Trail Dawg's kind of place. He forged ahead
in front of us, through rugged, rocky climbs and then down into
mucky lowlands where portions of the trail morphed into creeks.

As we scaled North Kinsman Mountain, Special Forces pointed
out a peak in the distance. "The backside of that one is full of the
nastiest scree you can imagine. It's just a slippery-slide of little rocks,
with plenty of trees and brush to crash into." He wasn't complain-
ing. Like Trail Dawg, he seemed to get *more* gleeful as things got
rougher. I didn't mind; I just hoped their joyful masochistic wisdom
would wear off on me. It was exactly the kind of crazy I needed to
finish this thing.

Fifteen miles in, and day thirty-seven was just getting started.

I had been on my feet for too much of the past twenty-four hours,
too many of the past ten days, and I was beginning to display the
signs of long-term wear.

Horty and Speedgoat had both been explicit in their directions:
get to Galehead Hut the first day in the Whites. They said it would
give me a psychological lift and then shorter daily mileage would
ensue after that. I followed orders even though I did notice my
mental state had started to warp. Since the Whites were completely

foreign to me, I was inclined to cling to whatever concrete advice I had. I needed to start breaking down the remaining and toughest part of the AT into smaller tasks anyway. If I focused on the impossibility of reaching Katahdin within ten days, I despaired. Focusing on Galehead made things smaller.

But I was fading, and day thirty-seven seemed to be whipping by. I wondered what I would do if I didn't make Galehead until sunrise. Would I just keep running? That sounded impossible and I had to avoid that at all costs. I needed to get to Galehead—I needed to sleep.

It wasn't supposed to be like this. As I'd dreamed this up, back home in Boulder, I'd imagined myself getting stronger as I approached Katahdin. Less Bilbo Baggins in Mordor, and more Galahad and the Holy Grail. But that wasn't happening.

I wasn't becoming more powerful, not at all. Instead I was being stripped down not only of fat, muscle, and nerve but also of my mental toughness. I was losing it, but maybe that's what I needed to do.

At Franconia Notch, I met up with JLu and the others who had hiked in a mile from the parking lot. We took our time carefully reloading my pack with absolute necessities for hiking through the White Mountains at night—headlamp, extra batteries, waterproof jacket, additional layers, space blanket, and as many caffeinated calories as possible. Trail Dawg was leaving and all I could hear over the waters of the Pemigewasset River was his proclamation "That's a twenty-four-hour day, my friend." This should have been a flashing red warning light, but the Horty-Speedgoat protocol of "Galehead or Bust" had me seeing only green.

A less-hobbled Timmy cycled back in and with Special Forces we all left Franconia Notch in the waning light. Even though I was buoyed by their comedic banter, we soon donned our headlamps to combat the gnarled and rocky terrain, and I felt the sinking repetition of here-we-go-again, another Late Late Show finish. I tried to utilize selective amnesia to the many recent twenty-hour days, as Frank Shorter rightly claimed that "your mind can't know what's coming," in reference to previous marathon trauma.

The night took on a surreal quality, as if we weren't consuming only miles and hours but also mescal buttons. When we finally reached the ridge of the bald granite mountaintops, it reminded me of a Martian landscape of stark and beautiful stone expanses with no other earthlings except for three alpine space walkers.

"Holy shit!" For the first time I had dozed off and almost catapulted down the granite trail. I was actually sleepwalking before I suddenly snapped to and caught myself as I slid down a series of cascading roots atop steep stone slabs. Timmy later told me that my movements resembled water sliding down the path of least resistance, as if I had surrendered to gravity.

As my trail compatriots traded laugh-out-loud anecdotes and parody songs, I realized how much fun I could have been having. I was like the boy in the bubble; I could see but not actually touch their world. I would laugh to myself in between head bobs. I had no idea what time it was. The hands on my internal clock slowed then sped up, and I couldn't determine if it was really late or really early.

A swirling fog suddenly appeared, as if a genie that had long been straining against its cork had finally wrested himself free from the bottle. It seemed as if the genie were showing me another dimension of the AT, one that would have me losing my mind as I had never done before.

And then I heard the tiny, almost secret peeps and chirps emanating from the bushes. "Are those the birds? No!" I was crushed to hear their songs, which signified the approaching dawn. Even the freaking birds were mocking me. Then over the next hill we saw it: Galehead! Even though we were close enough to make out the doors and windows, I saw that the way ahead curved down, around, and then back up. That mere mile appeared impassable.

"No, no way, how, what…I've got to sleep now," I weakly explained as I lay down on a perfectly flat rock.

Timmy looked at me like I was crazy. "But it's right there."

"I can't do it, dude, give me twenty minutes." I pulled my headband over my eyes and instantly fell asleep.

Timmy stood over me and thumbed *New York Times* articles on his phone as Special Forces went ahead to Galehead. Most likely by the time his head was hitting the pillow, mine was jerking awake. I snapped my head north and almost crowed, "Let's go to Maine!"

As the sun began to push above the horizon, I rediscovered my body and felt my limbs warm. I remembered how to use them. I remembered why I was there. I forced myself into some semblance of walking and stumbling. I'd been going for about twenty-four hours.

We pushed on. Or that's what Timmy told me happened, at least. I don't remember arriving. I have a vague memory of climbing up a giant ladder and Timmy spotting me from below. The bunk beds were stacked five high, and due to our late arrival, the only beds available were on the fifth level. I poured myself like wet concrete into the bed, and I heard him saying something about two hours.

That's it. I slept for two hours.

And then awoke to the smells of breakfast. Timmy was shaking me. The hut was a small dormitory run by the Appalachian Mountain Club and staffed by college kids, who sang wake-up songs and made tasty meals. One of them played the fiddle. I climbed out of bed, drank some coffee, ate some miraculous oatmeal, put on the same drenched socks and shoes, bade farewell to the young chorus of joy, and then Timmy, Special Forces, and I staggered off.

Almost right away I was on a steep ascent of South Twin Mountain, and soon we were climbing hand over hand, grabbing roots to pull ourselves over rocks and boulders bigger than we were. The rain had stopped; the sun was shining. I'd run all night and into the next morning, for twenty-six hours straight with only two hours of sleep. I had never felt this beaten. The cumulative stress and sleep deprivation were exacting a toll I never could have imagined.

It was a small moment, a few minutes after we began hiking on day thirty-eight, that crystallized how defeated I was. I didn't break down crying; I didn't fall asleep standing up. It was something simple and pathetic. A root. One of a trillion I'd seen and avoided over the past several weeks. But as I saw it coming, I didn't know what to do. Was I supposed to step around it or over it? I just couldn't remember. When it finally came, I tripped on it and stumbled forward. I'd forgotten how to raise my legs, how to run like a sane person. In Vermont, I'd thought I'd hit rock bottom, but the granite load of the White Mountains of New Hampshire pushed me even farther down, and then I broke. Just like everybody had warned.

Suddenly, running down toward us—almost floating—was a guy in a sleek running kit, breathing easily and lightly. He moved like a memory of myself, like El Venado had, once upon a time.

"Hey, Scott!" he said. I didn't know him. "How are you doing, man?"

I slowly tilted my head upward and then mumbled, "How... the...fuck...do you *think* I'm doing?"

Within a few steps, I was mortified that I had said that out loud. My censors were on break, having a smoke out back with that genie who had escaped from the bottle.

It wasn't like me to snap at someone out on the trail, especially someone who had simply asked me how I was doing. I realized almost immediately that my short fuse had to be a symptom of something deeper. I entertained the idea of turning around, chasing the runner down, and apologizing right then and there. But that just made things worse; it was hard for me even to imagine myself going fast enough to catch up to him.

The truth was, I was *crawling*. It really felt like I was on all fours, moving forward inch by inch. Of course I had known that I would go through stretches like this, but I had *also* known—known deep down in my bones and muscles—that by this point on the journey, I would have become trail-hardened like I always had before. *By now I should be stronger*.

That transformation wasn't happening. I wasn't becoming a sharper version of myself; I was getting smaller, slower, and weaker.

I consoled myself with the thought that my current state, equal parts escaped convict and mobile shipwreck, was not the worst state I could be in. I could be sitting still, either passed out or asleep. Back on that rock, in that motel, in Castle Black, or on my own couch, dreaming about throwing away the record. As long as I was falling forward and getting up to fall again, I wouldn't come in last in the race against myself.

I'd had some education in this kind of overreach before. Way back in 2000, back when I was really at my physical peak, I won the Western States 100. It was the second year in a row I'd won it. That would have been enough for almost anyone, but I got into the Hardrock Hundred that year too, and I decided I'd do that race right after Western. I'd have only two weeks off, two weeks to re-cover. There was no way I could win it, and I knew I'd be tired, but I figured I could at least cruise the race and enjoy it. Maybe get the lay of the land for the next attempt, the real attempt.

I dropped out of the Hardrock after forty-two miles. My legs were destroyed.

I had been young and naive and way too optimistic about how well I'd recover.

The truth was, and *is,* that mountains humble you. They humbled me. You can steal a performance or two, but you'd better be prepared to sit back and rest after your finish.

A decade and a half later, I was older and less naive. I hadn't thought I'd be blazing through this section of the White Mountains, but I'd thought I'd at least be *upright*.

By the middle of day thirty-eight, I was preserving what little energy I had left by avoiding decision-making altogether. I just pressed Play and let Timmy and Special Forces tell me when to stop.

There was one delectable moment that day in the Whites. We came to a little cabin called Zealand Falls Hut, an oasis for hikers. I was so spent it felt like I was taking a line of credit that I could never pay back and I slumped on a bench outside; I didn't want to be lured inside lest I lay my head down to sleep. But even outside, there was peace. I could hear hikers and the young staff cooking and laughing.

And it was where Timmy found a priceless treasure.

Later I learned that Timmy had left *twenty dollars* for a massive bag of potato chips, an absurd amount in the real world. But in the wilderness, it was worth it. I would have paid a hundred. The fat, the saltiness, the crunchy carbs—they were pure comfort. All three of us were shoveling them in with abandon. Timmy later showed me a picture he took of me with my little feast. I was guarding a pile of chips in my lap and looked pitiful. First I laughed, then I realized I barely recognized myself.

"You look like a fugitive emerging from a year in hiding," he joked. Timmy always knew how to employ the best gallows humor.

Nine potato-chip-fueled miles later, at 3:00 p.m., we stumbled into a clearing and a jam-packed trailhead parking lot. We had finally arrived at Crawford Notch. And I still had a disturbing twenty-four miles to go that day, including a five-thousand-foot climb up to the summit of Mount Washington.

The crowd waiting at Crawford Notch included JLu, who'd expected me to arrive there at 9:00 a.m. She had been sending runners up the trail to try to find me all morning—a wise tactic, since it also allowed her to have some peace and quiet there at the trail-head. Once I got there, she immediately tried to get me rested and ready. Maybe if I'd had Jenny back in 2000, she'd have talked me out of trying that audacious double dip of Western States and the Hardrock that had humbled me. Now, luckily, I had people who told me what I needed to hear. Timmy, for one. It was Timmy who'd seen me snap at the innocent runner we'd crossed. Like JLu, he realized I needed protection (from myself, mostly), so he leaped into action before I could reveal the antisocial depths to which I'd fallen. He became the jester of the Whites, cracking jokes and generally keeping people's attention off me, while Special Forces guided me down the path.

The key thing he did was create a buffer of approximately fifty feet of trail space between me and the people behind me. If a group started running faster or if I slowed down, he would hold the gang back until the fifty-foot cushion was restored. Under other circumstances, I would have felt bad about keeping myself so separate. I wanted to be a part of the jovial group of runners, but I wasn't in the right state of mind. It was the greatest gift anyone could have given me at the time, the gift of not having to be on.

Still, Timmy couldn't hide everything from the others. He later told me that at one point, at the head of a bunch of eager runners, I stopped so I could pee. I didn't even move off the trail. I just stopped, relieved myself right there, and then kept running. He said I was like a feral animal, unbothered by courtesies.

At Crawford Notch, Castle Black was practically in a ditch—it had been the only open parking space—but it didn't matter. When I got there, all I wanted to do was lie down and get some solid sleep. Looking back, I realize I should have spent the night at Crawford Notch or, even better, at Franconia Notch and ditched the Galehead goal. I probably should have killed the rest of day thirty-eight, called it good once I'd gotten fourteen miles from Galehead. I *needed* sleep. But JLu and I could hear Horty saying, "Stay on schedule!" I wasn't thinking for myself. I was in hurry-up offense mode. I didn't have time to recoup. So I passed out for just a few hours.

Timmy quickly joined a group of young yet seasoned thru-hikers and their parking-lot party and sparked a fun Q&A on the ways of the trail. After a handful of beers and a sleepless thirty-six hours, he was buzzing like a drunken gnat. But he quickly sobered when it was go time, and he went from being jester to king's soldier and started rounding up the troops. Special Forces helped too; he enlisted another stout local runner, Tristan, to hike into the night with us. Tristan was new to me, but I could tell he was wicked strong, and I was more than satisfied with the way our team was shaping up. That was the one positive I pocketed as we made our way out of Crawford Notch at dusk and set out for the next goal: the Lake of the Clouds Hut, the only hut in the White Mountains above tree line and one of the most stunning spots on the whole trail.

Around midnight, we had to make an unscheduled stop at another hut because it was dangerous to keep moving on granite slabs and rock piles when it was dark and I was so sleep-deprived. There was a scary moment when we were told there was simply no more room for us at the hut, but Tristan came through for us; he'd worked out here and was able to call in a favor. A small favor. We crashed on the kitchen floor.

It was quiet and warm in the kitchen, and just watching Special Forces inflate a sleeping pad made me groggy. I fell asleep instantly and got four or five solid hours, which felt like an illicit luxury. I did some math while I drifted to sleep, and the reality of how many miles I'd covered in the Whites sank in—and it wasn't good. I'd moved so slowly. I realized I had lost an entire day on the record in a matter of thirty-six hours. My one-day cushion was gone. There was no room for anything but perfection now.

The next morning was glorious, with blue skies and a fiery sun blazing behind the white tip of Mount Washington. It towered over us, rising 6,288 feet, making it the highest peak in the Whites and one of the highest on the trail. We started before sunrise and climbed a ridge as the sky behind the summit brightened to yellow. The sun's rays were invigorating, and the alpine terrain loosened my muscles and lightened my mood. We steadily climbed a couple of thousand feet in the next four miles and then the trail plateaued into a nice rolling stretch, finally giving me an opportunity to open up and run after days of fighting boulders, slabs, and roots. For the first time prior to the pits of Vermud, I felt a bit of ease.

Still, we couldn't count on the warm, clear weather lasting. Mount Washington is absolutely infamous for its unpredictable, overwhelming outbreaks of horrific weather, including blinding whiteouts that can occur at almost any time of year. The average wind on Mount Washington is thirty-five miles per hour, and there's a sign at the weather station on top that says THE HIGHEST WIND EVER OBSERVED BY MAN WAS RECORDED HERE—231 MILES PER HOUR. It can snow any month of the year, averaging forty-two feet annually, and there have been 137 fatalities on the mountain, mostly due to the constant collisions of powerful weather patterns. The mountain is widely known as the most dangerous small mountain in the world.

In 2006, a twenty-three-year-old hiker walked to the summit on a warm day. Suddenly, he was hit by a storm so severe that by the time he was rescued, he'd suffered massive brain damage. In 2013, an experienced hiker on the trail became so disoriented by the weather that she wandered in the cold and eventually died a short distance from the Lake of the Clouds Hut. It wasn't the hut's first tragedy. There was a solemn air to the place, reminding you that Mother Nature was a humbling force. A pair of boots hung from a nail in the hut. Legend had it that they had to be stopped from walking by themselves after the hiker wearing them died. There were so many ghosts in this immediate area that they weren't even named individually; they were known collectively as the Presence.

JLu met me at the summit of Mount Washington, and together we took it all in. We were on the roof of the long tunnel. It was a profound, peaceful reminder that we were out there together, and we'd come so far.

It was the Fourth of July, and with Jenny in our group, we rock-hopped and jostled along the boulders on the tops of Mounts Washington, Jefferson, and Madison to the bottom of Pinkham Notch, following the infamous Presidential Traverse. Even in my beaten-down state, I was able to enjoy this alpine path with JLu and our new friends. We hadn't been above the tree line together the entire trip, and this was welcome variety, more familiar to us than running in the low and woody peaks eighteen hundred miles south.

We finally ran out of the Whites, and we paused for a moment before plunging into the next range, the Wildcats. I had a fresh team of über-runners; I had JLu; I had Timmy. I also had my body, although I didn't know how much of it still functioned.

I think I had hope.

And I had a firm belief that I needed a lot more than hope.

On day thirty-nine, we pushed until 2:00 in the morning to stay on our razor-thin timeline. I was stumbling in the dark but there was no place flat enough to lie down even if my team would allow me to. In all directions, I saw rocks and boulders and roots carpeting the forest floor. We were out of the Presidential Range, but the lesser-known Wildcats were just as formidable. The night seemed to stretch into eternity but we finally made it to the only suitable place to sleep, the appropriately named Imp Shelter, as it seemed that a mischievous sprite (or two) was playing an exhausting, drawn-out, and disagreeable prank on me. Nocturnal rodents gnawed at our hanging packs and scurried over my nylon sleeping bag. I was frequently jolted awake by micro-bursts of nightmarish anxiety as I fretted about falling behind, falling down, and failing myself and JLu. I'd just as quickly cross back into the Land of Nod, and the visions of running late. I kept thinking Special Forces was trying to get me up, and then I'd realize that it was mice, or rats, or worse. I got three hours of sleep if you added all the pieces together.

I kept trying to convince myself it was all a bad dream.

When Jurker emerged from the woods near Gorham, New Hampshire, in the dawn of day forty, I realized I hadn't seen him any of the last three nights. They had taken their toll. He was unrecognizable.

His face had aged twenty years and he had a horrible patchy beard. His limbs looked extra-long and sinewy, and his fingernails were black with dirt. He didn't even smell like himself—he smelled like our compost bin back home. Timmy pointed out that he wasn't becoming *one* with the trail, he was becoming *the* trail. He speculated that if we sprinkled some seeds on Jurker, they would sprout.

It wasn't just physical. He had been drifting further and further away from the person I knew. He had a lifeless blank stare, like his mind wasn't all there. He reminded me of a soldier who'd gone off to war and came back the same, but different. His fine-motor skills were shot, and the tremors in both his hands had become almost constant. He'd also picked up an odd tic I'd never seen before, letting his lips flap as he exhaled, like a tired horse. He tripped on *everything,* the tiniest roots and rocks; I could swear he was even tripping on pine needles. Every misstep would pinch his sciatic nerve, and he would jolt upright and grab his lower back. Finally, one pesky blister on the top of his toe was infected, making him wince every time he stubbed it.

He asked me to grab his big shoes, the size 12 pair, that would accommodate the blister. I dug around in the shoe bin in Castle Black but couldn't find them. I asked Jurker if he knew where they went. He scrunched up his face and let out a long exhale. "Damn, I gave those to No Poles back in Tennessee when I thought I was done. Oh, well, such is trail magic." He looked too tired to care, too empty for regrets.

Before Jurker could sit down, Timmy whisked him away and walked him down the road to a nearby hiker hostel. The owner was kind, and she let Scott take a hot shower while she made him a smoothie and toast with peanut butter.

The hospitality was verifiably magical because, after three sleep-deprived nights, that morning of July 5, Jurker emerged from the hostel with new energy.

He was clean, fed, and ready to go.

It was also a moment of major changeover for our whole team.

Special Forces and Gabe had to head home, so we assembled replacement runners, some old faces and some new, to help Scott get into the Mahoosuc Range, the last part of the White Mountains and one that pushed all the way into Maine.

One of the stray runners who joined our caravan was a personal favorite. He had actually crossed our paths earlier, on day thirty-six, when he had left a vegan chocolate cake on the summit of Mount Cube for Scott. He reappeared in New Hampshire on day thirty-seven and got into the habit of placing organic cherries all around Castle Black, like blessings. He also wore very, very, very short shorts. We called him the Cherry Shaman. When he joined us outside the hostel on day forty, he told us he was supposed to run a race that morning but had felt called to be here instead. That was his word—*called*. He said he was a part of the team now, and then he handed us a lengthy typed poem with strict instructions. "This must be read to Scott in iambic pentameter, at a heart rate of forty-four to forty-eight beats per second, on every other footfall."

The last stanza read:

Perfectly normal, perfectly balanced, and perfectly equalized will be the condition when the being leaves the van each day. Namaste.

Nama-go running.

When Jurker left the van that morning, I don't know if he was balanced and equalized (and he certainly wasn't *normal*), but I think the Cherry Shaman's mantra did enlighten him, because he seemed to have regained a steady running pace.

MAINE

282 MILES

All of us have had the experience of a sudden joy that came when nothing in the world had forewarned us of its coming—a joy so thrilling that if it was born of misery we remembered even the misery with tenderness.
—Antoine de Saint-Exupéry, *Wind, Sand and Stars*

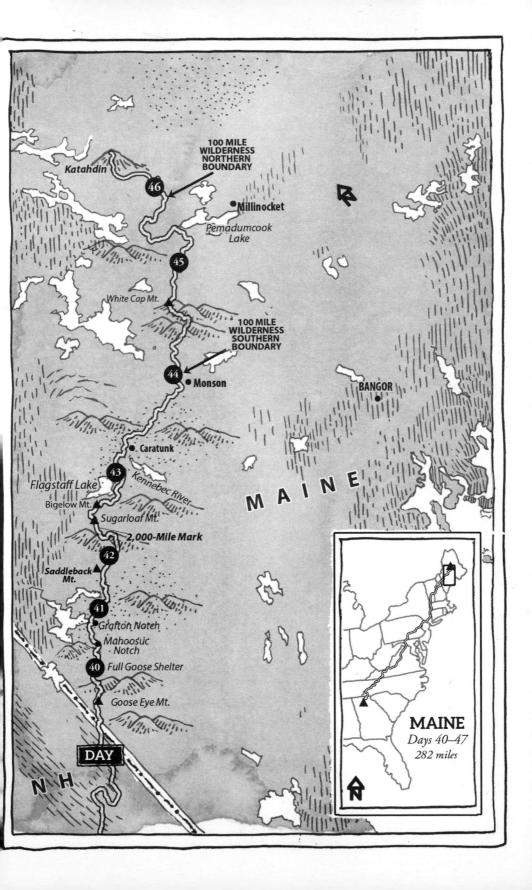

100 MILE
WILDERNESS
NORTHERN
BOUNDARY

Katahdin

Millinocket

*Pemadumcook
Lake*

White Cap Mt.

100 MILE
WILDERNESS
SOUTHERN
BOUNDARY

Monson

BANGOR

Caratunk

Flagstaff Lake

Kennebec River

Bigelow Mt.

Sugarloaf Mt.

2,000-Mile Mark

**Saddleback
Mt.**

Grafton Notch

*Mahoosuc
Notch*

Full Goose Shelter

Goose Eye Mt.

DAY

M A I N E

N H

MAINE
*Days 40–47
282 miles*

N

CHAPTER 14

DANCING WITH THE GENIE

Day Forty

THE MORNING'S DESCENT into Gorham mirrored the overall decline in my bandwidth, as both were gradual, rocky, and absolute. And by the time we had reached JLu and Castle Black, my mental capacity was fried and I was no longer transmitting any signal. It was as if I had placed my brain on airplane mode.

We can all relate to those annoying conversations caused by a wavering cell signal where you catch only every other word. Like those frustrating phone calls, I was unable to make myself understood, as if I were actually speaking and listening in fragments. It felt like my mind was coming in and out of reception.

When I had zero bars I would become withdrawn and incommunicado, equal parts off the grid and off my rocker. But then I'd round a turn, get to the top of a rise, and suddenly I'd be full bars. It was during these times, when I joyously crested the surface, that I'd reach out to connect, as I typically love to converse and prompt discussions. And just like when your multiple in-boxes noisily ping with each new notice, I would chime in to the conversations, catching the punch lines, sometimes even finishing them, signaling to my trail mates that I was back in service.

My new running partners were two of the greatest runners you've never heard of, Ryan and Kristina Welts, locals who knew Horty. It was a joy to watch them navigate the trail. They were like kids on a jungle gym, skating down slabs, hopping over gaps, swinging off branches and roots that they dubbed "cedar handrails."

Ryan held the FKT for the section of AT called the Mahoosuc Traverse, so this part of the state was his training ground. They were more than just happy; they were also well prepared. Along with their buddy Nate, they carried large backpacks full of lightweight camping gear and wonderfully nonessential comforts such as a giant Rice Krispies Treat the size of a pillow. They were into gutting it out—and laughing while they did it. They were a welcome change of pace from the heaviness and grandeur of the Whites and from all my depressingly slow miles there. I let myself forget about the miles and time altogether, and the feeling that the record had almost certainly slipped away from me.

I was fully present; I was moving. Moving *well*. But I didn't think too much about it. It was way too soon to start feeling confident again.

As we approached the Maine border—my final crossing—the excitement among the members of our group started to build. Timmy and JLu hiked in to meet us right before the border; there was no way she was going to miss crossing that line together. They brought sleeping bags so they could stay at the shelter with us. Right where the trail crossed the border, we saw a sign that read SPRINGER MOUNTAIN—1899.8 MILES. KATAHDIN—281.4 MILES. It was monumental. The fourteenth and final state. It had never grown old and tired; it hit me deep to my core. A Creamsicle sunset made the moment especially magical and ranked with the most memorable of times I'd cultivated on the trail since signing my name in the guest book and starting off into the Georgian darkness.

If I don't make it, or if I don't make the record, this will still be worth it. I kept that thought to myself, but those few hours made that clear to me. To be out here with JLu and Timmy doing what we all loved was enough.

The trail across the higher Mahoosuc ridgeline wove through the trees, and it was beautiful. When the trail wasn't rocky, we were walking on wooden planks to cross over bogs of mud and silt, moose territory. The views over the big north country were full of an untamed splendor. Pretty soon the terrain got so steep, we had to hold on to metal handrails drilled into the granite, what Timmy called "stone staples." Before it got totally dark, we'd made it to Full Goose Shelter and we were exuberant, just coursing with adrenaline. Thirty minutes later, we fell asleep like logs to the chainsaw snores of tired souls who were already tucked into the shelter.

We set off in the predawn darkness, with Timmy and JLu taking a side trail to peel off the AT while I dove deeper into Mahoosucs' bowels, a deep gully that looked like a glacier had dumped all its contents into a jumbled mess at the bottom. Massive boulders, crushed rock beds, and downed trees with gigantic root balls were littered everywhere. AT thru-hikers know it as the "hardest mile" and can take over two hours to pass through the mangled mess. I squeezed my body through fissures in miniature slot canyons formed by stacks of angular blocks. On all fours, I scrambled over the top of moss-covered rocks, grabbing onto roots and branches of hemlocks and balsam firs.

The genie that had escaped the bottle near Galehead Hut was back and I couldn't stuff him back in, so I had to wrestle with him under, over, and through this mile for an hour and twenty minutes before I danced through the Mahoosuc Notch with two left feet.

Seven miles later I hit Grafton Notch as the midday sun was baking the pavement parking lot. While reloading my pack at Castle Black, I heard a fellow NoBo thru-hiker shout out, "Hey, Scott, you're catching up to the badasses. It's time to start acting like one!" Even though I was starting to approach the strongest hikers of the AT Class of 2015, I sure didn't feel like I was much of a badass.

We looked at the numbers. On day thirty-nine, I'd done only thirty-two miles. Day forty had been worse: twenty-nine miles. Day forty-one was only thirty. I became painfully aware of the meager progress I'd been making. I'd been pushing myself to the limit, but the mileage wasn't reflecting that.

That thru-hiker made me reflect back to 2006 when Caballo Blanco tried getting under my skin in hopes of motivating me to venture down to race the Tarahumaran. In an e-mail he asked, "How *chingon* are you?" And for this venture, if I wanted the record I would need to be a lot more badass.

Day forty-two did not start auspiciously. I'd ended day forty-one by sleeping more hours than I should have, so JLu was already upset at me when dawn arrived, and I woke up dragging my feet, knowing I'd have to cover extra miles. Actually, I woke up to the sound of moose hooves galloping across pavement. Everyone else woke up too and scrambled to avoid getting trampled by the fatally powerful legs of the massive beast. As I dawdled in the van, doing my best to delay the start of another grueling day, Timmy joked to JLu that I left two tracks of ruts in the trail from my dragging feet.

Back in Boulder, I'd figured I'd be done with the whole trail by now. Instead, I felt like I was in a hamster wheel. I was running but my progress was a myth. Maine miles just seemed to keep going nowhere. Especially disheartening was how meandering the trail got up here, meaning that I'd sometimes be running due south in order to go north.

Eight miles into the day, I slipped on a slab of rock and landed on my hip. In the process, I snapped my hiking pole in half. The two parts were just barely connected by some carbon fibers. It was useless. I was so angry at the rock, I thrashed the remains of the pole against it over and over until it finally shattered completely. Luis had returned for one more AT tour of duty, and he stepped back. His face said everything. I was unrecognizable. Maybe I'd finally snapped altogether.

Still, everyone on the team and everyone who came out to see me kept saying encouraging things like "You're almost there!" and "Only four more days left!" Like it was the surest thing in the world. Perversely, their excitement for me made me feel worse. I was bending in half, hanging on by only a few threads, like my hiking pole.

It was on day forty-two that I morosely asked the local runners to run on ahead. They did, no questions asked. I needed space alone to face the numbers. There was an overwhelming sadness that I needed to process all by myself. I had to remind myself that the whole trip wasn't a waste, that the experience was greater than the record. I wanted to feel the emotions that came with accepting it was over. It would have been easier to bottle them up, but they were too heavy. This was what I came for, but it was still hard to stomach. I was dead in the water, floating facedown—FKT'd.

I walked forward and carried that burden with me; it was going to take more miles and more mud to process. Sure enough, almost on cue, I sank deep into some hidden mud. That was the whole Appalachian Trail in a nutshell. Just when you think you have the rhythm, it cuts you off at the knees.

Later that day, Timmy would be leaving. And a strong midsummer storm was headed our way. The hits kept coming. So I'd be running into wet, cold chaos with a crew made up of eager and fully capable runners but no one I had a deep connection with. The tempest would coincide with our push up Saddleback Mountain, which would inevitably stretch into the wee hours of morning. With Timmy leaving, it'd be like changing ship captains mid-hurricane.

It was too much. I called Jenny and Timmy over to the edge of the van, where I sat slouched in defeat, and told them straight up.

I've done the math. The math doesn't work.

I'm sorry, I fucked up. It's over.

There weren't enough hours in the day to break the record. I told them it was fine. I told them I wasn't quitting, that I'd get to Katahdin, but I'd just walk it in. There was no point to continuing with the sleepless nights of zombie marching

They didn't listen. JLu folded an entire pizza into one zip-lock bag and filled another with a smorgasbord of Clif Shots and Clif Bars and other staples. She packed my stuff for me like I was a kid going off to summer camp. Timmy peered into my eyes and looked straight into my soul, deeper than even old Horty had, and said, "You're so close. I've seen you go to the edge and back the last ten days. You've got this, Scotty!"

I didn't believe him.

All that full-bar connectivity I'd had in the Mahoosucs had disappeared entirely. I was out of service once again. Over the past forty-two days, I'd seesawed back and forth between really believing I could set the FKT and coming to terms with the fact that I wouldn't, but this time didn't feel like part of that cycle. This was permanent. This was it. The math was the math.

I was switching gears. I was starting to look forward to a leisurely hike through the rest of the Maine woods.

I looked at Timmy with clarity.

"It's not humanly possible. The nail is in the coffin."

I was in shock. What the hell was my crazy, blurry-eyed, scrawny-ass, shaky-handed husband talking about? It's over? And now we were gonna walk it in, just like Leadville 2013 all over again? Oh, hell no. I hadn't worked this hard and gotten this far to suddenly give up and cruise lazily through Maine on day forty-two. He didn't want to hurt anymore, and I didn't want him to either, but he'd have to wait until he got to the other end of this suffer-fest for that relief.

We were too close to quit.

"But I did the math. There's not enough hours in the days. I fucked up."

"What are you *talking* about? We have five days—you can do it!"

Visibly frustrated, he sighed. "JLu. Today is day forty-two. The record is forty-six days, so that's only four days."

"Jurker. Hello! We get the entire forty-sixth day plus another eleven hours on day forty-seven." He stared at me and I saw his mind sputter. I rolled my eyes. Was he kidding me? All this drama because he'd been spewing drunk math? They say not to drive or operate heavy machinery while drowsy; I think they should add arithmatic to that list. We packed a shit-ton of food, and sent him on his way with two strangers.

I said good-bye to Timmy. Like Speedgoat, he *really* didn't want to leave our team but he had work obligations back home. His imminent departure made me realize I had gotten dependent on him to help me strategize and keep morale up. Both those things had become harder in the past couple of days as we started to enter really wild territory. Thankfully, Timmy had been marshalling replacements.

It turned out that our friends Topher and Kim had understood how badly we needed them after all. It was great timing, because Toph had recently quit his job and was hanging in Mammoth Lakes with a bunch of elite ultrarunners when he received Jurker's SOS message. Jurker had sounded so dire, Toph later told me, that he'd replayed the message on speakerphone, and everyone winced from the palpable sounds of desperation. They immediately booked tickets to Portland, Maine, and they would be arriving that night. Best of all, the two of them with Timmy had been devising a game plan for what would be the most critical part of our trip and the biggest logistical puzzle: The Hundred-Mile Wilderness, the infamous stretch of central Maine that humbles thru-hikers every season.

Along with Toph and Kim, one other person was set to arrive, a total ultrarunning powerhouse who was as invaluable to Jurker as she was to me. I was so relieved to see Krissy. She looked much better than me—rested, clean, bright-eyed, and tanned. She was one of my best friends, and it felt like she'd brought a piece of home with her. I thought Krissy would want all the details on Scott right away, but she was more concerned about how I was doing. After forty-two days and nights of serving Jurker, I was unashamedly eager for some time for myself.

Krissy Moehl and I had met way back in 2001 when we were both new hires at a footwear company in Seattle and shared a cubicle. I'd never been a runner before and she was just transitioning from running track to going longer distances. It blew my mind back then. The thought of running a marathon (and beyond) sounded outlandish to me, but here Krissy was, a sweet, normal, even-keeled girl, about to run her first 50K race. Her enthusiasm was infectious. In two years, I went from not running at all to running a half marathon, a full marathon, and then my first 50K. I wasn't fast like her, but I could understand why she loved it.

Over the years since, we'd traveled around the world together, going to races from Hong Kong to France, and I crewed for her at some big ones like Western States and Wasatch. She'd known Jurker even longer than me; he was the one who got her into trail running when they worked at the Seattle Running Company. They were like brother and sister, so it was no surprise that she was a little grossed out in 2008 when I told her he and I had hooked up.

She had caught a ride out to the trail from a Mainer, and she managed to intersect with me near Rangeley Lake, a beautiful spot just west of Saddleback Mountain. Almost as soon as she got there, I asked, naturally, "You wanna jump in the lake?" A storm was brewing but it was still warm enough to swim. We changed in the van and caught the last rays of sunlight.

"Whoa! Look at all your bug bites!" She pointed to my arms and legs. I hardly noticed them anymore. They were reminders of the Deep South, which felt like a lifetime ago. I wondered what else had changed about me.

After drying off, we hopped in Castle Black and drove to Sugarloaf Mountain. On the way, I brought her up to speed on Scott's status and prospects. By the time we got to the mountain, it was really pouring, and we booked a room at the ski resort. Our room was total luxury, and I've got no regrets. I appreciated every bit of it, starting with the hot water and ending with the clean sheets and down comforter.

There was even an outdoor hot tub, and that night we got in it and gazed up at Saddleback Mountain. It was raining hard and the mountain was smothered in cold fog, and I wondered if Jurker had made it to his destination that night, a rustic three-sided lean-to. It was so nice to feel comfortable and clean, but I did feel a twinge of guilt in not even knowing where Scott was at that moment. My imagination began to run wild. Maybe he was out there in the storm, hunkered down in his greasy fart sack with two near-strangers while I was having a blast with my best friend.

Even in a queen-size bed with tons of pillows, I couldn't sleep more than six hours. I jumped out of bed as soon as I woke up and checked the tracker. Jurker was already on the move, which was good, but it crossed my mind that maybe he hadn't actually stopped that night. I hoped that wasn't the case—it'd *really* make me feel guilty about the hotel.

Topher and Kim met us that morning, day forty-three, at the hotel and we hashed out a plan. They came prepared with a map collection that would have made Speedgoat proud. Toph had downloaded a few AT apps on his phone, including one that gave him real-time GPS locations so he could calculate Jurker's pace when they were running together.

The plan that morning focused on the few—but serious—remaining obstacles.

The Kennebec River was thirty-six miles up the trail. If he was moving well, he would reach the river in the middle of the night. *Do not ford,* the guidebook warned. *Take ferry service.* I looked up the ferry service (which turned out to be a man in a canoe) and found that the hours of operation were from 9:00 a.m. to 5:00 p.m. We estimated Jurker could reach the river's edge just after midnight, so that wasn't gonna work for us. Everyone following our progress closely figured the same thing and debated online about what Scott was going to do.

Someone with the ferry service said if Jurker didn't use the "official" ferry, his record wouldn't be official. Other people quickly pointed out that previous AT FKT record holders, including Horty, didn't pay the fifty dollars to use the ferry. Horty forded the river. That was an option, but one I wasn't too psyched about. We had never been to this river before and had no idea about the currents or what lay downstream. I didn't trust Jurker in his sleep-deprived state to walk across in the dark. He was starting to resemble a piece of driftwood, and I pictured him floating away.

So when Mandy and John, the owners of a local adventure center nearby, volunteered to stash canoes for us to use when we arrived, we thanked our lucky stars (and a local runner, Gary) for that fortuitous piece of priceless trail magic.

The second hurdle was the Hundred-Mile Wilderness. I was impressed at how much research Toph and Kim had already done. It's a uniquely complicated section of the trail to support because it is crisscrossed by logging roads, and the entrances to the wilderness are guarded by locked gates that open and close at specific times. So once we got in, we wouldn't be able to leave until the gates reopened. If we took too long and got caught inside, we could be screwed. There were also no amenities of any kind once inside.

We studied the maps and entered the wilderness as soon as possible. Once we were inside, Topher suggested we drive our routes and scout out our meeting locations, just to make sure our vehicles could get to each destination. That stereotypical phrase (said with a northern Maine accent) "You can't get they-ahh from hee-yah" was invented for places like this.

Jurker would cross the two-thousand-mile mark this morning. Only a hundred and eighty-nine miles lay between him and Katahdin.

We were about to find out if we could get they-ahh from hee-yah.

CHAPTER 15

THE HUNDRED-MILE NIGHTMARE

Day Forty-Two

I PROBABLY SHOULDN'T have been crunching numbers in the state I was in. When JLu corrected me and pointed out I had an entire day that I'd overlooked, it was undeniably bittersweet. The FKT was still possible—but, man, did that leisurely walk to Katahdin sound good.

Not yet, though.

Day forty-two hinged on that moment. Before it—before JLu had brought me to my senses—everything was chaos. Up and down. Physically I was feeling okay, but mentally I was a basket case. Her talk braced me.

Ryan and Kristina had taken off. Timmy had just left us, and Toph was due to arrive tonight, but for the moment, I'd be running with near strangers. They joined me for the second stretch of the day, a nineteen-mile night run over Saddleback Mountain. It got me thinking about how my team had worked (and occasionally *not* worked) so far. It got me wondering about how teams come together or fall apart.

It made me nervous, as we ran through the night, that my current team consisted of me and two men I'd never met before. And we were plunging into the most challenging last step before the final ascent. This was the darkness before the dawn. John Rodrigue and Chris "Tarzan" Clemens looked stable enough, and I had heard they had toughness, but I was at the end of my rope and I didn't have anything left to manage a team. *I* needed to be managed. To give that responsibility to strangers was a risk I hated to take.

Could they motivate me?

Were they going to know when to push me and when to give me slack?

Were they going to know *how* to push me?

A few hours before, in the afternoon of day forty-two, I'd been ready to walk it in to Katahdin. It was a critical moment.

I was also a little worried Tarzan might think I was deranged. He'd seen me beat my broken pole into pieces earlier in the day. Not a good first impression.

John had come to us via the friendly and über-helpful Maine Trail Monsters running club, so I knew he'd at least have experience out here in the endless north country. Tarzan was here with Luis, and I trusted El Coyote's choices. It was comforting to run with them knowing that Tarzan had thru-hiked the AT in 2012, so he had recent memories of what I was going through.

Beyond those few details, I didn't know them. The FKT was at its most perilous—we were officially in make-or-break mode—and I'd be running with the equivalent of Facebook friends of friends.

But beggars couldn't be choosers.

The last goal of the day was to get in nineteen miles and spend the night at the Spaulding Mountain Lean-To. The miles would include a two-thousand-foot trek up Saddleback Mountain, then a drop back down, followed by another two-thousand-foot climb up Spaulding Mountain and everywhere in between, the countless mini-climbs the AT is known for.

After we'd climbed six miles through the dense forest, we popped out onto an open alpine ridge. As we neared the top, the fog was so thick I could feel its tendrils swirling around my face. It blotted out the sky, and as we ran, our packs and clothes were dotted by drops of rain that seemed to materialize out of nowhere.

With John motivating us, we made a steady push up and down the ridges of Saddleback—nothing spectacular, but our rhythm reassured me that I could still perform when I had to. I took the opportunity to interview them both (and hoped not to find out anything discomfiting).

John was an unassuming hard man, a single dad with a grown son who'd recently caught the ultrarunning bug himself. He was self-reliant and reserved, a classic Maine provincialist, who heard I would be running through the local trails and cleared his schedule to be available to help in any way.

Chris Clemens was paper-thin but quick as a whippet, with muscles like steel cords. Caballo Blanco had called him Tarzan because he had long brown hair and was perfectly comfortable in the middle of nowhere. Chris filled his pack with an outdoorsman's knack, jamming in a tent, sleeping bags, and more food than I could imagine us eating. It turned out to be just the right amount, but I could never consume enough calories per day. I'd still lost close to nineteen pounds.

I quickly dismissed my apprehension about whether these guys would help me perform. Having their fresh energy around me was as good as being with old friends.

It was still light when we summited Saddleback, a beautiful mountain with slopes covered in purple and pink midsummer wildflowers. We picked up the pace as the trail dropped suddenly into a steep decline—and there, to my shock, was Timmy with a can of Pabst Blue Ribbon in each hand. He had decided he wasn't ready to leave the adventure just yet.

Clearly in a party mood, he'd been up at the crest with a couple of guys who worked at the Saddleback ski lodge. They'd hiked up the ski run, and the three of them had started the party without us.

"Man," Timmy said boisterously, "when you guys were coming down the ridge, it looked like you were descending on a cloud!"

He was beaming at me, and I later found out why. He said that as I was running down the hill, he could tell from the look on my face that I was back in the game. He said it was the polar opposite of the look he'd seen less than twelve hours earlier, when I'd told him it was all over. Timmy's mood, as usual, was contagious, and the party at the top of the mountain felt celebratory, a harbinger of good fortune.

That night at the Spaulding Mountain Lean-To was wet and dreary, but on the morning of day forty-three, I dragged myself out of my sleeping bag at four thirty, squeezed as much water out of my socks as possible, and got ready by consuming the leftover pizza JLu had packed for me and a couple of Clif Bars. They broke down my tent, and I went ahead without them, knowing they would catch up.

I had four and a half days to reach Katahdin. I had slept a mere four hours for the second consecutive night. Each night was the same; as soon as I laid my head down, it felt like it was time to wake up. I needed to get more sleep, but I also needed to cover more miles. Despite the mist and fog, the air was balmy even before sunrise. I'd woken up warm, so I felt loose and just a touch rested. But the real reason I was feeling good was I knew Toph, Kim, and Krissy were about to join our team.

But as excited as I was for the arrival of one of my oldest and most trusted friends, I had no idea just how crucial he would be in the last, excruciating days and hours of the FKT.

The morning of day forty-three quickly warmed up as the storm passed. Just as we left the talus slope and reentered the Green Tunnel, I spotted an oncoming runner. Topher!

"Are you kidding me? This trail is crazy; it's so gnarly. Is it all like this?"

"You're in for a real treat!" I said as I gave him a solid hug.

True to form, he wasted no time. "From right now, we've got four days and five hours to get to the top of Katahdin. You'll need to average somewhere close to fifty miles a day. It should be doable, if we execute it right. The x factor is sleep. The y factor is your hourly pace."

Topher had the numbers. He had the authority. He had my ear. If he said it was possible, I believed him. I didn't have the energy to doubt.

Less than an hour later, as I was coming down a massive hill, the trees began to thin, the grade gradually leveled, and I could finally see the road that the trail crossed. As we got closer, I spotted Castle Black and several cars. More important, I saw the people who would determine my immediate fate.

JLu was there, with Krissy, a longtime ultrarunner friend of ours. And there was Topher's wife, Kim, herself an ultrarunner and a crew chief extraordinaire.

Walter was scheduled to rejoin us tomorrow, as was my Boulder friend Aron Ralston, who would both run the Hundred-Mile Wilderness with me. Ralsty famously amputated his own arm with a cheap multitool to escape death in a Utah slot canyon, so I hoped that his grit and determination would rub off on us all. There would also be a new guy from the Maine Trail Monsters club, Joe Wrobleski;

he held the self-supported FKT for the Hundred-Mile Wilderness AT section. Most skilled hikers spend about nine to twelve days traversing the Hundred-Mile Wilderness, but Iron Joe had run it in forty-three hours. I needed to do it in under forty-eight. Anything more and I could kiss the record good-bye.

In the past, the best moments in my life were when I reached down and found inner strength where I'd thought none existed. But I needed more than my own strength these days. I needed the strength embodied by the people standing by the side of the road, waving and calling out. This time, I really didn't have any strength left. But my team did. And even if they gave it to me, it still wouldn't be mine. It would be ours, collectively, just like the FKT would be—if we managed to get it.

Later, after Katahdin, I would look back and realize this moment was when the long "final day" began. A day that would combine many terrestrial days into one barely differentiated stretch of running and resting, split up only nominally by a few stolen hours of sleep. Night and day no longer meant anything other than whether or not we needed our headlamps.

I was disoriented, like in the floating state of consciousness during an extended hospital stay. Sleep deprivation makes time peel back at the edges; you can start to lose your bearings very quickly. You wake up at strange hours and never when you mean to. You doze off in the middle of conversations or during meals. Your sleep isn't quite sleep. Your waking isn't exactly waking. It starts to feel like you're living your life in a permanent twilight, where your circadian rhythms have lost their beat and you might collapse at any moment.

Topher set the pace, which, in typical Topher fashion, was precisely calculated. I was more tired than ever, but I could also feel the strength emanating from Topher and Krissy, two people who shared a very special gift for endurance and meeting almost impossible challenges. There was immense trust among the three of us; we knew we could function effectively as a single unit. The sport of ultrarunning cultivates perseverance in the face of pain, fatigue, illness, and anything else. For that reason, to the untrained eye, it might seem to reward the self-sufficient and punish any kind of weakness. But the most experienced and highest-achieving ultrarunners learn that without support, it's easy to wander aimlessly. And without a crew that you can honestly turn to for help, a crew that truly understands you, you won't be able to help yourself. Even the most eccentric among us—and, yes, I am referring here to Speedgoat—depend on other people far more than an outsider might suppose.

Of course, there's something else you'll always need, something that other people can never give you. *Sleep*.

Around 10:00 p.m. on day forty-three, we were running along the narrow edge of a cliff above a river. The sound of the running water lulled me toward sleep, and I felt myself drifting in and out of full consciousness.

In a desperate voice, I told Toph that I was falling asleep while walking, and I was worried I might sleepwalk to my death. He looked back at me and studied my face. Topher not only ran, he also ran businesses. I knew he was experienced in judging this type of situation, the situation being whether or not to believe me and then whether or not to give me what I wanted. Tough love meant pushing me on in spite of my protests. I had wanted Topher to come out here to support me, not to pamper me or serve as my butler. I got what I wanted.

"As soon as I find a spot," he said. And so we continued, and I continued to stagger on, half asleep. There was no room to pitch even our tiny tent, so we went another mile or two until we finally found a place where the trail opened wider than shoulder width. Topher and Krissy got the tent up almost instantly, directly on the trail, and I lay back and was suddenly asleep.

They set an alarm to go off in two hours, at 4:45 a.m., and hunkered down shoulder to shoulder in makeshift bivy sacks made from their down jackets and a bug net. They later told me they fell asleep making jokes about the definition of *friendship*. As in, this must be it, or why the hell else would they be lying on the trail under one sleeping bag for me?

The long last day continued two hours later. In the dark gray predawn light, Krissy and Topher woke me up and sent me down the trail by myself for a few minutes while they took down the tent and gathered our stuff. As I shuffled off, I remembered something that Speedgoat had told me about getting to the Hundred-Mile Wilderness. "You don't have to rally at that point," he'd said, "you just need to keep walking on the AT treadmill, three and a half miles per hour." So I kept walking, picked up the pace, and settled into the hurried quickstep that had carried me north for so many miles.

On the morning of day forty-four, we reached the banks of the Kennebec River, a clear, fast-moving, and deceptively friendly-looking body of water. Compared with the countless narrow rivers and streams I'd crossed thus far, the Kennebec seemed like a lake. It looked shallow enough to ford, but we understood that several people had died trying to do that, tempted by its apparent placidness. It was known to NoBo hikers as a kind of lock on the last door into the final push, and you couldn't open it without a key—or a crowbar.

Luckily my A-Team crew was already on top of this. They found the canoes stashed by the river for us and paddled across.

"We live in Maine," John said. "If we don't know how to paddle canoes, we don't deserve to be here."

When we got across, the last strategic meeting before entering the southern end of the Hundred-Mile Wilderness was convened with lightning speed. Walter and Ralsty would run the first leg of the wilderness with me, so they helped the Trail Monsters throw the gear we'd need into their packs, keeping mine as light as possible.

The Hundred-Mile Wilderness was like nothing that had come before it. For starters, it had the strange distinction of being a gated section of the trail, a wilderness that could be accessed by a labyrinth of logging roads with trapdoors. The gated roads had hard open and closed hours, which meant that my crew wasn't just running according to one schedule—ours—we were running on someone else's. It was a life-size video game that required precision skill and a lot of luck.

At the entrance of the Hundred-Mile Wilderness stood a sign that read CAUTION. THERE ARE NO PLACES TO OBTAIN SUPPLIES OR GET HELP UNTIL ABOL BRIDGE, 100 MILES NORTH. DO NOT ATTEMPT THIS SECTION UNLESS YOU HAVE A MINIMUM OF 10 DAYS SUPPLIES AND ARE FULLY EQUIPPED. THIS IS THE LONGEST WILDERNESS SECTION OF THE EN-TIRE "AT" AND ITS DIFFICULTY SHOULD NOT BE UNDERESTIMATED. GOOD HIKING!

In 2013, a sixty-six-year-old thru-hiker named Geraldine Largay stepped off the AT in Maine the recommended two hundred feet to relieve herself. Her body was found less than two miles from the trail. She had wandered, lost, for twenty-six days before dying of starvation.

She left a note in a Ziploc bag. It said: *When you find my body, please call my husband George and my daughter Kerry. It will be the greatest kindness for them to know that I am dead and where you found me—no matter how many years from now.*

The woods were so thick that her body wasn't found for two years.

We had two days and a few hours left. Every minute we could save would come back to us tenfold.

The trail began by bobbing up and down, making it nearly impossible for anyone to fall into a steady stride. Every hour, it seemed, we climbed a thousand feet over uneven piles of broken boulders, hopping over knife-edged rocks and struggling not to bruise and scratch our ankles and legs. The landscape, strewn with giant stones, looked like the site of a major earthquake. Then we'd go down, at least a thousand feet at a time. The trail sank into marshes and swamps with roots that reached up to our shins, forcing us into awkward stutter steps and causing plenty of falls.

Having Ralsty around really did make me feel better. His mere presence was a constant reminder of just how much a body and mind could endure without breaking. Not only had he gone 127 hours without sleep, he'd cut off his arm without anesthesia. And apparently, he hadn't suffered any lasting damage to his nerves, brain, or major organs. He was still extremely athletic, seemed to suffer no post-traumatic stress symptoms, and he didn't avoid taking calculated risks. I mean, he was out here, after all.

I knew that Ralsty was a good alpine skier, climber, and mountaineer. But I'd never known how supernaturally sure-footed he was until, as we were trying to make up time on a sharp descent, hopping and skipping over jagged rocks, he started reading a lengthy article to me on his phone to keep my mind awake. He read the whole thing, not even pausing as he leaped from rock to rock like a mountain goat.

But Ralsty, like Horty and the Speedgoat and many of my other friends, was full of contradictions. Maybe it's an ultrarunner thing. Maybe it's a human thing. In any case, my friends could sure be peculiar. Case in point: here was a man who'd endured something most people can't even imagine— yet he didn't like getting dirty.

He would take off his shoes and socks every time we crossed a stream so he wouldn't get sand in them, and he insisted on bathing as thoroughly as possible whenever it was even remotely feasible. Meanwhile, I was beginning to look semi-decomposed. Timmy, who was friends with Ralsty from their many wilderness outings, curiously maintained that "anyone who declares a war on dust obviously has too much time on their hand."

With Ralsty setting the pace, we seized every opportunity the trail gave us to open up and run. The afternoon stretched on for what felt like an eternity before suddenly sinking into the soft glow of twilight. We put on our headlamps as the deep-woods darkness brought the stars into stark relief, their points glittering so brightly that they looked almost artificial in their clarity.

We ran into day forty-six and beyond. The sun rose. My hands were shaking. My bones protuded.

At 5:00 a.m., we officially had thirty-six hours to break the record. I was sixty-three miles from the end of the line.

Later in the afternoon, Ralsty and I took a short side trail to reach the peaceful shores of Pemadumcook Lake, and finally there it was, the destination of this perpetual odyssey: Katahdin.

When I saw it for the first time, the realization was like suddenly seeing the glow from a lighthouse after floating hopelessly lost at sea: salvation. It hit me like a rogue wave. It was real, and it was near. Near enough.

Forty-eight miles to be exact.

We were about to find out if I had any El Venado left, if the Web Walker could break through the internal webs that had covered my fighting spirit.

JLu and Walter came out to do eight miles with me before the next crossing. I recall them running ahead and talking about how slow I was going as if I weren't there, the way you might talk about a baby or someone confused by dementia. I wasn't resentful. I understood. I was locked in a purgatory between dreamland and reality and couldn't function properly in either.

In addition to my hands and eyes and skin and bones all giving out, now my back suddenly decided to malfunction in a strange and horrible way. It spasmed and seized up almost constantly. For the first time, I didn't feel like I was merely in pain; I felt like I was actually losing my own body. Like someone or something else was taking over. More than the FKT, more than Katahdin, I just wanted to feel justified, even if that meant using up my body completely.

The night descended, for the last time on my journey. It was 9:00 p.m. on day forty-six and we were thirty-two miles from Katahdin. At Pollywog Stream crossing, my crew was wearing what looked like hazmat suits made out of bug netting because of the mosquitoes and biting flies. I didn't even notice the carnage the insects were inflicting on my bare skin.

I knew I had one more opportunity to sleep before we made the final push. I also knew I couldn't sleep just yet. Toph had scheduled seventeen more miles that night, but I couldn't do it.

Topher and Krissy were packed and ready for the night shift, and they had all of my stuff ready to go. Then my body just stopped working. I felt it coming on before it fully hit: "Toph," I said, "I need to sleep here. I've gotta stop. We can make up the difference tomorrow."

"Scott, I promise you we'll let you sleep, but let's get to Golden Road and then you can get a solid four hours."

I threw up my hands and tried saying no, but he quickly handed me a cup of cold instant coffee and I choked it down. I needed high-grade pharmaceuticals or a *Breaking Bad* barista, but the only other stimulant we had was yerba maté. Nothing put a dent in my sleepiness.

I suddenly got a crazy spasm in the middle of my back and couldn't stay upright. I hunched over while Krissy tried to massage it enough for me to stand. I felt like my whole body was breaking down, and whatever strength I was squeezing out of it now was the last I had. I had no idea what would happen when that was gone. I was all out of hidden reservoirs; there were no untapped resources.

We got to the crossing at Golden Road, near the base of Katahdin, at about 4:45 a.m. I'd done 47.6 miles that day. In the four days immediately following Galehead, I'd averaged twenty-eight miles a day. In the five days since then, I'd averaged forty-six. Not because I had any speed left—I didn't—but because I'd slept only seven hours total in the past three nights.

We were out of the Hundred-Mile Wilderness. All that was left was the fifteen-mile runway to the summit of Katahdin.

I could finally sleep now. All I'd been able to think about for the past twenty hours was sleeping four hours straight, something I hadn't done in days. Days that seemed a lifetime ago.

I was exhausted but couldn't sleep. On the night of day forty-six, we were at the flanks of Katahdin. It was amazing and awesome to finally see it, the previously abstract thing that had drawn us all the way from Georgia.

I couldn't sleep because Jurker was late—again. Although we were close to the finish, I was far from confident. Walter and I had covered 8 miles with him that afternoon in about four hours. He was moving ridiculously slowly, and every bathroom break seemed to take forever. It was as if he fell asleep every time his feet stopped moving. When the three of us got to Pollywog Stream, where the crew was waiting, it was already dark and well past the time we'd hoped to arrive. I knew Jurker wanted to crawl into the van, but he still had seventeen miles to go that night. I was starting to worry about physical limits.

But Toph told him he had to get those miles done. He promised him four hours of sleep once he reached Golden Road. Ralsty gave him an all-time inspirational pep talk, and if there was any guy who could speak on the topic of sleep deprivation, it was Ralsty.

I certainly couldn't be encouraging. I wanted to lock Scott inside Castle Black and drive him far away from this trail. I feared he was doing permanent damage to his body, to his nervous system, to his mind. He was a shell of himself; I had never seen him go this deep and this dark, ever. I remember telling him back in Boulder that I didn't want to see any half-assed effort, and apparently he took that to heart. More than anything, I just wanted him to stop here and sleep.

But that's why he had the A Team here. Toph and Krissy were the masters of triage, fully capable of managing any crisis. They knew how to motivate and push him better than I did. I didn't say anything; all I could do was let the others take control.

So late on day forty-six, when he asked for truck-stop-grade stimulants, I suppressed my instinct to yank him aside and tuck him into bed in Castle Black. He was delirious. I think he would have taken anything to keep him awake. Instead, he made do with two coconut-milk cappuccinos and caffeinated Clif Shots and hit the trail again.

It hurt me to see him go. It ripped my heart out. My high-priced thoroughbred had become a low-rent donkey. He had been on the trail around the clock the past four days. We didn't have time to talk, so I didn't know where his head was or if it was even still there.

Maybe that was for the best. I didn't know how much of his suffering I could handle.

I was also dealing with something of my own.

Right before we got to the crux of the Kennebec, exactly eight weeks after my D and C surgery, I finally got my period back. Dr. Flagg had warned me it could be heavier than normal, but I wasn't expecting this. It was like the Red Wedding scene from *Game of Thrones;* I was almost worried I'd bleed out in the middle of the wilderness. There was no prospect of finding a doctor or even a shower anywhere. I didn't dare mention it to Jurker, though. I knew he would freak out and end our trip immediately.

Thank goodness Krissy was with me. She drove off and found me some ginormous pads and a laundromat. Fortunately, over the next few days, the bleeding subsided and eventually stopped.

With my medical distraction behind me, I was free to focus all my worries on Jurker once again. Did something catastrophic happen? We'd been expecting him for hours, and I grew increasingly anxious. Here on Golden Road, Walter was already passed out in a tent, Kim and Ralsty were sleeping in their rental cars, and I was nervously organizing Castle Black. The sun had already started to rise when Jurker and the night shift finally arrived. I ran out to meet them. Krissy was in tears.

"JLu, we pushed him too far. He can't even move; he's tripping on everything. I've never seen him like this before." She was so obviously upset, it scared me. This was the no-holds-barred guidance we needed, yet it was something I couldn't bear to do: help Jurker hurt himself. Krissy and Toph's capacity to carry out the mission of all the people who came to help and all those who followed along online was damn near heroic. They were like torchbearers who just ran the final leg into the stadium to ignite the Olympic flame.

Jurker was so relieved to see me, he practically collapsed in my arms.

Topher calmly walked up to us, and his voice was all business.

"Here's the deal. You've got ten miles to the base of Katahdin and then a five-mile hike up. You have eleven hours to do that, so you only get one hour of sleep here."

"One hour?" Jurker balked. "You said I could have four!"

I nodded; I'd heard that too. Toph had said he could have those precious hours of sleep once he got to Golden Road.

"You don't believe in me, Toph? You don't think I can do it? You don't think I can sleep for four hours and cover the last *fifteen* miles in *seven* hours?"

I could tell Jurker was suddenly offended. How dare Toph doubt the Champ? But the Champ had taken eight hours to cover the last seventeen miles, so nobody knew what to expect from him.

"Do you want to sleep or do you want the record?" Topher asked. "You get *one* hour." With that, he turned around and walked to the rental car, where, he told me later, he started sobbing, worried that they had pushed him past his breaking point.

Jurker spun around and walked toward Castle Black. He looked me straight in the eye and said, "He's fucking crazy." He threw his poles down and I followed him to the van.

What the Champ didn't understand was the magnitude of the mountain he needed to climb. It was like he was looking at what the Penobscot tribe called "The Greatest Mountain" from the wrong end of a telescope.

"Toph's out of his mind," he huffed as he labored into the van. "Don't wake me up for at least two hours."

CHAPTER 16

DOWN TO THE WIRE

Day Forty-Six

TOPH'S WARNING ABOUT time must have wormed its way into my unconscious. It rang me awake as surely as any alarm clock, and I didn't even have to set it. My body wanted at least four hours, but some part of my mind wanted the record more, the deep, autonomic part that keeps the lungs expanding and heart pumping, the part that keeps each of us moving toward what we need rather than what we think we want. Toph was right. I couldn't spare more hours.

When I came to, I sort of blinked myself fully awake and took stock of my world as it came into focus. I could see JLu. She was there in the van with me, keeping quiet as she gathered up my stuff so I'd be ready to hit the trail. It dawned on me that today was her birthday. It was also the day I'd finish. But not yet. I couldn't think about finishing yet. Until I got out of that van, on the trail, and up Mount Katahdin, it was just another day of grinding.

There would be no premature victory celebration.

For one more day, I would have to be my primal self, alive only in the present. No futures, no pasts. No different from an animal. The real *El Venado* had to come out today.

I checked my watch as I got up. It was 6:25 a.m. We weren't out of the woods, not by a long shot. It wasn't any kind of smooth finish that lay ahead of me that day. For most NoBo thru-hikers who are finishing their journey, Katahdin is no cakewalk. There's a campground at the base where they stop to rest and get an early start the next morning. Mount Katahdin is the highest point in Maine; it's a monumental hike. This is why I wanted to finish here, for pure aesthetic reasons and ultimate thru-hike culmination. The climb symbolizes everything that the AT embodies: wildness, grandeur, and grit.

My desire to go north on the AT meant that the challenge would extend down to the last stretch, the last mile, the last minute. The path up the final mountain required full-on scrambling, the kind of hike you'd see out west in the Rockies, Cascades, or Sierras. Boulders and rocks cover the scarp. As I'd done through most of Maine, I'd have to pick my way carefully up the slope, one safe footfall after another.

As I got out of the van, I saw Kim and Toph studying a map of Katahdin and the surrounding area. The fact that everyone was still on high alert, still strategizing, reinforced what I already knew: We had work to do. And quickly.

My body reluctantly came to. Every joint felt a rusty stiffness with movements happening in slow motion. Running was an impossible notion.

Walking sounded better. Walking seemed more doable. Even on the very last day I thought about how sweet it would be just to walk it in.

Toph's sixth sense for slacking must have kicked in, because he came over to me and started delivering the hard facts of what I faced that day. I was struck by how calm he was, since what he was saying was so impossible-sounding—it sounded just as impossible as before my sixty-minute catnap.

"If you start in fifteen minutes," he said, glancing at his watch, "you'll have almost exactly ten hours to reach the summit. The base of the mountain is nine miles away, and then you'll have a five-mile climb. It's gonna be tough but it's not like you can't handle it. It would be awesome if you can keep three to four miles per hour. Even given how you feel now, that should be within your range." He didn't mention that my pace last night had been much slower than that, and he didn't need to. Toph was direct, always, but he never said more than he had to. However, there was one thing *I* absolutely had to say. With joy. JLu came over to me, and I embraced her. "Happy birthday!"

She hugged me back and looked at me like today was the best day of her life. I wished I could bottle her optimism so I could take sips from it forever.

I thought about something I'd said to her so many days and states and miles ago, back in Virginia. "If it comes down to hours, then you can get mad at me." I'd been so confident then.

But she wasn't mad at me. She just wanted me to get the record. I was suddenly overwhelmed with admiration for her, and with empathy for what she'd been through.

Not yet, though, I told myself. *Not yet.* There'd be time for feelings at the summit.

JLu had to drive the van to the park entrance to get the spot she'd reserved. We had one last moment before she took off. The next ten miles really were the linchpin to the whole FKT attempt, and none of us knew if I could actually do it. We were in totally unknown territory in terms of my body and fatigue. So when JLu asked me who I wanted to run with that morning, I knew my choice was critical. Krissy and Toph were out; they were too tired from the night before. What I really needed was a trail *boss,* someone to beat the drum and keep me moving forward no matter what. Luckily, Special Forces had arrived the night before—a total surprise—and he was more than ready for that job. So I picked him and Walter. It felt like I was choosing warriors more than runners. We were going into our last battle.

Jenny took off in Castle Black. Walter and Special Forces and I started moving. No theatrics, no rituals, no nothing. We just started moving, slowly, north.

We crossed the Penobscot River over Abol Bridge, an unforgettable milestone for every NoBo thru-hiker. The rushing water breathed life energy into me; it represented another passage to the end. But there was something better up above. Katahdin loomed. It was right there in front of us. All we had to do was keep moving forward, and then moving up.

I looked at Walter, and I could see that he knew the space my head was in. Like a soft suggestion, he asked, "Should we jog?"

I didn't want to, but his words fired up my legs and miraculously made them move. It was like when a song comes on the radio that stirs a certain emotion and you can't help but dance—he stirred movement in my legs. As I started *running,* everything started to click. *I know how to do this.* Without thinking, I let out a primal scream as I had before the start of so many races when the energy crested within. That's how I dealt with nervousness and excitement—I channeled it into a sound and released it.

My stride lengthened and quickened, and I fell into the strong, steady pace that had carried me forward over the past twenty years, and with so many good friends. I remembered something Topher had said to me two nights earlier, when it seemed like the suffering would never end. He'd said that what had impressed him most about me during this torturous challenge was that, even after the trail's two thousand miles had finally broken me, I'd still been kind to strangers and been a good trail steward.

I was in the shadow of Katahdin. Walter, Special Forces, and I had made it through the pivotal ten miles. I would have loved a burst of energy, but it was yet to emerge. What did exist was something more subtle and significant. I had exposed a primordial pathway to a part of myself that transformed my spasms of fear and pain into a fluid waltz of bliss. Broken and obliterated, I felt only ease. Having almost run 2,189 miles, I was hours from setting the new record and felt no worries, only calm, as I started the final ascent. It was the breaking down that built me up.

I didn't want to leave the scene at Golden Road. The momentum was building and it was powerful. But I knew the longer I stayed, the more likely Jurker would dawdle in the van. Plus I needed to drive to the park entrance to claim my parking spot. It was a bluebird midsummer Sunday morning, and I knew it would be crowded.

Speedgoat had warned me that Baxter State Park was, well, special, to put it nicely. I was about to find out what he meant. Technically, it's not even a state park; it's an independently funded land trust. Most hikers knew Baxter State Park had a long-standing love/hate relationship with thru-hikers. Before we stepped foot in the park, its director penned a letter requesting that the AT be diverted from Katahdin, claiming that thru-hikers were a bunch of rule-breaking, littering young partiers. It was a classic "Hey, kid! Get off my lawn!" kind of letter. Even old Warren Doyle had his beef with the park staff: in 1979, he was arrested for summiting Katahdin in the winter. Rather than pay the twenty-five-dollar fine, he spent the night in jail to call attention to the ridiculousness. In fact, most reasonable people seemed to agree that the park's attitude on this front was absurd; the *Portland Press Herald* wrote that the "park officials' statements on AT thru-hikers are the latest examples of overzealous park protectionism that is actually harming the park's reputation and, in turn, the local economy." Even so, we were mindful of their rules.

Kim had gotten us two parking permits, one for each of our vehicles, ahead of time, just to be safe. I didn't have a working phone, thanks to the water I'd spilled all over it, so I was grateful for the help. When we pulled up to the parking area, with Kim in front of me, two rangers eagerly jumped out of the booth, as if they'd been waiting for us. They talked to Kim for longer than I felt was necessary. I started to wonder if they weren't going to let us in. Eventually, they let Kim pass, and then I pulled up to the booth. The ranger standing outside held a clipboard and examined Castle Black. No *Hi! Welcome to our beautiful park!* or even a standard *Enjoy your visit!* I was greeted with: "Your permit expired at seven a.m."

I looked at the clock on the dashboard. It was 7:05.

"I could give your parking space away to somebody else," she warned. I looked behind me—there wasn't a single car in sight. Apparently, this ranger wanted to make sure I knew that she was doing me a favor. *I see how this is gonna go.* (El Coyote, Special Forces, Ralsty, and John Rodrigue were able to obtain parking spots later that morning with no problem.)

She grudgingly let me enter and I parked and got dressed to hike up that mountain. This was the day we'd been dreaming of for weeks. We couldn't have asked for better weather or a better crew.

I loaded my pack with extra snacks and layers of clothing because I knew this might take a while. I was so giddy; we all were. We eagerly gathered in the parking lot's picnic area, wondering when Jurker would arrive. And shortly after, we heard the roar of a wild animal right before it charges its greatest adversary.

The expression on Jurker's face was reminiscent of day one, when I'd seen him at Neels Gap looking like a kid again. Today, he looked like a man who had just walked away victorious from battle. He knew he'd just killed those ten miles in under three hours. Not fast by normal standards, but he'd basically just crushed it.

His face and body emanated confidence. He stood up straight; he didn't stumble, and he had no sense of urgency. The feeling of ease took over, as if he'd just removed his boxing gloves after twelve rounds. In his mind, he knew that he'd done it. The locals weren't as confident. They knew what lay ahead.

Standing among my best friends, old and new, as Jurker ran toward me was like all of the best moments of our journey rolled into one. It brought back memories of everything we'd been through. Even the bad memories felt precious, since those were the times that had made me and Jurker even closer. We'd traveled through so many different places and seen so many new things, in America and in ourselves, that we knew we'd never be quite the same. As I stood there feeling the sun on my face, I thought about all the people who had come to the crossings—even those who had driven me crazy—and I actually wished all of them could be here now.

But they were with us in spirit, glued to the live-tracker information. The tracking company later told me that they'd had more hits on their website than they'd ever had before as people constantly hit refresh. Jurker's phone was blowing up.

We got a message from Rickey, who was with Speedgoat and

other world-class runners at the Hardrock Hundred. They were all rooting for us. And there was a message from Scott's blind friend Thomas, reminding him to close his eyes and see the trail with his mind. People on Facebook were talking conspiracy theories, wondering if Jurker had cut it this close for entertainment's sake.

It was a preposterous idea, but I couldn't fault their thinking. To break the Appalachian Trail speed record by a mere three hours was highly unlikely. By way of contrast, the margin between the current world-record holder in the hundred-meter dash and the runner-up is four times as large. It was pretty nuts, but trust me, if we could have broken the record by four days, as we'd originally planned, we would have.

Looking back, I could see we were underprepared and naive. We'd thought we'd have this romantic and healing adventure for our tight family of two, but I realized that we would never be standing here if it weren't for the countless strangers who'd come out to help. They felt like family too, and I felt content. My heart was full.

I'd stopped thinking about my yearning for a baby, which had cast a pall over the drive out east. Jurker and I had everything we needed, and more. I had seen this man, who I spent practically every hour with at home, transform into someone I didn't know and then reemerge as someone better. He'd needed this journey; he'd needed to return to the edge. He had slowly transitioned from ultrarunning legend to my domestic dream, and he needed to once again feel what it was like to suffer.

Elective suffering is such a strange thing. At its essence, pushing his limits was a way for Jurker to learn more about himself and our relationship. Like Dean Potter once said, "I willingly expose myself to death-consequence situations in order to predictably enter heightened awareness.... And [it] often leads to a feeling of connectivity with everything."

Albeit less extreme, we had gone in searching for heightened awareness and connectivity with ourselves, each other, and the trail. I think that's what drew so many people to follow our journey. It was like Scott was in a fishbowl; people could watch him in his most vulnerable state and laugh at his humiliation and cry at his defeat. They had a feeling of connectedness to what Jurker was doing, as if they were a part of the journey.

Back on day two, Jurker had told a reporter that this would be his masterpiece. I'd cringed, but in a way, he was right. He'd gone to the graveyard and come back; he'd messed up and learned along the way; he'd pushed his body beyond what was possible and put it all out there for the world to see. In one sense, it was the most beautiful expression of his running career.

As we signed the logbook at the base of Katahdin and again were greeted by several rangers, we both felt that ease that comes at the end of suffering. Topher put away his phone and his apps; Jurker took off his pack and set down his poles.

He looked at me and his team and said, "I'm going for a birthday hike with my wife and our best friends."

CHAPTER 17

THE GREATEST MOUNTAIN

Day Forty-Seven

EVEN THOUGH I'D climbed higher mountains, explored more scabrous wilderness, and run under bigger skies, through more treacherous ground, these were all just lonely superlatives. The "best of" class is always exclusive, and like those singular experiences that seem to happen only in a world of their own, you can often find yourself there with no accompaniment.

This journey was anything but solitary, and, most important, it was this abundance that created such an intensely beautiful and magical experience. And it was not a beauty born of one image; it was like those expansive montages assembled using thousands of striking photos that coalesce to produce another, greater image— this was an all-inclusive portrait of every experience.

Over a lifetime of hard work and wins and close calls, I'd built a Wikipedia page's worth of accomplishments. Most of my records have already been broken. Some might never be matched. I say that with humility; I can't match them now. I'm not that runner now—

it's undeniable. My old self would smoke my current self almost anywhere in the world and under almost any conditions.

Maybe not on the Appalachian Trail, though. As I made my way up the slope, I felt like each step I took had been foreshadowed by the millions of other steps I'd taken. The long path north was about to end. Along the way, it had opened up and activated pathways inside me. If I got the record, it wouldn't be like my other victories. It was something deeper and, in a way, less remarkable. I didn't feel like an ultrarunner or someone particularly special. I felt like I'd taken a long route home.

It was the final leg on the final day on the Greatest Mountain, and I savored it. We couldn't have asked for a more bluebird day. I was with JLu, surrounded by our friends, and we climbed our way up, taking nothing for granted.

As we began the final ascent, I was once again happy for my decision to go north instead of south. The last five miles of the trail up to Katahdin are like a grand finale. It's incredible terrain all around, endless and spare and severe. People up in Maine have long thought that when the sun rises in the east, it hits the summit of Katahdin first. The Penobscot tribe puts the residence of its storm god there, and we'd learned that forty- to fifty-mile-an-hour winds are typical conditions.

Not today. Today was perfect. The higher I climbed, the stronger I got. The stronger I got, the easier my stride became. JLu laughed as she watched me. I was too tired to be exhausted, or vice versa.

We passed a crew of trail workers breaking up rocks with sledgehammers. I stopped and thanked them. Then a group of young hikers came along and giddily formed a human tunnel for me to run through. Others had gathered, having heard today was the day, and they high-fived me as I sprang up and onward.

When we passed the first false summit, we checked the time,

just to be absolutely sure. It was one more mile to the actual summit, and we had three hours and forty-five minutes. It struck me that Toph's insistence on one hour of sleep for me instead of four might well have decided the outcome. I scanned the mass of hikers for him and caught his eye just long enough to telegraph my absolute gratitude.

As we drew closer to the famous sign at the summit, I was reminded of the first time I'd seen it, in a photo. When I met Horty, back in the early 2000s, he'd taken me to his office, and hanging on the wall was a poster of a thru-hiker draping himself over the sign. His body language told a complex story not only of the exultant triumph that fills you with satisfaction and joy but also of the profound depletion that leaves you hollow and hungry. I'd wondered ever since what it would feel like to finish that same journey and touch that iconic sign.

There were tons of people on the peak. No wonder—it was a beautiful summer Sunday. I stopped, once, to soak in the atmosphere. JLu was right behind me, smiling. People started cheering and applauding as we got closer. She waved and motioned for me to keep going.

"Go!" she yelled. "Go!"

"No." I stuck out my hand for her to grab. "We're going together!"

It was 2:05 p.m. on July 12, 2015. I had run the Appalachian Trail in forty-six days, eight hours, and seven minutes. I had beaten the record by three hours and thirteen minutes.

One by one, our friends came over the top and joined the crowd of strangers, fans, and well-wishers. The summit magnet of Katahdin that had pulled me north was now pulling all of us together. I leaned my face against that weatherworn wooden sign that I had been dreaming about for thousands of miles. I hugged and kissed JLu. The area around the sign had suddenly become wonderfully, happily crowded, and people wanted to know how I felt.

I said, "Today is my wife's birthday!" and everybody burst into singing "Happy Birthday" to my best friend.

A year ago we had sought peace and healing in the California desert. We'd found just enough to make us want more. I'd had a wild idea, born out of frustration and stuckness, and JLu had responded to it with both confusion and understanding. Of course she had. She was the secret to my sauce, the salt to my pepper, and being with her had been my luckiest break. I was a better person because of her, and she was the reason I was standing on that mountain.

She was also the reason why I might never have begun this journey. JLu made my post-racing life rewarding and fun; I had lost the desire to push my body to the edge. I was content. But even complacency has a shelf life. I felt an urge to reconnect with my old self, the one that might not win but still kept fighting.

Up at the top of Katahdin, I realized some of the people who'd gathered there were just starting their two-thousand-mile journey south to Springer Mountain. One of them already had a trail name, Frisbee, and I signed her disc: *Get to Springer no matter what.* I saw something in Frisbee's eyes that mirrored what JLu and I had felt forty-six days ago. JLu and I had finished our pilgrimage, but we could only wonder what Frisbee would experience.

The point of a thru-hike is different for everybody. Some people assume thru-hikers are running away from something, trying to escape the real world. For me, it was transformation. I wanted to find something I thought I'd lost, to test strengths I didn't think I had anymore, to rekindle the fire I'd thought was long extinguished. The journey was the tool I needed to pry myself open.

I guess old Horty was right. *This is who I am. This is what I do.*

EPILOGUE

September 2016

THE WIND CAME gently through the old oaks high in Great Smoky Mountains National Park. It felt like an old friend, its sound and its feel and the memories it brought with it. It also felt new to me that day, almost unfamiliar. Our existence is always like this: the same but different, light then dark, found now lost, here and there and back again.

Other parts were entirely different. Above me, the nighttime sky held countless points of light and was wide open and cloudless—nothing like the gray waterlogged ceiling that hung over most of my days on the AT. All around me, the hint of fall was in the air instead of spring. I wasn't sleepy; I was fully alert. And most pertinent: I wasn't the poor soul just wrapping up Day 43 of a certain two-thousand-mile journey.

Speedgoat was already fast asleep in the shelter. I had just hiked in thirty pounds of food, water, and sleeping gear (including Speedgoat's pillow) eight miles to provide a few comforts. I knew that kindness. True to his precise planning, this would be his first and only night camping on the trail. He didn't like sleeping on rocks like I had become accustomed to. It was uncanny to have returned to the same grassy meadow where fourteen months ago I doubted myself as I drifted off for a quick nap, serenaded by these same rustling oaks.

A year had passed. I could hardly believe it. My AT trial had left me gasping for air and grasping for reality, but it had done so much more. Most important, it had tested—and honed, tempered, and steeled—my bond with JLu. I was still in awe of what she did for me last year, and suddenly I wanted to share my thoughts and feelings with the person who had joined me along the entire way. I called her that night from Spence Field Shelter. The modern cell signal, both amazing and unnerving in its ubiquity, was crystal clear as I heard her voice answer from across the country.

"Jurker! Where are you? What's it like? Is it raining yet? Are the bugs bad? Have you seen any SoBos?"

She loved for me to describe the places the two of us had been, and I indulged her with my observations on how things were the same, and how they were so different too. How the climbs and descents that I limped through in Tennessee were now dusty instead of muddy and how the hotel where we stayed with Horty in Erwin didn't look as depressing this time. One thing hadn't changed at all, though. The backroads were just as sketchy as she'd left them.

"Unless that rain dance you've been doing causes a hurricane, he's gonna break our record."

She laughed. "That lucky bastard! Third time's a charm. I'm happy for him, and I love that you're there, helping out. I just wish I could be there too. I was *so* looking forward to watching him suffer!" She laughed even louder. "Tell him to hurry up. I need you back here to help with the baby."

I could hear Raven keening in the background, and my heart went out to both of them as it always did and always would. She was born Ravenna Lynn Jurek on June 1, 2016, almost exactly a year after we'd started the trail.

"I miss you guys. It feels weird without you. I'll be home soon," I assured her, and hung up. I missed them both, but at the same time, I loved being out here. It was the middle of nowhere, as almost everyone would agree. But it was also something else for me. It was the middle of myself, the center of my existence, who I am and what I'm a part of: my tribe, my family, and myself.

I knew she wasn't worried about my peace of mind after losing the record. I've had all but one of my records broken. They don't mean anything; it's the acts that stand as moments and emblems for ourselves. I used Pharr Davis's record as a device to extract the best out of myself, a goal to keep pulling me forward. You train not to beat other people but to beat time and previous performances.

I've always thought of trails as veins on the surface of the earth. There was so much to learn from running and sharing these wilderness passages as they crisscrossed through ranges and canyons like blood vessels spanning the continent. Each section of the trail became a volume in my living body of knowledge that was drafted by Mother Nature. Horty and Speedgoat wrote a few pages too. As did everyone else who had shared even a moment of the AT with me. That's why I had to go help Karl. I had my piece to write for him as well. I had my own wisdom now, and it was my responsibility to pass it on. And like the progression from student to teacher, it is the passing along of that assistance, counsel, and perseverance that moves us all forward.

For several months after my run, my legs felt heavy, while I quickly regained the weight I'd lost—and then some, as JLu liked to point out. To be safe, we both took antibiotics for Lyme disease and checked to make sure no major damage had been done to my nervous system. Nothing to worry about. I bounced back and my energy returned.

In January I received a New Year's photocard from Frisbee, stating she'd made it to Springer exactly six months after she descended Katahdin and she'd carried that Frisbee the whole way. The runner I'd snapped at in the Whites caught me at the Boston Marathon Expo the next spring. As I apologized profusely, he just laughed and said, "I shouldn't have asked how you were doing, since the answer was written on your face." I grimaced again.

My body healed. I became what I was before I'd started running north. I returned to normal, physically. But I wasn't so sure about my intellectual and spiritual components. Could I ever be the same after such a pilgrimage into my deepest self? Doubt lingered on after we finished. Perhaps Timmy said it best when offering a pop-psychology assessment of my post-run state: "After such a beautiful and brutal odyssey, that white trail blaze is branded onto his soul forever." I had nothing to add to that. I still don't.

People often ask what getting to the other side provided and why I did it. And beyond the predictable and polite, I find it difficult to really say. Why would anyone volunteer for such suffering?

One theory that I embraced after a certain newcomer graced my life is that undergoing something like the FKT attempt was kind of like producing offspring: I wouldn't know what it was like until I went ahead and did it. On the other hand, I'm still figuring out fatherhood, so I'm not sure that really tracks either.

Maybe the whole thing was one long and muddy Zen koan, and only through considering it in the first place could I begin to comprehend the unanswerable. I remember Timmy telling me about a presentation he gave at a university where a professor's child suddenly raised his hand as an image of the yin and yang symbol appeared. When Timmy called on the precocious youth, he asked what color the line was between the black and white sides. The little Buddha was onto something. The line exists, but now I think I know that you have to start walking it to figure out what it really looks like.

Ultimately, it doesn't matter if I ever know exactly what it all was. The adventure was as much about what I saw and who I met while hiking on the trail as it was about the perceptions that I discovered within myself, and I suspect that those impressions will endure longer than anything else. Much more a life course than a race course, the entire two-thousand-mile line north truly was my greatest reward.

We've already taken Raven on lots of long hikes, including one across the Grand Canyon, and I'm sure she'll get interested in some of the outdoorsy things we do. As she gets older, we'll tell her about how we ran and hiked all the way up America, from the bottom to the top along a major trail artery, faster than anybody else ever had. She'll probably want to know why, but I doubt we'll be able to tell her in a way that makes total sense, because her own sense of why will be very different. That's how it should be. Out there in the wild, on a long journey, you hike your own hike, blaze your own trail, and only you can find what you're looking for.

ACKNOWLEDGMENTS

Like completing the AT, this book required a collective of talented, wise, and supportive individuals to get me to the end. My buddy Aron Ralston says it took me forty-six days to complete the trail but forty-six months to write about it. Not quite, but close. At a point when I was struggling with this project, a musician friend told me, "You have your whole life to write your first album and then you're expected to write the second one in six months." And I could relate.

Thank you to my literary agent, Richard Pine, for never giving up on me. Richard had been faithfully prodding me for years to write another book. Every once in a while, he would send me an email to check in. One afternoon while I was hobbling through Virginia, Richard wrote, "I've been following your trip. This adventure could very well be its own book."

Thank you to the crew at Inkwell Management. William Callahan, you are an alchemist and you helped turn my muddled thoughts into gold.

To Tracy Behar, Ian Straus, and the team at Little, Brown, I know we drove you nuts, but we work best under pressure! Thank you for always giving us one more day, one last tweak, one final edit, to make things right.

And to Timmy O'Neill: you have fought for us like no other human being ever has. You went to war with me in the Green Tunnel and in the writing pain cave. I am forever grateful to you for helping me remember and be able to describe the feelings and the sounds and emotions of the wild AT. I owe you a debt that I hope to repay when you write your book.

Thank you to Christopher McDougall for your guidance, as always. Somehow your abstract and wacky ideas make sense.

The beautiful maps are by Jeremy Collins, the only person we wanted to bring that two-thousand-mile line to life.

Luis Escobar, thanks for continually answering your phone when I call. You are a master of light, and your photos bring us back to the trail so we all can relive the emotions of every moment.

The heavy lifting happened at night. Thank you to all my trail compatriots who followed me into the dark, carrying camping gear and keeping me from sleepwalking off the edge: Andrew Drummond, Timmy O'Neill, Gabe Flanders, Tristan Williams, Ryan and Kristina Welts, Nate Sanel, John Rodrigue, Joe Wrobleski, Chris Clemens, Mark Godale, Aron Ralston, and Walter Edwards.

To Topher and Kim Gaylord and to Krissy Moehl: you guys were the missing pieces to the final act. You redefined what friendship means when you answered my SOS call and came to help.

David Horton and Karl Meltzer, your guidance and enthusiasm were taken to heart and I am fortunate to have had you on my squad. Even if your early morning "Let's go to Maine, boy!" wake-up calls and nickels and dimes drove me to the brink.

To everybody who did some miles with me, to my fellow thru-hikers, to the trail angels, to the people who came out to see me at trailheads, and to everyone following online, you got me 2,189 miles north.

To Dean Potter: I wish we had come to the Valley before you took your last flight, and I wish Raven could have met you and seen your magic. The world feels so much darker without your light. We miss you, a constant inspiration, even on the other side. Fly free, brother.

And to Jenny, this book is for you, because of you, and is you. There is no one else I'd rather walk through the fire with. You are my perpetually rising sun, my warrior, my endless source of inspiration and joy. I spent a lifetime wandering and when the path led me to you, I finally found my direction.

ABOUT THE AUTHOR

Scott Jurek, one of the greatest runners of all time, has claimed multiple victories in the historic 153-mile Spartathlon, Hardrock Hundred, Badwater 135-Mile Ultramarathon, and Western States 100-Mile Endurance Run, which he won a record seven straight times. He has been named a *National Geographic* Adventurer of the Year and one of *Sports Illustrated*'s Fittest 50. The *New York Times* bestselling author of *Eat and Run,* Jurek was featured in the book *Born to Run* and has appeared in the *New York Times, USA Today,* the *Wall Street Journal, Time,* and *ESPN The Magazine,* and on CNN. A passionate vegan, he lives in the mountains of Boulder, Colorado, with his wife, Jenny, and their daughter, Raven.